FRANCHISING

The Business Strategy that Changed the World

CARRIE SHOOK & ROBERT L. SHOOK

D0146885

PRENTICE HALL
Englewood Cliffs, New Jersey 07632

Prentice-Hall International (UK) Limited, *London*
Prentice-Hall of Australia Pty. Limited, *Sydney*
Prentice-Hall Canada, Inc., *Toronto*
Prentice-Hall Hispanoamericana, S.A., *Mexico*
Prentice-Hall of India Private Limited, *New Delhi*
Prentice-Hall of Japan, Inc., *Tokyo*
Simon & Schuster Asia Pte. Ltd., *Singapore*
Editora Prentice-Hall do Brasil, Ltda., *Rio de Janeiro*

10 9 8 7 6 5 4 3 2 1

Library of Congress Cataloging-in-Publication Data

Shook, Carrie.
  Franchising: the business strategy that changed the world / by
Carrie Shook & Robert L. Shook
    p. cm.
  Includes index.
  ISBN 0-13-065608-9
  1. Franchises (Retail trade)—United States—Case studies.
I. Shook, Robert L., 1938-   . II. Title.
HF5429.235.U5S56 1993   92-39398
658.8'708—dc20   CIP

ISBN   0-13-065608-9

PRENTICE HALL
Career & Personal Development
Englewood Cliffs, NJ 07632

Simon & Schuster, A Paramount Communications Company

Printed in the United States of America

Contents

Acknowledgments

The authors are grateful to many people who made valuable contributions during the course of the preparation of this book.

From beginning to end (and beyond), our dear friend Jim Trethewey, a past chairman of the International Franchiser Association (IFA), and franchising expert, gave us guidance and support. Jim, in our book, you're the greatest—we couldn't have done it without you.

The present president of IFA, Bill Cherkasky, also toiled closely with us from start to finish. It was a delightful experience to work with such a professional, and we greatly appreciate your interest and cooperation, Bill. Likewise, John Reynolds, the IFA's extremely capable executive vice president of marketing, was always available for support and advice. Thanks, John, for always being there when we needed you.

We were fortunate to have some very good legal counsel from Lewis Rudnick and Ross Blair, attorneys in Chicago who are considered the best in their franchising speciality. Our appreciation also goes to another fine attorney, Philip Zeidman, a talented person who even gave a hand with the editing work.

We thank the following people for their help and insights: Don Anderson, Richard Armstrong, Mark Arnold, Henry Bloch, Richard Bloch, Tom Bloch, Hugh Boesett, William C. Bond, Bud Brooks, Terry Burke, Carlos Cantu, Dan Carney, Frank Carney, Burt Cohen, Mike Dart, Joe Davis, Mike Davis, Dick Dole, Jim Dora, Charles Ebeling, Alan Feldman, Frank Flautt, Robert Goff, Jr., Bob Groff, Jerry Grossman, Ken Hansen, Val Hanson, Robert Hutchinson, Robin Johnson, Tom Kanawyer, Akira Kojima, Shigeharu Komai, Terry

Komai, Michael Leven, Steve Losorwith, Richard Loughlin, Helen Marchick, Seiko Masuda, Clark Matthews, Jim McCauley, Wes Mitchell, J. R. Moore, Duane Mora, Cecilia Stubbs Norwood, Melissa Frick Oakley, Lonnie Orns, Dan Paxton, Robert Perkins, Bill Pollard, Steve Reinemund, Russell Richards, Elie Rivollier, Lori Roberts, Anne Rosenberg, Bill Rosenberg, Bob Rosenberg, Tadashi Sasaki, Charlie Simpson, Richard Spencer, Gaines Sturdivant, Jere Thompson, Randy Vest, Bill Walsh, Glenn Waslien, Richard Weiner, Ken Wessner, Larry Whitt, Pat Williamson, and Kemmons Wilson.

In Columbus, Ohio, Mary Liff performed wonderfully as a transcriber of taped interviews and organizer of our extensive files. Thanks, Mary, for your usual cooperation and ever-present good-natured spirit.

Finally, we thank our friends in the publishing aspect of our endeavor. Al Zuckerman, our longtime agent and good friend, whom we think is the best in his field; we deeply appreciate his belief in our writing projects. And it was our good fortune to have worked with two exceptional editors at Prentice Hall, Phil Ruppel and Drew Dreeland.

When writers are blessed with so many supporters and friends, the task of writing a book is indeed a pleasurable one.

Dedication

This book is dedicated to a man who made enormous contributions to franchising—Bill Rosenberg, the founder of Dunkin' Donuts.

Perhaps no other individual has done so much to make franchising what it is today. At the time when Bill first began to franchise his Dunkin' Donuts stores, it was not a popular way to transact business (*The New York Times* and *The Wall Street Journal* did not accept "franchising" ads).

Since then, Bill's commitment to the promotion of franchising has become legendary. In 1960, he founded the International Franchise Association and today serves as its chairman emeritus. He is the first person to be inducted into the prestigious IFA Hall of Fame. Through generous personal contributions, Bill has launched educational programs at several universities. He is also the Honorary Founding Trustee of the IFA Educational Foundation, Inc.

It was Bill who planted the seed for this book, and he too consented to be our first interview. Throughout the course of preparing and writing the manuscript, Bill served as our mentor and dear friend. Admittedly, it is unusual for a dedication to honor someone who is also a major subject of the book. But, then, Bill Rosenberg is an extraordinary man.

Thanks, Bill, for everything you have done.

Carrie and Bob

Foreword

Carrie and Robert Shook bring the wonderful story of franchising to life in *Franchising: The Business Strategy That Changed the World*. As its title suggests, franchising has reached out and touched hundreds of millions of men and women around the globe.

The franchising method of distribution has been hailed by experts as the most successful business strategy ever created. In 1982, when the best-selling book, *Megatrends*, was released, author John Naisbitt described franchising as "the wave of the future." A decade has passed that has proved him right.

In *Franchising*, the Shooks present an in-depth look at ten of the most successful franchise companies. Here the authors portray their founders, the entrepreneurs who built these ten companies into modern-day marketing giants in their respective industries. Here, too, the executives who operate these far-flung franchising systems with business locations from Minneapolis to Moscow reveal what goes on in today's corporate suites. And still other entrepreneurs are introduced: the franchisees themselves, many of whom are as competitive and driven as the very founders who, years ago, started these enormous enterprises that have since become household words in many languages around the world.

The International Franchise Association is deeply grateful to Carrie and Robert Shook for the many months of effort, research, and extensive interviewing that went into the creation of this work. It is our sincere hope that *Franchising: The Business Strategy That Changed the World* will both inspire and educate many young entrepreneurs with new business concepts to help launch their dreams upon the foundation of franchising. And, upon doing so, they will follow in the footsteps of the trailblazers described in this book.

William B. Cherkasky, President
International Franchise Association

Introduction

More than 540,000 franchised businesses dot the American landscape today, with sales totaling more than $758 billion, which equals about one-third of the nation's retail market. It's no wonder that you see them on main streets and highways and in shopping centers across the country. More than 7 million Americans draw their paychecks from a franchise. With a new franchise opening every 17 minutes, these numbers keep growing and growing.

The appeal of owning a franchise attracts Americans in all walks of life. Above all, owning your own business is the epitome of the American dream itself. It represents the opportunity to attain financial security and, for the most successful, the accumulation of wealth. Then too, to many, it provides independence—the freedom to be your own boss.

Interestingly, the word *franchising* literally means to be free. In this sense, franchising offers people the freedom to own, manage, and direct their own business.

During recessionary times, being an independent business person is particularly appealing because it relieves the anxiety of being laid off when the economy is soft. To scores of middle and upper managers over age 40 who are unable to secure a comparable job to the one they lost, owning a franchise is an attractive option—and to some, it is the *only option*.

Of course, there are no guarantees for an entrepreneur. Along with the rewards of the free enterprise system are the risks of failure. In this area in particular, owning a franchise is enticing. The Department of Commerce claims that less than 5 percent of franchised outlets have failed or were discontinued each year since 1971. By contrast, the U.S. Small Business Administration reports that 65 percent of all business start-ups go belly up within five years. With odds like these, it's no wonder that franchising is such a phenomenon in the 1990s.

With the collapse of the Soviet Union, and the demise of communism in Eastern Europe, for the first time, millions of people on foreign shores are anxious to participate in what has previously been reserved for citizens of a free society. It may well be that franchising will be one of America's chief exports during the remainder of the twentieth century.

Here, at home, franchising also offers wonderful opportunities to minorities. Millions of disadvantaged youths are provided with entry-level employment by franchised businesses—often their first jobs—and starting at the bottom lends itself to learning the business from the ground up. Many of today's leading franchisors are structured to develop these young people from within and, when appropriate, will give assistance in financing them to own their own franchises!

This book features in-depth profiles of ten of the most successful players in the history of franchising. Each chapter begins with the early struggles and obstacles that its founder had to overcome. You will also be privy to how these small enterprises were able to make the difficult transition and eventually expand into international corporations.

Most important, you will observe what happens on the inside— something which we believe is essential for every would-be franchisee. This viewpoint provides rare insight—one not readily available even to the experienced franchisee. Why is this exposure so important to you? Because it allows you to witness how the managers of the most successful franchisors operate. As you will learn, the relationship between a franchisor and franchisee is a vital factor in the success equation. As a franchisee who must work with a franchisor on a regular basis, what you learn here promises to be invaluable.

Also, you will meet dozens of successful franchisees with years of experience under their belts. These men and women speak candidly about franchising and, in this role, contribute convincing insight to the ins and outs of owning a franchise. As you will discover, all franchising opportunities are not equal!

Ten of the most successful franchising operations are profiled in this book.

- *H & R Block, Inc.*, is the largest income tax preparation, electronic filing, and tax return preparer in the world. It has 4,837 franchised outlets and 3,994 company-owned offices.

- *Century 21 Real Estate Corporation* is the world's largest real estate franchising organization, with over 7,000 franchised outlets and $68 billion in annual sales volume.

- *Dunkin' Donuts* is the largest coffee and donut restaurant chain in existence, with more than 3,000 franchised outlets around the world.

- *The Duskin Company, Ltd.*, is a Japanese conglomerate of various American franchises, with exclusive territorial rights on the Pacific Rim, the Philippines, Thailand, and Indonesia. The company's franchising interests include Continuous Towel, ServiceMaster, Linen Supply, United-Rent-All, and Mister Donut.

- *Holiday Inn, Inc.*, is the first hotel chain to franchise, and since its beginning in 1952, it now has 1,400 franchised outlets and 190 company-owned hotels in its worldwide operations.

- *Midas Muffler* is an automobile exhaust, brake, and suspension service company with 1,675 franchised outlets and 118 company-owned stores in the United States. Combined with its international business, it has 2,410 shops.

- *McDonald's* is truly a fast-food phenomenon and synonymous with franchising. Starting with a single hamburger stand, founder Ray Kroc turned McDonald's into a multibillion dollar corporation. The company's innovations set many of the standards for franchising and the food service industry, and in doing so, McDonald's influence has had a tremendous impact on American culture. Since the corporation began to franchise in the mid-1950s, McDonald's has grown to an enormous size with over 13,000 restaurants in all 50 states and 65 foreign countries. Approximately 80% of its outlets are franchised.

- *Pizza Hut* was established in 1958 and introduced pizza to millions of Americans. There are over 8,000 locations in all 50 states and over 1,500 units in 64 foreign countries.

- *ServiceMaster* is a residential and commercial cleaning service company with over 5,500 franchised outlets around the world. The required cash investment for a ServiceMaster franchise is among the lowest in the industry, thereby providing many opportunities to individuals with modest means.

- *7-Eleven (The Southland Corporation)* is the largest convenience store chain in the United States with approximately 3,000 company-owned units in the U.S. and Canada; 3,100 franchise-operated stores in the U.S.; and over 7,350 7-Eleven stores owned and operated or franchised by area licensees in parts of the U.S., Japan, and 17 other countries. In business since 1927, it has been franchising since 1964. Here is an interesting story about how a company has made many changes over the years to adapt to the times.

The diverse products that these ten companies deal with range from tax preparation services to cleaning services and doughnuts to real estate. These companies are clearly the leaders in their respective industries. Yet, despite their size and international scope, as you read on in *Franchising: The Business Strategy that Changed the World*, you will meet many of the most interesting and successful men and women in the field of franchising.

Chapter 1

H & R BLOCK

Turning Taxes into Profit

As a student at the Harvard Business School in the mid-1940s, Henry Bloch stumbled across a speech in the library archives that had been given by one of his professors. In this lecture, Sumner Slichter told a group of executives that business is divided into three parts—big business, small business, and labor. The professor went on to explain that big business and labor are both extremely powerful but that the American economy is based on the free enterprise system and, without small businesses, there would not be a democracy.

Henry Bloch took these words to heart, and on that day he began to think about what small business he might enter into; one that would find a unique niche in the marketplace.

Shortly after graduation, in 1946, the 24-year-old aspiring entrepreneur secured a $5,000 loan from a wealthy aunt and convinced his brother Leon to be his partner in forming the United Business Company in their hometown, Kansas City, Missouri. The brothers decided their business would provide advertising, bookkeeping, accounting, collection work, temporary help, administrative details, and legal services for small companies that could not afford to hire their own in-house professionals—clients would pay a monthly fee for these comprehensive services.

The Blochs pounded the pavements of Kansas City, knocking on doors in search of clients. They faced the age-old problem of prospective clients wanting references, which the struggling enterprise did not yet have. The first year in business was so disappointing that Leon abandoned the partnership to enroll in law school. "I have always been very persistent, so I refused to give up," says Henry Bloch.

Having served as a combat navigator in 31 bombing missions with the Eighth Air Force during World War II, Henry received $50 a month provided to him by the GI Bill of Rights. Still living at home, this $50 was his entire income in those early days, just enough to pay the office rent.

Slowly, the business started to grow, which prompted the young entrepreneur to place an advertisement in the local newspaper for an assistant. Upon reading the ad, Henry's mother, Hortense, urged Henry to hire his younger brother Richard to be his partner. "Mom was strong-willed and I ended up taking her advice," Bloch confesses, "but I wasn't sure how Richard could live on what he'd make. He was married and had young children."

Upon joining, his brother, Richard sat down with Henry to evaluate their business. The brothers decided that its focus was too broad, so they narrowed down their services to bookkeeping.

"In addition, we did tax preparations out of courtesy for some of our customers, employees, and friends," Henry tells. "When other people found out about us, they offered to pay us $5.00 for doing their returns, too. We accepted the extra work and earned about $1,800 just from doing 300 returns during the 1954 tax season. However, we felt the extra money wasn't worth our trouble because the returns were taking up too much of our free time. Dick and I were working seven days a week and nights, between our bookkeeping and the tax preparations, and it was simply too much. At the time, tax season ended on March 15. I had a family by then too and felt we weren't spending enough time at home. Our families have always meant a lot to both of us." As a consequence, the Blochs refused to do the extra tax returns, and only for their clients did they prepare returns.

After nine years in business, the United Business Company developed a solid foundation of clients with plenty of bookkeeping to keep busy, so the Blochs were planning to get out of tax preparing completely. "But our customers asked us where they would turn if we stopped helping them," recalls Richard, "and we were concerned about letting them down." One of their early customers, John White, an ad salesman for the *Kansas City Star*, the local newspaper, tried to convince the brothers to stay in the tax preparation business. He suggested that they run two ads to advertise their service, and if there was no response, they should drop this entire segment of their business completely. He also recommended that they create an eye catcher for the ads, and this prompted the Blochs to offer tax preparation for as low as $5.00 a return. The Blochs idea of $5.00 charges was a unique marketing approach—they determined the price first and then designed the system that would allow them a profit at this price. The two ads ran on January 23, and 24, 1955.

"We weren't sure that filing returns at this low price would be profitable to pursue because in those days," Henry tells, "the government was preparing returns for free! But luckily, before the first ad ran, many people received their W-2 forms, and they wanted and needed help. Also, the IRS announced it was discontinuing its free preparation service except for people who could not read or write English."

The day after the first ad ran, the United Business Company was never to be the same again. "Dick arrived at the office early, and to his delight, found that it was filled with people," recalls Henry.

That winter, the Bloch brothers grossed a sensational $25,000 from tax preparation, and they knew that there was no turning back. The $200 the brothers spent for advertising in the *Kansas City Star* was worth every penny. In this one season, they had earned nearly a third of the annual income that their business had taken a decade to develop.

Henry and Richard recognized that the need for professional tax assistance was an untapped market. Realizing that average middle-class people could not afford to hire a certified public accountant or attorney for assistance with their taxes, the Blochs decided to drop their other services and prepare tax returns on a full-time basis.

Henry believed that since his company sold a service and not a product, it should bear their name. Accordingly, the firm was named H & R Block. They dropped the "h" and added a "k" to their last name to avoid mispronunciations. "We didn't want people to say we 'blotched' their return," Dick grins.

In 1956, Henry and Richard decided to expand their business outside of Kansas City and chose New York City as their first venture. On October 1, Henry moved to New York and opened seven store-front offices which were planned to be operating by January 1. "Even then we knew that if we could make it there we could make it anywhere," chuckles Henry. But there was one problem: neither brother wanted to leave Kansas City permanently, so they alternated spending three weeks living in New York. "We never saw each other and I was lucky if I passed by Henry at the airport," says Richard.

"I immediately placed an ad in *The New York Times* and was able to hire enough people to work in all seven offices," Henry adds. "Unfortunately, when January 2 rolled around, not one person showed up for work. I had made the mistake of hiring them too early and apparently they had all found other jobs.

"Luckily, on January 2, business was slow, and I was afforded the time to place more ads. When I found enough new people, I set up a school in the store and taught them what to do. I believed that good tax preparers must have two important qualities: they should like to talk to people and work with figures; I would teach them the rest."

The first year in New York was very successful. "We had built up a good business, except we were not making much profit," says Richard. "We had a budget of $65,000, and the first year we grossed $65,782.50! I will never forget that. It was a solid operation, but we were not making any money! We gave our employees all the profits we earned."

The Blochs realized that one of them was going to have to stay in New York to run the business, but neither brother volunteered to stay. "Our wives wanted to raise our children in Kansas City, so we chose to sell the business," explains Richard.

The Blochs placed an advertisement in *The New York Times* and two local accountants responded.

"Richard and I sat down to interview them," Henry explains, "and after hearing us out, they offered us $10,000 to buy our New York operations and the right to use our name.

"Do you mind if we talk it over?" I asked them, and with that, Richard and I went into the next room.

"It's worth a lot more than $10,000," my brother said.

"Yeah, but that's all the money they can afford," I replied. "If we want to sell it to these guys, we have to accept what they're offering."

"We could always run another ad and see what other offers we get."

"Yes, but that means we have to spend more money advertising, and besides, who knows if we'll even get another offer," I said.

"So what do you say we take the $10,000 and we can both go home to Kansas City," Richard suggested.

"As things turned out, it was worth a lot more than $10,000 and was one of the biggest mistakes we ever made," Richard comments.

The Blochs accepted the offer in exchange for a fee of 5 to 10 percent of the future gross revenues as ongoing royalty. In return, the Blochs agreed to provide various support services. The Bloch's didn't sell their first franchise. They had sold their existing business and gave the territory away for nothing to the qualified accountants.

"We didn't call our offices operated by others 'franchises' back then, because we had never heard of franchising! We told the accountants that we would give them New York, Connecticut, and Long Island. Today, this area is worth a fortune!" exclaims Henry. (In 1967, H & R Block bought back the New York operation for over $1 million.)

The New York business grew rapidly, and soon significant royalty payments began pouring in. The Blochs realized that selling territories was profitable, and furthermore, it allowed expansion without capital requirements. They also knew it was impossible to operate all offices personally, but they could contract with qualified local people and train them to operate H & R Block offices on a franchise basis. In turn, the opportunity to operate an H & R Block operation was a good investment for aspiring entrepreneurs because there was no inventory, a small unit of sale, no large capital requirement, and it was a business spawned by the government. What's more, over 75 percent of their customers return every year.

Henry and Richard began to seek accountants around the country who were willing to prepare income taxes under the name of H & R Block instead of their own name. The Blochs promised that they would accept royalty payments only on returns that were brought in under the H & R Block name but not on existing business. Prior to joining their company, to assist their associates, with their business, the brothers wrote a book called *The Policy and Procedure Manual*, which described to potential franchisees what was needed to know how to run an H & R Block tax preparation business successfully.

"We would put an ad in the newspaper and Dick would go to a hotel and interview people, but nobody had ever heard of the company," Henry says. "Many of the applicants were local accountants who had their own practice. They would say 'I am already too busy. I've got more tax work than I can do now, so why do I need you?' They failed to see what business we are in. They were in the business of preparing tax returns and ours is really *the business of the business of preparing tax returns*. There is a big difference. You've got to know what business you are in to be successful. In other words, we didn't want our franchisees to do the returns personally. We wanted them to own the franchise and hire and train other people to do them, which is what we did."

Richard remembers, "When I went to Denver, for example, I interviewed 30 or 40 people and I ended up with only 1. But that is all I needed. We experienced a lot of rejection because a lot of people didn't believe in us. Then, too, there were some who wanted to join us, but we didn't feel that they would do a good job."

Joining the Bloch's growing enterprise presented a no-risk situation for potential franchisees. But in spite of this, the brothers had a great deal of trouble convincing people to come aboard.

"It was a hard sell for Henry and Richard," explains Vice Chairman of the Board Jerry Grossman, who has been with the company since 1966. "We were an unknown company back then, and all they had to sell was the success story of the company-owned operations and how they were going to grow. They were very fortunate to attract several excellent entrepreneurs early on who actually helped the Blochs expand the company."

In January 1957, H & R Block opened its first offices in Columbia, Missouri, and Topeka, Kansas. The following year, offices were added in Des Moines, Iowa; Oklahoma City; and Little Rock, Arkansas.

Pat Merriman, one of the earliest franchisees, signed his franchise contract with H & R Block in 1958 and was given nine districts in metropolitan areas within Texas. "I was already in the tax business when Henry and Richard heard about me through the Chamber of Commerce in Lubbock, Texas. They got my address and wrote me a letter explaining what they did. Six weeks later, I was paid a visit by one of their company representatives who explained the Blochs' system to me and elaborated on the success they had already achieved. I decided I would try it out and see if it would work for me," he recalls. "They promised me that all my existing business would be excluded from royalty fees and I would have to share only the receipts of any new business with them."

Other accountants were also attracted to the unique structure of the H & R Block system. Ross Angel of Greensboro, North Carolina, was an accountant who joined the Blochs in 1960. "I was desperate. I was in the accounting business, and our personal returns were running out of hand. We had so many returns to prepare that it was taking up all my time, leaving none for the rest of my accounting practice," explains Angel. "So when I saw the Block ad, I thought that perhaps they had a program for doing individual tax returns that could help me run my business. I thought if I joined H & R Block I would be able to handle all the returns and the rest of my business, too. It didn't work out that way. I finally sold the accounting business."

The Blochs gave Angel several territories in North and South Carolina where Angel currently operates 73 units. "The system worked for me immediately. My first year as a franchisee, I anticipated my business to do 100 or so returns, and we did over 400! The tax preparation business was something that was needed because taxes were beginning to get more complicated."

In 1960, the Blochs decided that additional capital was needed for further expansion. They offered to the public a limited amount of their stock in the company, but it was by no means an easy task. "To go public we needed a lawyer, an underwriter, and an accountant. At the time, we were using the biggest underwriting firm, the largest law firm in Kansas City, as well as one of the Big Eight accounting firms," recalls Henry.

"We were all ready to go until one day the accountants didn't show up to audit our books. When we called them to ask why they were not here, they said 'Well, we received word from our headquarters in New York to pull off your account. They won't let us audit your books because they think you are a competitor.' They thought we were a competitor because we both did tax work."

"So our underwriter tried to engage other big eight firms, but they too turned us down. Then our lawyer decided to pull out because we didn't have a big eight accounting firm. They only wanted a first-class offering. Anyway, it all fell apart!

"We did end up going public a couple of years later, but it was a very small offering. We hired a small underwriter and a local law firm, and they put together a 'Regulation A,' which limited us to a $300,000 offering. Our advantage was that with a small offering, we were still able to keep much of the company. We kept it instead of selling it to the public.

"Keeping most of the company for ourselves turned out to be a great thing for us, because soon after, the business grew enormously!" Henry says with a smile.

During the early and mid-1960s, the firm expanded rapidly. By 1968, there were over 3,286 offices throughout the United States,

Canada, and Puerto Rico with an annual volume in excess of $56 million. One year later, the stock was listed on the New York Stock Exchange. By 1978, H & R Block was preparing more than one out of nine of the tax returns filed in the United States. Since then the original stock has split 120 shares for each original share and a $10,000 investment in 1962 would be worth well over $12 million today!

According to Henry, H & R Block has endured only one down year in its history. "In 1972, the same year after the company opened 1,000 new offices, Johnnie Walters, the Commissioner of the IRS, headed a tremendous publicity campaign advising the public to do their own taxes and not to seek commercial help. He told the public 'A fifth grader can do a return.' "

"This campaign was so big that elementary schools all over the country were teaching their fifth grade students how to prepare tax returns," Henry says with a frown. "Of course, the children couldn't do it adequately! Business did not increase in proportion to expenses. We ended the year with 15 percent decline in profits compared to 1971. We were still making money, but it was less than before, so our board suggested that I call on the Commissioner and tell him that we are a good company with services beneficial to both the IRS and the public."

"I went to his office and sat down with him. I said, 'Mr. Commissioner, we think we are helping you. The returns we prepare make it easier for your people to check the returns and to audit them. We think that we know as much about taxes as anybody in the country, yet you are advising the public not to do business with us. We think you are hurting us unjustifiably as well as the IRS.' "

"His response to me was, 'Mr. Bloch, you don't understand. You don't know what we are trying to do.' I thought with friends like him, who needs enemies! 'You will get by because you are legitimate.' He was right. The industry was a mess because unlike today, it was completely unregulated. Our competitors were anybody that wanted to prepare tax returns. No one had to be licensed to practice tax preparation. Anybody could prepare tax returns, even a mechanic or hotel clerk!

"The Commissioner told me that he intended to clean up the industry. 'We know your work is good, but we can't live with some of the fly-by-nights who prepare returns and disappear when their customers need them to answer questions.' The Commissioner was absolutely right because anyone could get into the tax return business back then. The Commissioner weeded out the industry, and while we were hurt, the others were killed!"

H & R Block pushed for federal regulation that provided the credibility it needed and, in the process, eliminated the competition that was giving the industry a bad name. Even so, H & R Block temporarily suffered smaller profits, and the company's stock plummeted in value. "Before 1972, because of our tremendous growth, our stock was selling at a multiple in excess of 100. In 1972, the price dropped to around $7. It took years for our stock to jump back up to where it had been before," Henry adds.

That year, the company sustained another setback. Richard was diagnosed with lung cancer and told he had only six months left to live. Determined to overcome the cancer, Richard vowed that if he did, he would retire from the company. He would dedicate the rest of his life to inspire and help others afflicted with the dreadful disease by devoting his full time to educational and support programs. After a year of radiation treatment and the removal of the top lobe of his right lung, two ribs and part of a third, as well as affected nerves in his right shoulder, Richard was deemed cured.

No longer a cancer patient, Richard was overwhelmed with joy and began his work to help others. He initiated a cancer hotline, staffed by volunteers who had suffered from cancer to help patients who had nowhere to turn. Using office space within the H & R Block corporate headquarters, the hotline was a huge success; a survey revealed that 99 percent of the callers felt satisfied with the help received when they called. As a result, similar hotlines were established across the country.

In 1982, the R. A. Bloch Cancer Management Center opened, its goal being to organize oncologists, cancer surgeons, radiologists, and numerous other specialists to review cases as a group. Together, a team of physicians suggests treatment free of charge for cancer victims unable to pay; fees run several hundred dollars for those who can afford it. The center's specialists who come from different disciplines review cases by using the patient's medical records, X rays, reports, slides, and any other available information. Thereupon, the panel recommends treatment to the patients personal physician.

In addition, Richard has built a "Survivors" park in Kansas City and plans to build others across the country to serve as an inspiration for cancer patients. Each is beautifully landscaped with sculptures and flower beds.

Now in its fourth decade, H & R Block offices are located in nearly every town, large and small, throughout the country. By 1991, there were over 8,995 offices around the globe; over half are franchised operations; the remainder are company owned. H & R Block employs approximately 2,800 people year round, while during the busy tax season, more than 45,000 are hired.

H & R Block may be one of the few franchisors that is not looking to expand its major franchise operations. "There's no more room," says Henry. "Everything has been taken. We haven't invited a major new franchisee to join the company for over 25 years. We would like to buy out our major franchise holders, but most don't want to sell. There has never been a single failure."

There is no competition between the franchisees and the company-owned operators, since each territory, which may be a city, town, or a state, is exclusively owned by either a franchisee or the company. There are two types of franchise operations: "majors" and "satellites." There are 22 major franchisees with exclusive rights generally to large metropolitan areas. The major franchisees pay up to a 15 percent royalty fee. These franchisees were the early pioneers with H & R Block.

According to Grossman, "All the major franchisees date back to the early days. Once the company was off and running, we quit franchising except in satellite areas where it didn't make sense from an operational standpoint to run a company-owned office. It would be difficult for us to run a company-owned office in a town of 15,000 in a remote area and make a profit."

Pat Merriman, one of the system's largest franchisees, owns 170 offices and subfranchises another 180. "The year I joined H & R Block, there were 39 offices around the country. So I've been with them since nearly the beginning. When the Blochs were first starting to give away territories, they had two needs to fill. First, they didn't have the personnel required to manage company-owned offices, and second, they lacked the capital to open offices. So to fill this need, they gave away franchises until they overcame the obstacles of needing people and capital. When this happened, they stopped granting the major franchises," Merriman exclaims.

The majority of the satellite franchise operations are located in small towns, some in communities with as little as a few thousand people. There are approximately 2,200 satellite franchises, described by Henry as "mom and pop" offices. Since tax season is so short, a satellite owner-manager often has an opportunity to pursue another activity that provides an additional source of income.

A satellite is subfranchised by either the company or a major franchisee depending on its territory. The company-owned satellites report directly to company owned operations, while the others report to the major franchisee. In some cases, a satellite operator may personally service the entire community's population. This personal touch may be more difficult to achieve for either the company or a major franchisee.

Generally, the satellites pay a 50 percent royalty rate for the first $5,000 in gross revenues which decreases to 30 percent thereafter. In return, the franchisor, who may be the corporate office or a major franchisee, furnishes the satellites facility with almost everything from training and tax preparation supplies to equipment.

"We also provide them with advertising," says Grossman. "And we feel our satellites get $1.10 for every dollar they pay us in royalty fees."

Satellite offices are open at least one day a week during the off-season, while the major franchises keep a few offices open year round, strategically located in each geographical area. These offices are open to answer questions on tax returns and to assist and accompany customers audited by the IRS.

In the 1970s, H & R Block expanded into retail stores around the country, and by 1990 there were 925 such outlets. H & R Block signed a contract with Sears in 1972, and today the giant Chicago-based retailer has 800 outlets in operation. The affiliation with Sears gave H & R Block more creditability, which added to its phenomenal growth. In return, Sears is able to offer its customers an additional service.

"Our stores in Sears represent some of our most terrific locations," explains Grossman. "And the endorsement by Sears is a big plus.

"We were the first independent company allowed to use its own name as a concession in Sears," Grossman points out. "As far as our reputation for integrity was concerned, this has been very valuable to us.

"Our Sears' stores are company-owned in the company-owned territories and franchised in franchise areas," Jerry adds. "In return for the use of its space, Sears receives a certain percentage of our gross sales."

One of the major reasons H & R Block has been successful for almost 40 years is because the company paid a great deal of attention to training its preparers properly. In the early days, it was easy for Richard or Henry to teach employees how to serve the client adequately and prepare tax forms. But, as the business grew, it became apparent to the brothers that the number to train had increased to hundreds, and it was not possible for them to conduct all training sessions personally.

In 1962, the Blochs established the H & R Block Income Tax School, with classrooms located all over the country. The school's tuition today is approximately $250 to $300 and covers 27 three-hour sessions, conducted over a 13-week period. The "basic course" is equivalent to an estimated two full college semesters. In addition, to keep current with changes in tax legislation, the company offers four advanced courses, each consisting of 40 to 45 hours of additional training in areas of individual, partnership, corporation, gift tax, and fiduciary returns.

Currently, approximately 100,000 students attend the training sessions each year, with thousands returning to take the advanced courses. Each year H & R Block hires approximately 40 percent of the graduates. The school is open to the public, and people can take the courses to learn how to prepare their own return, although most people take the courses to work for the company. "We don't guarantee employment, but we offer it to the best graduates," explains Henry. The company figures the more people learn about taxes, the less they're really going to want to do them on their own—and where better to take them than to the tax experts at an H & R Block office.

H & R Block depends a great deal on retired or semiretired homeworkers and part-time workers. "Such individuals are the backbone of our operations," admits Henry. "We're lucky that our business is seasonal so we can attract people with diverse backgrounds and for whom seasonal work is so appealing." H & R Block pays its tax preparers a salary against a percentage of the fees they generate. Each year, the percentage goes up—a simple device that rewards both productivity and loyalty. Retaining a large percentage of tax preparers from year to year provides each office with a pool of experienced employees from which to draw and is very attractive to customers who prefer to return to the same preparer every tax season.

The training department has written a guide to preparing income taxes which is updated and reprinted each year. The *H & R Block Income Tax Guide* is a *New York Times* best-seller, with over a quarter of a million copies sold each year. The book is an easy-to-use guide complete with tax forms, worksheets, and a tax encyclopedia with answers to most tax questions. The purchase price of approximately $9.95 is tax deductible, and H & R Block guarantees satisfaction or refunds the entire cost of the book when it is applied toward tax preparation services.

"At one time, our franchisees felt that we were cannibalizing the business with the book. We are convinced that we don't because people who will buy it to help them do their own returns are going to do their own returns regardless," Grossman tells. "There are many books like this one on the market, and we felt we might as well get our fair share of that business because we know tax preparation as well as anyone. Of course, we share the proceeds of the book with our major franchisees so the book isn't in competition with them. And we feel that the book has helped make H & R Block a household name."

As a service business, H & R Block always realized that, if it ever began taking its customers for granted, offering less than satisfactory service or discourteous treatment, word would quickly spread, and business would deteriorate. Repeat business is essential to H & R Block, which today, represents approximately 75% of its customer base. Franchisees who don't meet company standards are dropped or bought out, despite the cost to the franchisor. For example, the company spent $1 million dollars in the mid-sixties to buy out a franchisee that was operating unethically according to the Blochs' standards. This particular franchisee was raising rates the closer it got to April 15 and charging customers to accompany them to an audit. Had the Blochs let this practice continue, it could have been disastrous to the entire system.

Henry Bloch's goal is to provide consistently good service and quality to all customers. It has always been imperative to him that his employees produce high quality returns. "Customer service is paramount for our business just as it is in any service-oriented organization. Our tax preparers must be accurate and courteous. They are the representatives of our company," Henry explains.

Richard adds: "We've always had a requirement that, upon leaving a preparer's desk, a client should voluntarily say, 'Thank you. That is the best job of tax preparation I've ever had.' When that happens, there's a good chance there will be repeat business. If it doesn't happen, we haven't done a good job for him—or for ourselves."

"I believe the reason we are so good is because we have such an excellent interview process. Our preparers are trained to sit down with customers and find out what their situation is. They will un-cover everything they can about the client which aids them in doing the return and also saves the most tax money. In a nutshell, this is our whole objective," explains Henry.

No appointments are necessary for return preparation, but it is a good idea to call ahead to find out what information is needed to bring to the interview. Customers are taken on a first-come, first-served basis, but they also can make an appointment.

|One key to their terrific success is due to the way the Blocks stand behind the quality of their company's work.| The written guarantee H & R Block offers to its customers states that if an error is made on a return, the company will pay the interest and the penalty that is assessed to the customer due to the error. The second part of the guarantee is that an H & R Block representative will accompany a customer to an IRS audit at no extra charge. Needless to say, these customers are far and few between. Only 1 percent of all H & R Block customers are audited every year.

Henry and Richard not only started a tax preparation company, they also created an industry. Before H & R Block, tax preparation was a sideline business for accountants and a luxury for the few people who could afford it. H & R Block believes that its preparers are more practical for the average American than CPAs. The Block preparers are specifically trained to do returns while CPAs and accountants are not specialists in tax preparation. H & R Block's biggest competitor is not the private, large accounting firms, it is the individual who prepares his or her own return.

"Our preparers enjoy working for H & R Block so much that most of them keep coming back year after year," Henry says with pride. "Some of them find full-time jobs that are better paying during the off-season but as soon as January 1 rolls around, they quit those jobs and come back to work for us.

"We have never tried to compete with the Big Six firms for business. They don't want to prepare the average taxpayers returns, and, in fact, today they send business to us. Why would an average taxpayer want to pay high fees which can be in the hundreds of dollars range when they can come to us for the same job for around $52.00," says Henry.

"The market we want to attract is the 53 percent of the U.S. taxpayers who still prepare their own returns every year," Henry points out. "Our goal is to provide an excellent service to the millions of taxpayers who still prepare their own income tax returns.

"Our customers are paying for peace of mind. They don't want to overpay or underpay. What they fear most is that they will be audited. Our customers want to make sure that if they're in that position, they will have us behind them."

"If a customer comes into one of our offices and pays $50 for a return, and it is audited, we will go with him or her and explain to the IRS how the return was prepared," Grossman states. "Often, the IRS will pick returns to audit at random. There might be nothing in the world wrong with the return, or any information on it, but we will still accompany the customer and explain things to the government.

"We are frank to admit that a small percentage of our returns are audited, so we can afford and want to go with our customers," he adds.

A chip off the old block (no pun intended), Henry's son, Tom, has been a full-time employee of H & R Block since he was 22 years old. In 1976, fresh out of California's Claremont Men's College, Tom came aboard, beginning at the bottom of the corporate ladder.

" It was almost a nondecision," Tom proudly says. "I never seriously considered doing anything else. In the beginning, I was placed into a custom-designed training program and I worked in one of our standard tax offices as a tax preparer. Later, I taught at one of our tax schools and was responsible for ordering supplies like paper. Then, at one point, I was even involved with the internal audit department. The training program was wonderful and exposed me to all facets of the operation. It was really the only way to go."

Now the president and chief operating officer, Tom shares a successful working relationship with his father, though Tom is the first to admit that, "I think dad has been very careful in making sure that we have a very professional relationship at the office. Of course, it is sometimes a special challenge when it is a father and son relationship, and I believe we both always felt it was important for me to earn any promotion I received. Jerry Grossman has played a very important role in our working relationship because he has worked very closely with my dad for many years and I have worked closely with Jerry since the beginning. It has been rewarding to have Jerry involved as our third person in the office of the chairman."

Tom was instrumental in the recent computerization of the business and helped coordinate a program with the IRS to file returns electronically. First introduced in 1986, H & R Block has been filing tax returns electronically to the IRS ever since. "This happened only after lengthy discussions with the IRS," Tom explains. "Electronic filing, I think it is fair to say, is really a revolutionary development insofar as the tax preparation business is concerned. It started as a pilot program in three cities in the United States, and in 1990 we took it nationwide into all our offices. We didn't realize the potential and the demand for this kind of service. We learned that many taxpayers not only love big refunds, but they also love to receive them fast. Electronic filing is a tremendous stimulus for our company."

Electronic filing is a benefit to the customer because it enables the government to process the return and issue the refund within a period as brief as three weeks. "I remember there was some skepticism initially as to whether the concept could in fact work. After being so accustomed to filing returns by mail, it is understandable why some initially reacted to the idea of electronic filing almost as if it were like something out of the science fiction movie *Star Wars*. We learned that not only can a tax return be filed via telecommunications, but such a process produces advantages for taxpayers, the IRS, and tax firms as well.

"Thanks in part to the acceptance of electronic filing, I believe we are now in the position where we can justify fully computerizing all our tax offices. Automation allows us to enhance further the service we provide our clients. A computerized return is a quality product: it is accurate, and the appearance of the paper output is first rate," adds Tom.

A popular option offered in conjunction with Blocks electronic filing program is Rapid Refund—a refund anticipation loan. A loan provided by one of four banks allows customers to receive their refunds within three or four days of the filing date. To accomplish this, the participating bank collects a flat fee of about $30 from the customer. In return, the bank opens an account with the customer and advances him or her, through H & R Block, the entire expected refund amount less the bank's and Block's fees . Later, the customer repays the bank by designating it as the recipient for the refund, and the government sends via direct deposit the refund into the account. This program has been very popular with the customers, and it has been a major draw for new customers to file their returns through H & R Block. And the bank benefits because it receives a fee for the loan.

In addition to electronic filing and Rapid Refund, H & R Block has still another new service that appeals to a distinct group of taxpayers in higher income levels. Its Executive Tax Service is offered exclusively in Block's own offices around the country, separate from the rest of the H & R Block units. The service is geared toward higher-income customers who have more complex returns. ETS has experienced tremendous growth since its inception, increasing in size every year.

"With the advent of the 1986 Tax Reform Act, there were two classes of taxpayers," Henry points out. "There is the low-income taxpayer who has a relatively simple return, and there is the high-income taxpayer who has a return which is much more complex than it formerly was.

"Generally speaking, the fees a customer pays to someone to prepare his or her tax return are no longer deductible unless the miscellaneous deductions exceed 2 percent of adjusted gross income. As a result, very few people can deduct their income tax preparation cost, and the fee must be paid with after-tax dollars. A Big Six accounting firm may charge up to several thousand dollars for their services, while our Executive Tax Service does as good a job for an average of $102."

Approaching its fifth decade, H & R Block's variety of services has continued to be very successful as a direct result of the millions of dollars the company spends each year. Its annual advertising budget is in excess of $10 million, and for the past 20 years, Henry has served as the key spokesperson for the company. Through this exposure and repeated appearances, the founder has become a national celebrity while making H & R Block a household name.

"One of our early advertising people came up with the idea that we should have a theme of 17, 27, or 37 reasons why a customer should go to H & R Block," Grossman explains. "It ended up being

17 reasons. They said we needed a spokesperson who would represent the company. One of the advertising people turned around and said, 'Why, we've got the guy right here—Henry. He ought to do the commercials!' That is how it happened. The commercials were not originally designed for Henry to be the spokesperson. His first words were: 'I don't think I would be very good at that.' The advertising people told him that he would be perfect for the task."

Henry explains that the reason why he agreed to represent the company is because he was convinced it would be best for the company. "A marketing consultant from Harvard told us that I should do the commercials because we were selling a personal service and it is better to use the person whose name is on the door than an outsider. So I was drafted."

H & R Block has traditionally used local spot TV advertising in lieu of national network TV advertising. In this way, its commercials are fed directly to local television stations for airing. "Our commercials stress quality tax preparation, peace of mind, and our ability to help taxpayers get the biggest refund they're entitled to," emphasizes Tom.

"Many people still think that we are local," Richard explains. "In the beginning, no one had any idea we were anywhere but local and that was the impression we wanted to give. Even with television advertising running in most major markets, people still think that we live in their hometowns of Milwaukee or Sacramento. They think we are a local operation. That is why I think Henry's advertisements are so effective."

Henry Bloch has the sincerity that the public wants to see. "Henry is no made up thing. He is exactly the same in person as he is in the commercials. He is not an egomaniac and has never lost sight of where he comes from. His affluence has not changed him at all," says Grossman.

Franchisee Merriman believes that Henry Bloch "is the grandfather you would always like to have. He has been a fabulous spokesperson for the company. I am really appreciative of Henry for donating his time for this purpose. Eventually, I hope that Tom will be a spokesperson for us. He's handsome and wholesome and comes across as effectively as his dad."

Richard explains that the commercials adequately reveal the company's principles. "Our principles are pretty straightforward. I really believe that we do the finest possible work, we charge fairly, and we stand behind our work. And believe me, these principles are just as important and true today to our customers as they were 30 years ago.

"H & R Block is a fabulous business that has helped millions and millions of people. I am very proud of it. It is a business that has allowed me to hold my head up high, and whenever I walked down the street, I knew whenever somebody said, 'I know you. You did my income tax return,' it was a compliment. I am proud of the business we helped build."

In addition to advertising, another reason why H & R Block has been able to maintain a high level of success is the result of a positive and close relationship it has developed with its franchisees. In the beginning, Henry and Richard communicated with their franchisees on a daily basis, and as a team, the two brothers developed the road map for their company. According to Henry, many of the improvements to the system came about through suggestions made by the franchisees.

Grossman admits, "Communication is the name of the game in franchising. In 1974, we initiated a franchise council with two representatives of our major franchisees who came to Kansas City and met with our operating committee. Through this direct contact, the franchisees were able to have input and be a part of our management team. In 1980, we initiated a council for the satellites and selected representatives from all of our smaller operations. We got this idea from Elmer Winter, founder of Manpower temporary services, who was a leader of the International Franchise Association. I attended an International Franchise Association meeting when Winter gave a speech which extolled the advantages of having a franchisee council. He said, 'Those of you franchisors who have not yet established a franchisee council will someday have one, but it will probably be initiated by your franchisees and it won't be so friendly.' We decided that we wanted to maintain a positive relationship with the franchisees, so we immediately organized and supported a council for them. We want to be sure our franchisees are informed at all times of what is going on with the company," says Jerry.

In addition to the H & R Block Major Franchise Association's annual national convention, several meetings during the year are held at the corporate office in Kansas City. Franchisee Pat Merriman, the current president, explains, "Basically, our association discusses operational and future plans. Management participates and reviews events that have occurred during the previous tax year and what is anticipated in the future. We have a positive relationship with the corporate office, and, above all else, they listen to us.

"I have been with H & R Block for so many years that I don't even consider myself as a franchisee. I participate fully with the company in all national and local meetings that the company holds. They give me as much of a voice as most of their corporate employees. They invite me to be present when decisions are made on a national level, which is much better than reading about them in a newsletter, and if I have any qualms about a decision, I want them to be known immediately rather than trying to change something after the fact.

"I have had a very positive experience with H & R Block throughout my career, and when I say 'we,' I am talking about the national company, not only my organization," exclaims Merriman. "The company and I have grown up together. I was 24 years old when I joined H & R Block, and over 32 years later, I am still a part of the team. H & R Block has brought me more success than I ever dreamed was possible. What I am and what I have today is directly attributable to my affiliation with the company. I love what I do, the people with whom I work, and serving the general public. My goal is to be with them for 50 years!"

Since its modest beginning in 1955, H & R Block has enjoyed unprecedented growth. It is highly probable that its future will continue to be fruitful, and similarly, franchisees like Pat Merriman will continue to prosper. After all, our voluntary tax system is here to stay. Henry chooses a quote from Ben Franklin to describe the security that his business has in its marketplace: "Nothing is certain except death and taxes."

Chapter 2

CENTURY 21 INTERNATIONAL

Franchising the Real Estate Industry

Signing up the first CENTURY 21 franchisees may have been the most difficult sales job of all time. The company's founder, Art Bartlett, vividly recalls those early days back in 1971: "You can just imagine the reaction we got when we'd ask a real estate broker for $500 to become a franchisee of CENTURY 21. The prospect would look at us like we were crazy and say, 'Now, let me get this straight. I've been in the business for 30 years, and this business belonged to my father before me. We're known throughout the entire community. And what you want me to do is this: You want me to take my name off the sign and put up your brand-new name that's unknown, and you want me to pay you $500 to do that. And, you want me to pay you 6 percent on my gross revenue for the rest of my life. You know, Art, you've been out to a long lunch!' "

In what seemed like an impossible task, Bartlett and his partner Marshall Fischer did convince real estate brokers to sign up, and in doing so, CENTURY 21 became the largest real estate franchisor in the world. In 1990, CENTURY 21 brokers and sales associates assisted over 800,000 families in buying or selling properties, translating into an estimated $80 billion in real estate sold worldwide and approximately $2.2 billion in commissions.

No other real estate network in the world handles more real estate transactions, has more offices or more sales associates, or is represented in more cities and communities. Independent research has also shown that the CENTURY 21 name continues to be the most recognizable and most preferred name in real estate.

Extraordinarily, this incredible growth occurred within a relatively short period. The success of CENTURY 21 has convinced many disciples of the franchising industry to name Bartlett as the Father of Conversion Franchising.

Bartlett began his sales career with the Campbell Soup Company in 1955. Five years later, he entered the real estate industry as a salesperson for the Forest E. Olsen Real Estate Company in Southern California and later was promoted to district manager. In 1965, with three partners he founded Four Star Realty in Santa Ana, California. While still a partner with Four Star, he formed Comps., Inc., a publishing company that provided computerized sales and building statistics for the real estate industry.

The idea behind CENTURY 21 was born during a meal at a fast-food restaurant in Orange County, California, back in 1971, when Bartlett and another real estate broker, Marshall Fischer, discussed plans to develop a franchised real estate company. Between the two brokers, they had pulled together $8,000 in investment capital which they planned to use to start their enterprise.

The first step in developing the business was signing up brokers as franchisees. Bartlett knew many brokers from his previous business, Comps, Inc., but he confesses that it was even more difficult to sell the CENTURY 21 concept to his friends and acquaintances than to strangers. "Without a doubt," he grins, "those guys were the toughest for me to sell. I couldn't sell anybody whom I knew well.

They just thought it was a dream. They'd say, 'You already have a nice thing going, Art. Why don't you stick to it?' We never sold anybody on the first call. It was impossible! When we first started selling CENTURY 21 franchises, we were selling nothing more than a dream. We were selling what we were going to do!"

During the first year, the fledgling company began to fly. Although there was a negative cash flow, 100 brokers became affiliated with CENTURY 21. "We were still operating off our loans," Art reveals. "I had a very good relationship with my banker from my past business experiences. Originally we had to put only an $8,000 investment into this business, with no personal signature required. We started with a $25,000 line of credit, and by the end of the first year we had built it up to a million-dollar line of credit. And, although we weren't generating any operating profits, we were making progress, with new offices coming in every day. Within the first 90 days of operation, we developed our regional concept and divided the country up into regions.

"When Art first started, he was selling a dream," recalls Richard Loughlin, an original master franchisee who is now the chief executive officer of CENTURY 21 International. "He approached brokers and said, 'You are going to pay us on an ongoing rate of 6 percent of your profits, and in turn we will bring to you a big powerful image—advertising and marketing know-how that you need to be successful. We are going to be able to draw sales associates to your office that you could never draw before because they want that power of marketing.' This was a very difficult sale. He had to convince brokers to sign a five- to ten-year contract with nothing more than the hope that various services of CENTURY 21 would be worth the money.

"Art's first goal was to sell franchises, it was not to back it up with a lot of maintenance and service programs," Loughlin continues. "Art wanted to get the numbers out there, so that we would have an awareness factor by the public and later do mass marketing and advertising. Art looked for quality people in every region who had superb vision. Every master franchisee, called a regional director, was selected because he was well known in the real estate industry in his community, so when he went out and told the CENTURY 21 story, he had credibility. It was because of these strong regional directors that this company had its tremendous growth and was able to sell the dream of market dominance. The CENTURY 21 story is one in which a dream turned into reality."

Bartlett asserts that his company's decentralized system was a major factor in determining its record growth. "Our concept was to bring into the company smart business people who had an entrepreneurial desire. Franchisees are the kind of individuals who are willing to work around the clock," Bartlett states. "We recruited top real estate brokers in a given area, and when we sold them the regions, they gave up their real estate business to work with us. Some of them kept their businesses and delegated the managerial responsibilities.

"But it was a traumatic thing for a broker to become part of the CENTURY 21 system," Bartlett adds. "Most of our franchisees were already very successful brokers when they joined us, and, in general, real estate is a very entrepreneurial business. It was a major change for an individual to take his name off a sign in front of his establishment and replace it with ours. I'm sure most of our franchisees had a lot of trepidation when they first came aboard."

Loughlin agrees and believes the CENTURY 21 franchisees realized that the real estate business was changing and their future as an independent operation was limited. "But this doesn't mean the franchisees were happy about it. Still, it was a traumatic thing for franchisees to convert, and it generally took them six months to a year to get the feel of CENTURY 21. At this point, the franchisees understand that they are still an entrepreneur, running their own business. We have proved to the franchisees that we don't constantly interfere with their operation. Since the beginning, the vast majority of our brokers has been absolutely thrilled with the CENTURY 21 system.

"Art knew that the biggest problem in the real estate industry was the broker's inability to recruit and keep top agents," Loughlin tells. "So, in the beginning, he offered franchisees recruiting programs where the corporate office ran full-page ads in newspapers, did the interviews, and hired the agents. Then, the corporate office trained the agents and finally relocated them to one of the franchisee's offices. At the same time, CENTURY 21 was also running a licensing training program for our brokers.

"We emphasized that the real estate business is changing," Bartlett proclaims, "and that the small independent broker is going to disappear. He isn't going to be around. Of course, we knew that back in 1971, although the country as a whole was not aware of it. But we knew it. Many regional firms were getting bigger and bigger, and with companies like Merrill Lynch in the business, there was a great need for independent brokers to band together. There was a tremendous need for the services a franchise company could offer the independent broker. We fulfilled that need."

Bob Hutchinson, executive vice president of regional services since 1990, is a 13-year veteran of the CENTURY 21 system. Hutchinson recalls how difficult it was for Bartlett to sell the franchises. "Many people were joining the system while others were laughing at them for doing so. 'Why would you do that? Why would you make your name only this big and this CENTURY 21 name is so large, above your own? It will never last.' "

Loughlin agrees that franchising in the real estate industry was not an easy task for Bartlett in the early days, and it is still not easy now. "We have to convince people that they are going to have greater productivity by converting—affiliating with us and using our name, system, tools, services, and training than they could manage on their own. We told them: 'We would like you to adopt the CENTURY 21 franchise system. To do so, you must change your business cards, your office sign, your letterhead and stationery, and your yard signs. Plus, you must pay us 6 percent on top of that!' We had to prove to them that we offered real value.

"I think the timing in the early 1970s was perfect for Art because many of the local chains and large regional operators were getting larger, while the medium-sized offices were having a difficult time competing to attract sales associates," Loughlin tells. "In addition, one of the keys to success in the real estate industry is having strong marketing power and having a company name that is presold to the public, creating consumer preference. It made a lot of sense to those independents who were competing with giants in their particular marketplace to want the collective power of a name that was becoming a household word. They didn't want to have to go out and explain, 'I am Joe Smith with ABC Realty on the corner of 4th and Main St. Have you ever heard of us?'

"Most of the smaller to medium-sized offices were unable to offer good training programs," the CEO continues. "An office that had 10 to 15 sales associates usually doesn't have enough capital to support a full-time trainer while some of the larger operations could. Each region hires its own trainers who can train the sales associates in 8 to 12 offices in sales and marketing. So really what happened was, as a group, with CENTURY 21, the franchisees were collectively able to take advantage of what the larger firms were doing."

Loughlin and Bartlett met a number of years before CENTURY 21 was founded. "I was impressed with Art's leadership and his vision. When he started his company, I was familiar with a few of his regional directors, and I was impressed with the caliber of those people. Art had an ideal strategy for building a trademark through the United States at this time. It was something that I knew had great chances of being successful," Loughlin tells.

The track record of CENTURY 21 brokers has been outstanding since the beginning. "Our average office grew dramatically," Bartlett stresses. "The very few who chose to leave the CENTURY 21 system were those who didn't follow the system. They wouldn't use our program and weren't geared for growth."

Generally, there is one reason why such a young company can expand so dramatically in such a short period of time: *CENTURY 21 had a concept that worked!* "The whole concept of CENTURY 21 was based on Art and Marsh's belief of where the real estate industry was at that time and what they thought would work," recalls CEO Loughlin. "Their concept was an idea whose time had come. They chose to franchise real estate offices through a regional concept, which had never been done before in real estate. They divided the country up into geographic regions, called 'master franchises'—serviced by individuals who had entrepreneurial skills and real estate backgrounds.

"The contract gave each region the licensing rights to sell franchises to individual real estate brokers throughout its territory," explains the CEO. "The CENTURY 21 system was successful because it was strategically organized into independently owned regions throughout the country. Art sold regions to individual entrepreneurs, who in turn sold franchisees to local brokers. This gave the company the opportunity to expand quickly and made the entire system responsive to the needs of the franchisee."

Bartlett's belief was that all regions and franchisees should be independently owned. Originally, each one of the domestic regions with the exception of Orange County was sold to investors around the country. This generated a substantial amount of capital for the corporate office and energized the system with strong, diversified leadership. Orange County served as a model region, where new systems were tested before being implemented around the country. In 1976-77, the company changed its strategy and decided to acquire these regions after they were developed and were financially successful entities. By the late 1970s, CENTURY 21 began purchasing back the regions and now owns and operates 13 of the 21 regions in the United States. "We are still in the process of trying to repurchase as many domestic regions as we can," acknowledges Loughlin.

Both the company-owned and the privately held regions operate autonomously from the corporate office. The company's objective is to provide services and support to the regions. "The fact that they own some of the regions is an investment reality, it is not an operational reality," comments Bob Hutchinson.

Yet, to this day, CENTURY 21 has never owned a franchise. "We have never competed with our franchisees. We want to maintain a strictly franchisor-franchisee relationship with no conflicts of interest," adds the CEO.

Richard Loughlin, along with two partners, purchased the Northern California region, the sixth master franchise sold in the system, for $30,000 in 1973. After a year and a half in the business, the region was operating at a profitable level, and it continued to grow until it became one of the largest and most successful territories in the entire CENTURY 21 system. Loughlin served as president of the independent corporation and regional director until 1978, when the partners decided it was an appropriate time to sell the region back to the company, which made an offer of several million dollars. Loughlin stayed on and served as regional director until his appointment in 1981 as president and chief executive officer of CENTURY 21.

Loughlin explains, "While the first few regions sold for $500, just two years later, we bought our region for $30,000, and the last domestic region in the system sold for approximately $250,000! Each time Art went out to sell a region, it was worth more money because he had a proven track record of the success enjoyed by the established regions. This enabled Art to attract stronger people who had access to more capital to use to develop regions. Now, CENTURY 21 is in the process of buying back the regions, whose values have skyrocketed—going as high as $20 to $30 million each! The regional owners were largely responsible for the success of the system, and in return, CENTURY 21 has made these master franchisees very wealthy."

The CENTURY 21 operational network consists of 21 domestic and 7 international regions.

The company-owned regions are operated as separate corporations from International. Many of the regional managers who operate the company-owned regions were the original owners. The company-owned regions continue to operate as they did when they were privately owned. "We give them a lot of autonomy because we believe that is the best way to build the asset and be responsive to local marketing conditions," explains Loughlin.

"Each CENTURY 21 region has a staff of 40 to 60 employees whose function is to counsel its franchisees, improve their marketing power, train their sales associates, and help them develop a good business plan to operate in a profitable and productive manner. Every customer region is alerted on every dissatisfied customer by surveys, so they can try to rectify the situation and help the franchisee eliminate the problem," explains Loughlin.

While the regions were invaluable in developing the CENTURY 21 worldwide network, the lifeblood of the system was and continues to be the franchisees—independently owned and operated offices. The franchisees are able to retain their independence while benefiting from the CENTURY 21 national image, extensive sales, management and training programs, referral networks, and access to ancillary services. In addition, broker-to-broker referrals continue to be one of the hallmarks of the CENTURY 21 system. In an increasingly mobile society, the referral opportunities available to CENTURY 21 brokers and sales associates are a lucrative income source. And, with over 6,000 offices worldwide, referral capabilities are a valuable benefit to buyers and sellers.

Today, CENTURY 21 regions search for franchisees in much the same way as did Art Bartlett in the 1970s. According to CEO Loughlin, "Each region looks at numerous brokerage operations and decides which ones would be most appropriate for our system. The regional representatives approach the brokers and offer them the opportunity to convert to our system with the hope that these brokers see value in our service, agree with our strategies, and are willing to take down their own sign and replace it with the CENTURY 21 name.

"The preponderance of our franchisees today are coming into our system as conversion franchisees," Loughlin continues. "Periodically we have what we call a 'start-up.' This is somebody who is a manager of an existing brokerage operation and has the experience, and what we believe to be the knowledge, commitment, and management ability, to handle a franchise. We may even allow the person the opportunity to start a franchise from scratch if we think he or she is well qualified, but only on rare occasions."

Because of Loughlin's experience as a master franchisor, he can relate to the regions. "I have an empathy for how regions operate, what their priorities are, and I think I was close enough to the franchisees at that level to understand them, too. We continue to use a tremendous amount of task forces consisting of appointed franchisees, sales associates, and regional directors who assist in developing programs.

"Our regions meet on an ongoing basis with all of their franchisees. They have what are called broker councils, and they meet regularly with the regional director and his staff. They sit down and talk to the franchisees about what is needed in that local marketplace, what they should be doing in advertising, in training, in marketing, and in developing new systems. They review what is happening with the competition and where our system can be better and stronger. They get this continual dialogue going. We meet with our regional directors three times a year. It is a top-bottom, bottom-top type of communication that continually shapes and reshapes our services and activities," adds Loughlin.

The CENTURY 21 network is divided into 28 U.S. and foreign regions. Each region is responsible for attracting successful real estate brokers to join the CENTURY 21 system as franchisees. Additionally, these regions are primary providers of franchisee services.

"The regional concept has cemented the team spirit that has made us successful," says Loughlin. "Franchisees look at their regions and corporate as teammates. We don't operate by directives. Instead, we try to lead by valuing quality, knowledge, and honesty and being responsive to our franchisee's needs."

The CENTURY 21 system that was started July 28, 1971, was the industry leader in fewer than five years. On October 11, 1977, the company went public to generate more capital for expansion. Seven years after Alex Bartlett and Marshall Fischer's lunch, on October 31, 1979, TransWorld Corporation acquired CENTURY 21 for $93 million. TransWorld owned CENTURY 21 for seven years, at which point, according to Loughlin, TransWorld decided that it wanted to change its strategy.

"When TransWorld chose to change their strategy in 1985, they decided that they wanted to stay primarily in the food, vending, and retail business. So they sold us to MetLife. It was a very comfortable sale. We knew all along that they were going to sell us, and fortunately they involved me in the interviewing process. I met with dozens of the 83 potential buyers.

"TransWorld took secret bids, and said that they wanted nothing less than $200 million for our company," recollects Loughlin.

"When Metropolitan purchased us in October 1985, for $251,200,000 in a closed-bid process, the second closest bidder was at $251,000,000. The other firm missed it by $200,000! That is quite a growth rate, from a few thousand dollars to start the company in 1971 to $90-plus million in 1978 to a $251.2 million sale 14 years later."

MetLife is one of the world's leading insurance companies, with more than 45 million policyholders and assets under management totaling in excess of $132 billion. The MetLife family of companies includes insurance, real estate, mortgage, investment, and other service companies offering an array of financial services.

"Our organization, being a system of over 6,000 franchisees around the world, provides MetLife with a great distribution network for its products and services," admits Loughlin. "When we sell a home, often the buyer needs homeowner's insurance and other ancillary services, and in turn, insurance clients need to purchase real estate from time to time."

In 1990, CENTURY 21 Insurance Services merged into MetLife Personal Insurance to streamline operations and begin the expansion of the customer base for both organizations across the United States. Participating in CENTURY 21 franchises may now offer a full range of insurance products to their clients. Franchisees can earn insurance commissions for writing an insurance policy or performing certain field underwriting prior to the policy's issuance.

Currently, there are over 5,000 offices in the United States. The company's success in the United States has been translated to a number of foreign markets and is now the only U.S. based real estate brokerage with a substantial overseas presence. There are over 300 offices in Canada and nearly 100 in Mexico. As are the U.S., Canadian, and Mexican offices, each overseas CENTURY 21 franchise is independently owned and operated.

One year after its overseas drive started in 1987, 100 franchisees were sold in suburban Paris and 35 in the United Kingdom. Despite the differences in language and operating styles, the CENTURY 21 system travels remarkably well. There are 275 offices in Japan and 150 in Australia and New Zealand (combined region).

The concept has been exported with excellent results. In 1975, the Canadian region was opened, the first of the international ventures. Then, in 1983, CENTURY 21 moved into Japan and, in 1987, into the United Kingdom and France. At present, CENTURY 21 is operating in ten countries around the world.

Richard Spencer, vice president of international expansion, explains that the company looks at several conditions before expanding into a foreign country. "We look for countries that have economic viability and a real estate culture that can accept an organization like ours. Our expansion plans are to try to open up one country each year to 18 months. In searching for international subfranchisees or regions, we look for people or corporations of quality, who have an entrepreneurial spirit and real estate experience in their country, and who have a business mind.

"Our plan for going into international expansion was to sell regions to people already involved in the real estate industry. In addition, we are always looking for a corporation or an individual who also understands the local culture. We are not interested in owning regions outside the United States, even though we find ourselves owning two international regions," explains Richard Spencer.

The relationships between the corporate office and the regions and franchisees are strong. When a new region opens, support staff from corporate headquarters remains on site for an extended period of consultation. Afterward, there is a series of meetings—between master franchisees and corporate personnel; master franchisees and franchisees; and twice a year, corporate personnel and elected representatives of franchisees. These meetings are designed to keep lines of communication open.

CENTURY 21 has the unique experience of being a franchisor to its parent company, MetLife. Spencer recalls what led to the purchase of a region by MetLife: "MetLife bought an insurance corporation headquartered in London. They told us they were also interested in developing CENTURY 21 in the United Kingdom. When we told MetLife we would send over a representative to find someone who might be interested in buying the master franchise, they told us 'Why would you want to sell it? You are buying back regions in the U.S., so why not just own it?' We responded by explaining that we don't operate the same way internationally. We look for an entrepreneur who has to go into his or her own pocket or a major corporation to put up the money and the energy to develop the business.

"But MetLife thought it would be better to own it and hire people. Since that was not our design, and we weren't interested in owning it, they said okay, we will buy it! So our parent company bought the United Kingdom from us," explains Spencer.

CENTURY 21 has had one international venture that was not successful. Spencer recalls the sale of the master franchise for Australia to a group of investors. "We sold the region to a group who had already franchised 200 offices for another real estate company. We thought we had a good group of people who were knowledgeable and capable of successfully franchising CENTURY 21. They had a strong net worth and a line of credit at the bank, and everything seemed great. But they had designs to open up everywhere at once—contrary to our recommendations, they entered Perth while opening up in Sydney, Melbourne, Brisbane, and all the other major areas—this is like covering a territory from San Francisco to New York.

"They were just so fast—they sold franchises at a tremendous rate with little infrastructure, and their expenses were outrageous," adds Spencer. "All of a sudden, the economy in Australia went downhill. Interest rates shot up to 18 and 19 percent. Some values of property went down as much as 40 percent during the time they were building. There were dozens of other real estate companies going out of business. One company that went out of business had a line of credit at the same bank as our Australian subfranchisee. All of a sudden, the bank stopped our subfranchisee's line of credit, and unfortunately, they didn't tell us until they were nearly insolvent. At the last minute, our master subfranchisors told us they ran out of funds and their real estate holdings became of less and less value. We sent our people over there to evaluate the situation and immediately tried to find a buyer for them. We ended up having to take it over ourselves, and we are currently operating it as a company-owned region.

"Eventually, we were able to build business back up. We now have 150 offices over there, and it is operating smoothly.

"We plan to manage this strategy until we have strengthened its value and we will then search for qualified buyers," explains the CEO. "Our long-term strategy is to have all international regions owned and operated by local master franchisees while we hope to own the domestic regions."

Spencer believes the international sales will one day surpass the domestic totals. "Certainly, we are never going to be in every country in the world, but I receive inquiries from people all over the world who are interested in buying a franchise. Currently, we are concentrating on South East Asia and Western Europe.

Although the real estate industry may operate differently in foreign countries, basically there is always a buyer and a seller. "How you put the two together varies from culture to culture, but inevitably someone accomplishes the task," says Spencer.

Each international region has its own advertising fund. The regions collect fees from each of their individual franchises, and they buy whichever media that works best in that particular country. They design their own strategies, and their own advertising agencies create their campaigns.

"We provide the international regions with whatever knowledge we possess on how they can help their franchisees develop better offices. What they use is basically up to them and will reflect their housing market and real estate traditions," explains Spencer. "We allow our master subfranchisors a great deal of flexibility in running their regions, and internationally, we want them to be able to accommodate their services to their culture. We are not going overseas with our system and saying, 'This is the way it is. You can't change it.' We wouldn't get very far that way, so there has to be some flexibility, but in the use of the name, the logo, and some of those other things, we are very strict. They all have clear obligations in the contract with corporate and a policy and procedure manual that they agree to abide by."

The same basic rules and regulations apply to the domestic franchisees, who also receive training and assistance in marketing from the company.

"Our job is to provide training materials, training programs, marketing programs, marketing materials, and any kind of support and guidance that will help our regions develop and sell franchises," explains Duane Mora, vice president of franchise sales, who has been servicing franchisees in the CENTURY 21 system since 1977.

Education continues to be a top priority for CENTURY 21. In 1990, the company introduced a Quality Service Course. This course, offered to brokers and sales associates, teaches quality service skills. Also introduced in 1990 was the Personal Career Management Course, created for experienced sales associates. This course focuses on image, personal marketing, time management, and business planning.

"We were the first real estate organization to offer training on a large scale. From the beginning, we stressed quality of service and ethics, the foundation of what we believed professionalizes the business. We also taught thousands of agents the principles of fair dealing and that the concept of quality service brings income," says CEO Laughlin.

"If you provide good quality service and fulfill a person's real estate needs, you automatically have a strong income flow," the CEO adds. "We taught this to tens of thousands of agents across the country. We were the pioneers in this area, and it benefited the entire industry by elevating the standards of quality service.

"We also pushed our brokers to offer a better, more complete and competitive service," Loughlin reveals. "The real estate business down the street had to compete with us because our market share started to grow. To compete with us, it had to attract sales associates by offering the same types of programs as ours. I believe we instituted an escalation of the quality of training and expectations of the agents. We set this standard," exclaims the CEO.

Bob Hutchinson, executive vice president of regional services at international headquarters, began his career in real estate in Flint, Michigan, where he was an executive vice president of the board of realtors. Later, he began his CENTURY 21 career as the regional director for the state. After four years, Hutchinson relocated to New England where he served as president and regional director until 1990.

Hutchinson claims that CENTURY 21 was the first in the industry to provide these valuable ancillary services to brokers on a broader scale and that this is what attracted many potential franchisees. "Independents who heard about CENTURY 21 were willing to spend money to continue operating their business, but under our name because there was a real feeling that it would provide them with an advantage. We are selling them the opportunity to be a small business and also a part of a large organization. As a franchisee, they could make an impact in the marketplace with terrific advertising and promotion just like the larger real estate operations in town."

CEO Loughlin believes that the company would not be the success it is today if it were not for the superb training that it has provided to its franchisees. "However, there is another issue in the real estate business that has been advantageous to us, and this is the fact that brokers are natural joiners," Loughlin explains. "They belong to multiple listing services and real estate boards so they realize the power of numbers and advantages of trade associations. Accordingly, when we came to them with our concepts, they comprehended quickly the concepts of 'strength in numbers' and the 'value of association.' You don't find that in many other industries. With this in mind, our philosophy, numbers, and synergy made sense to them."

CENTURY 21 also brought realtors the recognition and support that weren't yet prevalent in the real estate industry. The company offered training and monthly sales rallies that were well received by the real estate community. "People in the industry enjoy achievement and recognition," tells Hutchinson. "Our agents want to provide the best possible service, and they want to do their best. They also want to make as many sales as they can while helping families find the right situation. And they want to be properly recognized for their accomplishments. On the one hand, CENTURY 21 provided the training; on the other, we also provided the environment to recognize them."

Another tangible benefit to being a part of the CENTURY 21 system is the collective buying power the franchisees have when purchasing supplies. The company has approved suppliers who offer brochures, business cards, stationery and "For Sale" signs at considerable savings.

Contrary to many other franchising operations, CENTURY 21 has no interest in these suppliers and accepts no fees for what is sold by vendors to its organization. The company assists in the negotiation and requires that the prices remain competitive because products are being manufactured in mass quantities. The firm also provides franchisees with a legal and research department as well as an information system that performs research, surveys, and analyses. The information system calculates numbers and statistics, which assists the marketing department with the quality service program.

One requirement for owning a franchise is that of participating in the day-to-day business of the operation. "The broker who thinks he is buying a franchise, is going to put up a sign and send his people to training, but is not trying to grow and build the business is going to fail," says Duane Mora, vice president of franchise sales support. "I don't care what franchise he or she has or what business he or she is in; it doesn't work if there's no commitment and follow-through."

In addition, the franchisee must maintain the standards set by international, and this responsibility rests on the region that monitors the franchise's methods of operation. Strict guidelines spell out how the franchise may use the CENTURY 21 trademark and logo, but according to Mora, "We allow the franchisees to operate autonomously. We offer the franchisees as little or as much service as they want. Primarily, the only two areas that we strongly enforce is the use of the logo and that assurance that the franchisee is operating an ethical business. We expect the franchisees to be honest and deliver a high level of service."

Perhaps the most recognizable symbol of CENTURY 21 is the gold jacket worn by its thousands of brokers and sales agents around the world. But, according to Executive Vice President Hutchinson, as the 1990s approached, it became clearer that CENTURY 21 needed to take a hard look at its longtime symbol. "We found out from a study that some of our identifiers were outdated," he confesses. "We are a company that started in the early 1970s when earth tones were very popular. Since our beginning, brown had been one of our basic colors, until 1991 when at our convention, we unveiled our new colors—which are now black with white and gold. We changed our identifiers—our logo, colors, and career apparel. This change should come as no surprise to CENTURY 21 followers. The company, in spite of its enormous size, has always been very quick to adapt."

To join the CENTURY 21 franchise system, a broker must pay his or her regional office an initial fee that provides the broker with the right to operate as a company franchisee. "We allow the regional director or regional owner to decide the fee when selling a franchise in his or her region," states Vice President Duane Mora. This fee varies around the country depending on the location and is likely to be more expensive in a more mature region.

"Our objective is not to make money on the initial franchise fee," he continues. "Our objective is to bring them in, to be a part of the system; the money is made jointly as that organization begins to grow and pay royalties (service fees). This is how the regions and international make money—on the long-term affiliation and the royalty fees that are paid." The franchise start-up costs range between $14,999 and $30,000.

The franchisees also pay 6 percent of their monthly gross closing commissions to the region, and each domestic region contributes 15 percent of what it receives in start-up fees and royalty payments to International. These payments pay for the operating system, the ongoing support, and training the franchisees receive from the company. This is the only domestic source of earnings of the company. Outside of the United States, regions pay an additional 10 percent service fee to cover the cost of translation, and language changes of the various programs that are offered. The domestic regions contribute 10 percent of their earnings to the National Advertising Fund each month, which in 1990 had receipts of approximately $40 million. The company's powerful national and local advertising and marketing programs have led to a name recognition rate of 91 percent, nearly twice that of its nearest competitor. Loughlin credits founder Bartlett for initiating the successful advertising campaign: "One of the greatest accomplishments that Art achieved was to go back to all the regions in 1976 and convince them to rewrite their existing contracts with their franchises to provide what we call the National Advertising Fund.

"Early on, the vision wasn't there to realize that we might have the numbers to enable us to go on television," tells Loughlin. "Art knew that we could have mass marketing and advertising in local newspapers by collectively bringing our people together. In the mid-1970s, Art and Marsh announced that regions had enough numbers across the country to collect a portion of the franchisees' income toward advertising. Then they visited each of the regions around the country and spoke to the franchisees at meetings to convince them to amend their contracts and pay an additional 2 percent for advertising.

"This was not an easy task," admits the CEO. "When the contracts came up for renewal, 80-85 percent of the franchisees voluntarily accepted the additional payment rate, but the balance had to be convinced of the benefits. This was an incredible sales job that had a lot to do with the growth of this company. From that point on, we were able to support advertising on a national network basis. Our awareness and our image took an immediate and dramatic jump. By the late 1970s, we had an 85-percent-plus awareness factor throughout the United States."

Since then, CENTURY 21 advertising has been extraordinarily successful. "We have two messages to get across," says Bruce Oseland, senior vice president of marketing and advertising. "The first is that CENTURY 21 is number one; the second is that the CENTURY 21 agent is a person whom the consumer knows—someone from his or her hometown." Because the message is conveyed so successfully, brokers contribute each month for this strong national ad support.

Additionally, a substantial portion of the advertising budget is spent to help brokers recruit sales associates. "In fact," Oseland adds, "this might be the most important thing we do." Hiring and retaining good salespeople is a major objective of CENTURY 21.

The strong sales force of CENTURY 21 is the envy of the real estate industry. When compared with other real estate franchisers, Mora points out that while CENTURY 21 is a full-service real estate firm, Remax, the Denver-based firm, is a example of a competitor that offers limited services to its sales associates.

"ReMax's focus is different from ours, because we operate as a conventional real estate business and our agents' commission splits range from half to 60/40 and 70/30 percent. ReMax hires sales associates and pays them 100 percent of the commissions, but the sales associate must pay the office a fee for working there each month. The fee ranges from $800 to $2,000 a month. Sales associates rent a desk and receive very little service or assistance. The ReMax agents must pay for their own secretarial support, advertising, phone bills, and so on. The type of agent who works at a ReMax office is someone who has been in business for a period of time.

"We have lost some sales associates to ReMax, but people do return to us," Mora adds. "The ReMax concept is one that has a lot of high-powered agents competing within an office. We believe that this strategy creates a cut-throat climate that turns off a lot of agents. At CENTURY 21, we created a more supportive network within the office, which inspires teamwork."

Mora believes the real estate business has changed dramatically since 1971. "The competition has become tougher," he points out. "The things we pioneered have been copied by other people. When they said they wanted to design a better mousetrap, they said 'Let's see what CENTURY 21 has done and copy their strengths' or 'Let's see where CENTURY 21 is weak.' We have a lot of national competitors; however, our primary competitor in most marketplaces, is the very strong, large independently owned operator, not the big national chain. The large independents who have a recognized name and a stable base of past clients, and are active in their communities maintain a strong market presence."

Bob Thomas, regional director for the company-owned CENTURY 21 of the Pacific concurs: "Our competition literally takes place at the neighborhood where the homeowner is selling a house. A typical homeowner in my Southern California territory will interview 6 to 12 agents before making a selection about whom will list his or her property.

"We have an edge over our competition because we have established the market position as number one," notes Thomas, "and our product is better known and more widely accepted than any other in the marketplace."

The company conducted a study that concluded that in many different areas CENTURY 21 consistently had a 5-to-1 preference ratio over those of other national organizations. "People recognize that CENTURY 21 provides superior training and quality service," points out Hutchinson. "We have done a good job both in our marketing and in delivering what we have said over the years."

Loughlin believes one factor that contributes to the success of the CENTURY 21 franchisees is their involvement in their communities. "Many of our franchisees are active with the National Easter Seals Society—CENTURY 21 is one of the top corporate contributors to the organization—and many serve on the local Easter Seals board of directors. Our franchisees are involved in all sorts of fundraising events.

"We have successfully encouraged our people to be active in their local real estate boards, state associations, the National Association of Realtors, government, and any service organization that has worthy objectives and goals," Loughlin notes.

Another contributing factor to the success of the CENTURY 21 franchise system is the array of services each office provides to its customers. According to the CEO, "Because there is a natural tie between financial services and the real estate transaction, we are assisting our offices to offer full-service insurance—investment opportunities, property management, corporate relocation, and so on." Many of the CENTURY 21 brokers are already full-fledged agents who sell insurance along with real estate.

"We have dedicated the organization to providing the highest-quality and most professional service in the real estate industry in the 1990s," notes Loughlin. "We will provide a level of service that establishes the benchmark in the industry, and we will continue to be the dominant company in the next century."

The CENTURY 21 mission statement reveals the company's commitment to its franchisee's success: *CENTURY 21 is an international franchisor whose goal is to enhance its leadership position by provid-*

ing high-quality services, systems, and products, through regional or-ganizations, to affiliated independent real estate brokers so that they may profitably offer a full-range of real estate and related services to their customers in the most professional manner.

Into the future, CENTURY 21 plans to emphasize customer service. "We are the biggest, and we want the customer to know that we are the absolute best," admits Loughlin. "In order to be the best, we want continually to increase our preference rate. We already have five times the preference rate of any national competitors in the United States, and we want this same rate throughout the world. We want all consumers to want to do business with our franchisees and to do it because of the quality of service and the ability that they bring to their customers.

"Consumers are becoming more sophisticated and demanding over the years," the CEO adds. "They expect a higher quality of service, and we believe that the real estate company that fulfills this demand will be the big winner in this decade and beyond. We have instituted a lot of programs that will absolutely assure us that quality service is provided by all our franchisees. We survey every buyer and seller in our system to be sure that they were satisfied. This relatively new service is unique to CENTURY 21 and is a huge undertaking by us—between 600,000 and 800,000 people are sur-veyed each year to determine if they were satisfied with their trans-action.

"We feel it is extremely important for us to find out just exactly what type of service our franchisees are providing," explains Lough-lin. "Since we don't have a product—we can't provide a recipe for a hamburger as McDonald's can—and because we are dealing with a service, we must be sure it totally satisfies the client. The results of our surveys come back to our regional directors for their review and notification as to which franchisees and sales associates are provid-ing exemplary service as well as those who are not. For those in the latter group, they will be given an opportunity to improve their level of service, or they will no longer be a part of our system. We have a clause in our contracts that the franchisees must meet certain stand-ards and comply with our *Policy and Procedure Manual*. We are in the process of establishing certain criteria that determine what is considered unacceptable levels of service, and we have the authority to terminate a franchise for this reason," says Loughlin. "This has never been done in our industry before, and it is a huge undertaking, but we believe that it is what is going to win the competitive battle."

According to Duane Mora, vice president of franchise sales support, "The company has set a ceiling on market penetration of 25 percent in a given area. We feel that this is a reasonable market share and we want to leave our brokers ample room to grow and expand.

"We would like to think that our CENTURY 21 offices are not competing with each other but they are competing collectively against the others," the vice president says. "If there are two CENTURY 21 offices in Long Beach, I don't see them as competitors but instead as joint forces to compete with the other companies that are in the same marketplace.

"We place our franchises based on population and market share," Mora continues. "Our guideline is no more than one office per 15,000 population within a region."

Mora points out that offices will often consolidate. "A franchisee who owns two or three branches many close down one or two and consolidate expenses into one location," he remarks. "We lose weak offices when the marketplace is soft, but this is indicative of the industry."

Bob Thomas, regional director for the company-owned CENTURY 21 of the Pacific, manages a large territory that includes San Diego, Orange County, most of Los Angeles County, the states of Alaska and Hawaii and the U.S. territories of Guam and Saipan. This area has 250 offices and 9,000 agents. In 1991, the Pacific Region's sales totaled $1.8 billion.

Thomas, who has been a part of the CENTURY 21 system since 1978 states: "Our real competitive advantage is our consumer awareness and preference. We are preferred by homeowners 5 to 1 over our nearest competitor.

"Brokers know that our trademark includes all these advantages as well as all the tangible operational services and support programs, both on the management side (how to build and run a real estate office as a business) and on the sales side (how to hire, train, and support agents)," Thomas adds.

International's job is to take advantage of national marketing opportunities and to create programs and services that will support regions in servicing brokers," tells Thomas.

Franchisee Gloria McGurk began her real estate career in 1974. Two years later, she opened her own agency, and in 1978, she converted her agency to the CENTURY 21 system. She now owns three CENTURY 21 offices in Richmond, Virginia, and employs 80 agents who, in 1990, had sales in excess of $75 million.

"CENTURY 21 provides a lot of opportunity for people to make good incomes without requiring college degrees or a lot of background experience in the business world," says McGurk. "The company played an important role in liberating women. If it weren't for CENTURY 21, I probably would have been a secretary. I had a lot of talents that would have never been exposed.

"My interest in real estate started with my father who dabbled in buying and selling properties. Later, I found I was always going out with friends and family members to look at houses and help them decide whether to buy them or not. I realized I could be paid for doing what I really enjoyed. So I entered the industry and made a career out of it.

"When I operated my own agency, it was very small, with only four or five agents at a time. I realized the future of the industry was with a large company with the power to market. I was well aware that we needed a bigger image to succeed.

"I looked at every franchise opportunity available at that time," McGurk recalls. "I knew that I was going to get what I paid for, and even though CENTURY 21 was a more expensive franchise, it had a lot more to offer in terms of services for brokers and agents.

"I don't believe my company would have grown much beyond five to ten agents if I hadn't converted to CENTURY 21," concedes McGurk. "I didn't have a college degree or a management background. CENTURY 21 taught me how to make management decisions. To me, this was the biggest advantage to me for joining the system.

"The national image that I now have with CENTURY 21 makes the job for my agents so much easier," she adds. "Ordinarily, when independents go to an appointment with a client, they spend the first 30 minutes trying to explain who they are and how they can help them. As part of CENTURY 21, the agent can walk in the door as a presold product. The clients know who the agent is. They see that nice, friendly person they saw on television who loves kids and dogs and sells homes. We have instant credibility."

McGurk credits the National Brokers Communication Congress (NBCC), the organization's national communications and planning group, as the backbone of communication with the corporate office. The NBCC is a body of franchisees from across the country, either elected by their peers or appointed, depending on the geographic makeup of their region. The members of the NBCC represent the franchisees' voice to the company. The NBCC has a membership that includes approximately 75 to 80 brokers who meet the international executive staff twice a year in two- to three-day sessions to discuss business strategy. The group acts as a recommending body for the company. It discusses their feelings about the system, services, and organization with the corporate officers.

"The consistent and regular dialogue between the franchisees, the master franchises, and the executives is rare," Thomas points out. "As a result of this dialogue, many issues have been decided at these NBCC meetings, including the recent change in the logo, company colors, and sign configuration."

Gloria McGurk has served as a representative for the NBCC and feels that the meetings are very effective. "We give management feedback on what is going on in the system, and they listen to us."

"The NBCC is instrumental in maintaining a strong relationship between the corporate office and the franchise community," the CEO Loughlin concurs. The NBCC allows us to have a greater understanding and to be responsive to our franchisee's needs. Furthermore, this approach to concensus building creates a team with unified ownership in our strategies, values, and mission.

"They have given us clear direction when undertaking new activities and have helped us refine our training programs, our image and all of our marketing systems," adds Loughlin. "Our meetings are very intense. The franchisees establish the agenda because every franchisee across the country can contact his or her NBCC representative with any question that he or she wants answered. 'Why aren't we doing this?' 'Why are we doing that?' and so forth. We address every one of those questions and place them in a binder for each NBCC representative to have at the meeting. The NBCC has been a wonderful experience for us and has helped us have a terrific rapport with our system."

Additionally, franchisees also serve on a National Advertising Fund Advisory Council. This council, which is automatically part of our NBCC, meets biannually and provides input on the advertising and public relations strategies.

CENTURY 21 is the story of a small business—Art Bartlett's dream—that translated into an opportunity for thousands of aspiring entrepreneurs to own a successful business. CENTURY 21 brokers have come a long way from the "mom and pop" businesses they once were; today the company is the world's largest real estate organization. At present, the company accounts for 10 percent of all U.S. residential real estate transactions.

Perhaps the company's vision statement best describes the direction CENTURY 21 is going in the twenty-first century. It states: *The CENTURY 21 system, in all of its operations, will epitomize not only professional real estate knowledge, but a dedication to honesty, integrity and responsiveness to every customer whom we have the privilege of serving. This "service culture" will be promoted, integrated and expected throughout every level of our system and no deviation from this high ideal will be accepted.*

Chapter 3

DUNKIN' DONUTS

Dollars from Doughnuts

In 1946, shortly after World War II, Bill Rosenberg started an industrial catering company. Later, he opened a doughnut and coffee shop, and by 1953, working with his brother-in-law, Harry Winokur, there were five Dunkin' Donuts shops in the greater Boston area.

"There were many doughnut and coffee shops, but none like ours," Rosenberg tells with pride. "Our merchandise was baked daily, and nobody made a cup of coffee like we did. I figured that if Howard Johnson's could offer 28 varieties of ice cream, we could do the same thing with doughnuts. In fact, we expanded that number to 52 different doughnuts—one for every week of the year.

"Then I started to think, 'If Howard Johnson's could sell ice cream across the country, we could do the same thing with doughnuts. So I said to Harry, 'You watch the business, while I take my car and travel all over America looking to see what's out there.'"

Driving southeastward, then heading west, and coming back on a northern route, Rosenberg visited hundreds of doughnut shops. "I stopped in small towns and big cities like Houston, Dallas, and Los

Angeles, and everywhere I went, I recorded what I observed on a tape recorder sitting next to me in my car. Everybody was selling four kinds of doughnuts—plain, yeast-raised, jelly, and crullers. Nobody was even selling coffee. There was no seating or eating on their premises, which were generally located near a streetcar or bus stop in the downtown areas. Nobody was out on the highway like my shops in Boston. Just the same, everyone seemed to be making a living at it."

Six weeks after his return, Rosenberg went to an advertising agency to create a brochure that he could use to enlist potential franchisees. The brochure, "Dollars from Donuts," detailed Rosenberg's ideas for a franchise operation, including royalty and advertising fees, training opportunities, and general information.

Rosenberg enthusiastically reported back to his partner. "We are sitting on a potential goldmine," he recited, rambling through his transcribed recorded notes. "We don't have the money or the work force, so before some big bakery or coffee company does it, we've got to franchise our business and start opening stores.

"Here is a program I had designed that should explain how everything will work," Rosenberg continued. "You're the account-ant, so you figure out if I'm right on these numbers and see whether we can make money as a franchiser.

"This is ridiculous. We're not going into franchising," Winokur responded. "Bill, you're going crazy again. We've got a very successful catering business and five doughnut stores, and now you want to sell doughnuts all over the country. I think you're losing your mind."

With that note, Winokur, who was five years his partner's senior, summoned two of the company's suppliers and told them to "talk some sense into my kid brother-in-law."

"So they came over to straighten me out," Rosenberg explains. "One of them sold us flour and the other sold shortening. Both of them advised: 'Use your head, Bill, you can't franchise doughnut stores. If someone wants to open a doughnut store, he'll come to us and we'll set him up in a doughnut store. We'll sell him the flour and the shortening. What the hell do you have to sell him?'

" 'The same thing that Howard Johnson's has to sell,' I replied.

'A person can go to the ice cream supplier and buy ice cream, can't he? So why does anyone go to Howard Johnson's? You see what I mean?'

" 'What do you mean, Bill?' The men asked, staring at me as if I had gone off the deep end.

" 'Everybody who works in our organization,' I insisted, 'beginning with me to the guy who sweeps the floor, focuses on selling doughnuts and coffee. We spend all our time at it, and that is why we can do it better than people like you in the business of manufacturing mixes. You don't sell retail to the consumer. Just as you know your business, we're the experts in this end of the business. It's what we do.' "

Rosenberg pauses briefly and adds, "They couldn't see it my way. Harry and I fought about it for nearly two years. I wanted to expand and franchise, and he didn't. I'll buy you out then, or you buy me out,' I finally told him. But he wouldn't budge. He didn't want me to go nor did he want to get out. Finally, I hired an attorney, and the day before we were to appear in court, I made one last appeal to Harry.

" 'I made you a proposition a long time ago,' I said. 'I'll take it or you can take it. If you take it, I want the right to go into the industrial catering business and the doughnut business because I don't want out. And nobody's going to stop you from doing the same thing.' Harry finally agreed to allow me to buy him out. I was elated! The total book value of the company was $350,000, and that is what I gave him for *his* share. I paid him its entire value to be the sole owner of the business that I originally started. To do it, I had to mortgage my home."

Mortgaged to the hilt, Rosenberg went to his bank with full confidence that he would secure the necessary financing to begin a successful franchise business.

"Only coffee and doughnuts? Why would you want to carry only these two products? It simply won't work," he was told.

"Yes, sir," he retorted, "you may be right. But look at the Coca-Cola Company. It only has one product, and it's a refreshment. Doughnuts and coffee are breakfast items, desserts, picnic items, *and* refreshments. Not only that, but we will have a retail store, and in the back, we'll manufacture our own product. This way, if we don't draw enough customers into our retail store, we'll go out and take them to where our competition is selling machine-made doughnuts at the same price."

However, the bankers considered Rosenberg a poor risk and turned him down. Eventually, he was able to assemble a group of nine investors, who each put in $10,000, and this money was used to finance the franchising of new stores.

A product of the depression, in 1930, at age 14, Rosenberg dropped out of school in the eighth grade to help support his family. "Quitting school broke my parents' hearts," he tells. "My father, who slaved away in his small grocery store, was forced to close its doors. I felt as though I had to do my share and make some extra money to help the family pay the bills. In those days, you could get your work papers when you turned 14, and that is exactly what I did."

Shortly after that, Rosenberg landed his first full-time job as a delivery boy for Western Union telegrams. "We were paid a commission for each delivery, so the faster I peddled my bicycle, the more commissions I made. And if people liked me, I'd get tips, too. Well, I peddled and peddled and became the highest-paid kid working for the company in the Boston area. I was making $22 a week, which, except for some pocket money, was turned over to my mother."

During the winter months, working conditions in the Northeast were harsh, and especially so for a boy on a bicycle. But this didn't stop young Bill Rosenberg. One Christmas, while most of the other children chose to take the day off to be with their families, Rosenberg viewed the holiday as an opportunity: In spite of the depression, people would be in a Christmas mood that would result in more tips. So, at 7:00 A.M., when the temperature stood at 10 degrees above zero, he began making deliveries. "I was in agony," he recalls. "When I arrived downtown, my hands had frozen to the handlebars. They were so stiff, they had to be pried loose. I put them in cold water to get the circulation going, and then, once I felt some sensation, I was back on the job." His determination paid off. By the end of the day, his earnings had equaled a full week's paycheck.

Once the young man was able to obtain his driver's license, he sold Jack and Jill ice cream from a refrigerated truck for the Simco Company. Here, too, he worked on a commission basis. Applying the same principles that made him successful with Western Union—long hours and hard work—Bill took an undesirable route and converted it into the second most profitable in the Boston area.

His productivity resulted in a promotion to the position of assistant manager, and at age 20 he was transferred to New Haven, Connecticut, where he was employed at the company's first out-of-state branch. The following year, he was named manager. "That is when I asked for a raise," Bill explains. "By then, I was married and had a wife and son to support. The company's owner refused my request so I resigned. Still, I learned a lot from my boss. He was bright and ambitious. However, he had one major fault. He wasn't a sharer. What a shame! He had some good people working for him, and eventually, they all quit. Ultimately, he rehired me at a higher salary, and five years later I returned to Boston as the company's national sales manager.

"I learned a very valuable lesson from this man," the square-jawed, striking man continues. "If you have good people, you have to share with them. If you don't, somebody is going to steal them away, or they're going to do something on their own. Had that man shared with me, I would have probably stayed with him for the rest of my life.

"If a business succeeds, your employees are going to want to participate in that success. This was so obvious to me when I worked for the ice cream company that I made up my mind that if I ever owned a business, my people would have profit sharing and equity sharing. To this day, I still believe that this is the foundation of success behind franchising. Individuals own their units, and they have equity. Success is shared by everybody who is involved in the business. Yet there is no such thing as a free lunch. It takes a lot of hard work to succeed."

During World War II, Rosenberg worked at the Bethlehem Steel shipyard in Hingham, Massachusetts, where he was elected union delegate and later served as a contract coordinator for management.

After the war ended, he became a full partner in a box lunch company in Bridgeport, Connecticut, where he increased the business substantially. The budding entrepreneur resigned to begin his own industrial catering business in Boston.

With $1,500 in war bonds, $1,000 borrowed from his mother, plus $1,250 borrowed and $1,250 invested for 25 percent of the business from his brother-in-law, Harry Winokur, Bill rented a small building in Dorchester, Massachusetts. He purchased a panel truck and started a route selling sandwiches, pastries, doughnuts, and coffee at factories. Winokur, a C.P.A., stayed in his practice and kept the new company's books.

Each morning at 3:00 A.M., Rosenberg would climb out of bed to go to the commissary to make sandwiches. Sales dribbled in slowly, and the orders were small, until one day when Rosenberg came rushing into the office, out of breath and red-faced. He had just landed his first big account, the Tubular Rivet and Stud Company, with 1,500 employees. A few months later, more big accounts were opened and Industrial Luncheon Service began to expand.

"When we first opened Industrial Luncheon Service, the Boston area was still a 5-cent coffee market, and for that price, you had to serve a mediocre product," Rosenberg recalls. "Against the advice of the coffee company, I decided to sell a 10-cent cup of superior coffee. No one thought we could sell the more expensive product, but we did! We broke the coffee market against all the leading chains and restaurants, and we did it from a catering truck!"

Rosenberg believes that people appreciate quality. "People were willing to pay 10 cents because it was unbelievably great coffee. That was my beginning and never-ending dedication to the 'world's finest cup of coffee.' This resulted in our forever-after motto, 'Never compromise with quality.'

"You can ask anybody in the world today where to find the best cup of coffee. They will tell you to go to Dunkin' Donuts. This has been our reputation in the industrial catering business, and the same holds true with our doughnuts and other products."

In the end of its first year, the fledgling enterprise proved to be a lucrative business, having a 21 percent profit margin. Two years later, Winokur left his accounting business and became a 50 percent partner. It wasn't long before the company outgrew its headquarters and moved to a 144,000 square-foot building in Quincy. The new headquarters were completely renovated using state-of-the-art equipment, making Industrial Luncheon Service the most efficient company in the New England area. Other branches soon opened throughout New England and New York.

Industrial Luncheon Service continued to grow. "Soon we had 144 trucks to add to our canteen, cafeteria, and vending machine business. As we started more businesses with a variety of names, we grouped them under a new heading, Universal Food Systems," Rosenberg says. In nine years, starting with little more than the knowledge that workers needed a better way to purchase a hot cup of coffee and a fresh sandwich, Rosenberg developed a thriving business.

He credits his success to several philosophies that he held from the beginning, which were illustrated on signs that were displayed on the walls to remind his employees of his beliefs. One such sign reads: "A man does not build a business, he builds an organization. An organization builds a business." Others stated, "Thank you for maintaining our fine reputation" and "Quality, Service, Cleanliness and Value." Rosenberg stressed the customer is paramount. He instilled high ideals in his employees, which in turn, permeated the organization and are adhered to by present employees. Soon, Rosenberg began a profit-sharing and stock option plan that he believes helped him attract and retain talented people, who in turn built the business.

One day, while analyzing the company's financial statement, Rosenberg discovered that 40 percent of the company's gross earnings was from the sale of coffee and doughnuts. His kitchen was baking hundreds of dozens of doughnuts a day and brewing over 25,000 gallons of coffee. Both were by far the most profitable part of his business.

"I had the best doughnut baker in the city of Boston working for me," Rosenberg says. "His name was Alvin Johnson and he was running our commissary's doughnut department. Alvin ran a doughnut company for his former employer, and he told me that his old shop made more money selling retail doughnuts and coffee than the combined total of 12 catering trucks that his previous employer operated. I wanted to utilize him at his fullest capacity, so I went to Harry and told him I was going to open a retail doughnut store. He said, 'You have to be kidding! You are a gambler! We have enough business as it is!'

"I said, 'Look, Harry. I want to open a store, and I think this is a great idea. You know that coffee and doughnuts represent 40 percent of our gross earnings.' Even with these numbers, it took me six months to convince Harry that we should do it."

In 1950, the first doughnut store opened in Quincy, Massachusetts. It was named "Open Kettle" and became an overnight success. "There was only one problem," Bill says, "I didn't like the name. 'Open Kettle' wasn't catchy enough. So I called in several people for a brainstorming session. I told them to suggest anything that came to mind. Names like Hot 'n Fresh, Donut Land, and Donut World were mentioned, but nothing appealed to everyone. Finally, our architect, Bernard Healy, blurted out, 'Gee, what do you do with a doughnut? You pick a chicken . . . and you dunk a doughnut . . .' That is it, I exclaimed. Dunkin' Donuts!' " It wasn't long before Rosenberg planned to open more units.

Bob Rosenberg, Bill's oldest son, grew up watching Dunkin' Donuts evolve. Now the chief executive officer, the younger Rosenberg has been involved with the business since childhood.

"I remember when I was 9 or 10 years old going to wash coffee cans after school," he recalls, "and on weekends I would go out and take traffic counts with my dad for possible locations for new doughnut stores. We would have to sit in his car with a counter and push the button every time a car went by. One summer during my high school years, I held three jobs at once!"

Bob Rosenberg grew up learning a strong work ethic with his father as a prime example. "My dad always used to say he worked from 'can't see to can't see.' He would wake up when it was still dark out, at perhaps 3:00 or 4:00 A.M. and would work sometimes until midnight," he says matter-of-factly.

"I was always intrigued by my dad's business, and that is a credit to him," Bob says. "He always shared information with me. When it came time for him to buy out my Uncle Harry, my father solicited my opinion. I advised him to buy and that's just what he did. I am not sure he took my advice because I was still in high school!

"But the fact is that it was very flattering to be involved. I was asked to participate in an important decision, and he treated me as a responsible person. The respect he gave me was instrumental in making me enjoy the business and wanting to follow in his footsteps."

Although the elder Rosenberg was an eighth grade dropout, he encouraged Bob to pursue a good education. "He was always advising me, coaching me, to make sure that I got a fine education," Bob states. "I got my bachelor's degree at Cornell's Hotel and Restaurant School in 1959 and later received my Master's in Business Administration from Harvard Business School."

Bob hasn't only been "dunkin' donuts." For two years between undergraduate and graduate school he worked at McDonald's. "At the time diversification and expansion was an important part of Universal Food System's strategy. My dad was getting into several different businesses," he explains. "I thought I could learn a lot from McDonald's success. I helped McDonald's with its first operation in New England, and then came back to Universal to work at "Howdy's," our venture in the hamburger business. At one time we had as many as 26 Howdy restaurants. After we got the chain going, I went to Harvard for my graduate work. Universal later got out of the hamburger business when we sold Howdy's to concentrate on doughnuts."

Bob graduated from Harvard Business School in May 1963, and two months later, he joined Universal and was named president; Bill became the chairman.

"When I became president in 1963, Universal Food Systems had a fleet of trucks, mobile canteen services in factories, cafeterias in large companies, a vending division, Howdy Beefburgers, and Dunkin' Donuts. By then, we had a substantial organization with an executive vice president, vice presidents of finance, operations, and real estate; and an office manager." Several Harvard classmates were recruited by Bob to join the existing organization, including Tom Schwarz who served many years as executive vice president and later as president when Bob progressed to his role as chairman.

With the knowledge he gained from business school, Bob initiated an important discipline of strategic planning. He taught the rest of management the importance of setting goals and objectives. He adhered to evaluating the performance of the business against specified objectives and continuously measured the effectiveness of established goals.

In 1963 Dunkin' Donuts had about 100 stores and was doing $10 million in sales," Bob reports. "It was a nice-sized business. We had a good deal of success and were consistently expanding from then until 1968 at an almost uninterrupted 40 percent compounded rate of growth." By then, the chain numbered 300 stores and sales added $44 million to the parent company.

This is when Universal Food Systems decided to go public for the purposes of capitalization and extensive expansion. Because the name Dunkin' Donuts was so well known, it became the new corporate title. Going public also gave the executives a chance to capitalize on the stock option plan that began many years before.

"When we went public, our stock came out at $20 and it rapidly climbed to $66 a share. We then split, and the stock was valued at $33 and quickly rose to $36," states Bill.

The company continued to enjoy a sustained period of growth, but soon, there were problems. "Unfortunately, we were becoming too aggressive, and we outstripped our people." Bob admits.

In 1973, an indication of trouble at Dunkin' Donuts occurred in the Midwest. The territory had expanded at an abnormally rapid rate, and sales were extremely low. Bob asked Bill to accompany him to tour the Midwest franchises so the two executives could see firsthand why these franchises were doing so poorly.

"What we found was approximately 100 stores that had to be closed down. They were not in the right locations, the sales were poor, and they were falling behind on their rent," explains Bill. "Since the corporate office owned the leases, we were responsible for sub-leasing the locations to other kinds of businesses."

"As a result, we had to write off $3 million. Suffering our first loss ever, we were no longer one of Wall Street's darlings. Consequently, the price of our stock began to tumble," says the elder Rosenberg, "and it continued to fall until it was as low as $1.75. In the process, our personal net worth dropped by millions!

"So some members of our board came to me with our bankers to ask me to change our management," Bill continues. "They said Wall Street had lost faith in Dunkin' Donuts, and unless the company let some of our top officials go—including Bob—the price of the stock would remain depressed.

"I had a decision to make. I decided that I had excellent people working for me, and sure, they had made some major mistakes. But they agreed that they wanted to solve our problems. I had faith in my son and I had faith in the organization. I refused to let them go.

"I went back to the board and the bankers and I said to them, 'Look, I have faith in these people. If I let them go, I must start all over, hiring other people and teaching them all the things I have already taught our current management. If you were a father and you had a son who had the education and the background that Bobby has, and you had the faith that I have in him, how could you let your son go through the rest of his life thinking that he was a failure?' There is no way I was going to do that. I couldn't let Bob and the others go through life believing that they hadn't succeeded." Bill tells. "I had to give them the opportunity to come back. Well, they proved me right!"

In time, the company bounced back and returned to a profitable status. It wasn't long before Dunkin' Donuts had again become a favorite of Wall Street. Accordingly, the price of the stock spiraled.

"In my case, adversity was a far better teacher than success," Bob professes. "What I learned from this experience is fundamental. I became more outreaching to others. I started to look at the franchisees as partners and invited them to participate in the decision-making process of the business," Bob explains. "Today, Dunkin' Donuts' communications network includes advisory councils, district meetings, task forces, and newsletters. The organization is divided into 65 districts, and franchise owners within each district choose a representative to attend one of six zone advisory councils in the United States. Then, goals for sales and profits are discussed between management and advisory councils, and are then communicated to all owners via meetings, shop visits by company field personnel, and newsletters. District meetings are held regularly to discuss such things as district and national marketing plans, methods to improve shop operating profits, and task force recommendations. Task forces composed of both franchise owners and company executives convene as required to address specific needs. The representatives for each district sit with senior management at least once each quarter to discuss how we can achieve unit profitability for the owners."

Besides increasing communication with its franchisees, the company decided to increase its effort in properly preparing new franchise owners for the business. To accomplish this, it formed Dunkin' Donuts University, located at its present headquarters in Randolph, just outside Boston. Here, franchise owners and their personnel train for their new responsibilities. Every new franchise operator is invited to attend this six-week program to receive basic instructions necessary to run a successful operation. Owners and managers are taught to produce and merchandise all Dunkin' Donuts products. They are shown how to recruit, train, and manage employees; how to use equipment safely; and how to control inventory. The course includes a basic system of accounting.

In addition to intensive classroom work and hands-on instruction, franchise owners receive a complete set of operations manuals to be followed daily. Dunkin' Donuts believes that training is the key in the process of achieving high quality; by teaching its personnel the proper skills and abilities, franchisees will be able to operate a profitable business. The company spends millions of dollars every year operating the university; franchise owners and their employees attend free of charge. Due to international expansion, Dunkin' Donuts University branches have opened in the Philippines and Japan.

Bill Rosenberg has continued to serve as an inspiration for Bob and the rest of the Dunkin' Donuts team in its quest for improvement. "Everybody says that I can be difficult at times and I agree with them," Bill explains. "They say 'You are never satisfied. No matter how good we are, you are never satisfied.' I always maintain, 'Of course not. How can I be satisfied? If I am satisfied and you are satisfied, and the next person is satisfied, how are we going to get better? When that happens, our competitors will surpass us. We must believe that there is always room for improvement. Although Dunkin' Donuts is the best, there is *still* room for improvement."

Ralph Gabellieri experienced Bill Rosenberg's quest for constant improvement when Gabellieri was a manager at a Dunkin' Donuts franchise in Providence, Rhode Island, in the late 1950s. "It was the day after a hurricane," tells Gabellieri, today a Dunkin' Donuts executive. "There was no power in the city, but I had the shop open anyway. I was brewing coffee on a gas burner. We were having our busiest day ever, because no one else was open. Bill Rosenberg came into the shop and was disturbed that the windows were dirty. Of course they were dirty! It was the day after a major hurricane! Although he praised me for my innovativeness with respect to having the business operating, he was also critical because the windows were dirty. He believed that there was always room for improvement. I have the highest respect for him."

"Well, people think that I am a person who is difficult to satisfy, and I tell them that progress is the result of enlightened dissatisfaction. If you are satisfied, you will never get better," Bill insists.

The fast-food industry is highly competitive, and all businesses, even the big companies, must be able to adapt to continual change and consistently improve their operations. So, for good reason, according to Bob Rosenberg, "Every five years, we redesign our business and redefine our strategy. Presently, we are focusing on broadened distribution. This is a redesign of what we did five years before when we emphasized remodeling and expansion of menu items. Right now, our current strategy calls for contraction of the menu. Each period of time requires a different adaptation of the basic business that is constantly evolving."

One success for menu innovation occurred in 1974, when "Munchkins," the holes cut out of the center of the doughnuts, were introduced. Previously, the company had been unsuccessful in marketing the holes because whenever they were sold, the holes cannibalized doughnut sales; customers were purchasing the holes instead of doughnuts. "We hired Bob Kamersham, a great marketing man who came from the Revlon Company," Bill tells. "I told him that I thought the doughnut holes were a good idea and asked him to think about a way to sell them with our doughnuts. The next thing I knew is that Kamersham reserved the rights to the name "Munchkins," the little people Dorothy befriended in the film, *The Wizard of Oz*, giving us exclusivity in the food industry to use the name."

Dunkin' Donuts tested the "doughnut holes" without special packaging in three stores in Providence, Rhode Island, and in three other stores, the same product was called Munchkins and displayed in small bags with a picture of a little person from Oz on the front. The Munchkins sold *in addition* to doughnuts; parents took them home for their children. In the other stores, the holes were purchased instead of doughnuts, bringing sales totals down. With the success that the market test envisioned, Munchkins were soon offered in all Dunkin' franchises and accounted for a whopping 10 percent increase in the company's total sales.

"In the first year, our sales increased 10 percent as a direct result in using the name, 'Munchkins'! Today, Munchkins represent tens of millions of dollars in additional sales, and they cost us no additional overhead. It was just a matter of knowing how to repackage and reassign the product to the public," states Bill.

Everything at Dunkin' Donuts is subject to change and improvement. This includes a store remodeling plan and constant product development. "We have routinely improved our juices, cookies, and fillings, and according to consumer surveys, our products are the best in each of their categories. Of course, the quality of our coffee and doughnuts is acknowledged number one," Bob says matter-of-factly.

Dunkin' Donuts' quality control department monitors every

ingredient used in each of its products. The company hires independent laboratories to conduct tests to ensure that the products, such as flour, sugar, and coffee beans, meet a consistent level of quality.

"We have hot lines for both the franchisee and the consumer, so we are constantly monitoring all products," Bob continues. "Furthermore, Dunkin' Donuts University serves as a quality control vehicle to train our people," Bob explains, "so each franchisee is aware at every stage of the process if he or she receives or produces poor ingredients and products. Poor quality adversely affects the franchises! It hurts every franchise because a chain is only as strong as its weakest link."

According to Bill Rosenberg, quality control is essential to a prosperous business, and the quality of products, service, cleanliness, and store presentation must be uniform at every franchise. "If five people keep dirty stores and produce greasy doughnuts, it is a poor reflection on our entire system. If they are overlooked, our other franchisees will complain: 'I bought into this name, and it is not fair that a few poor stores are destroying business for the rest of us.' A few bad apples can hurt everyone's business. We must maintain the power to control all our franchisees in a positive direction; otherwise, our name means nothing. We are all in business for the same reason—to satisfy the customer. If certain people are doing something wrong, word will spread that we operate a bad chain. This will hurt everybody in the company, many of whom have their life savings invested."

"If we have one strength that is superior to our competition, it is our ability to continue to redesign our business to suit the needs of the current market," Bob says. "Of course, any changes we decide to make are done in very close concert and in partnership with our owners.

"This is a highly competitive business," Bob adds. "And we have to continue to improve to grow. America's change in life-style over the last 20 years has severely affected the per capita coffee consumption. People are on the go, so they want cold drinks, and they don't want to sit and spend time drinking a cup of coffee. Sixty to 70 percent of the adult population used to drink 3 to 4 cups of coffee a day. Now, it is down to 1.75 cups a day.

"And our doughnuts are competing for a share of the 2,500 calories that the average American consumes each day. Still, we sell more doughnuts than all our retail competitors combined," Bob says. Because people are eating less food these days does not seem adversely to affect Dunkin' Donuts. This is true because the company's market share has steadily increased in recent years.

"Our mission is to be the dominant retailer of high-quality doughnuts and related bakery, snack, and beverage products in each market in which we compete," Bob stresses. "In addition, we hope to be the leader in these categories as measured by total sales throughout the world."

In conjunction with its philosophy to adapt to change, Dunkin' Donuts has changed its menu in response to America's health craze. "To appeal to the more health-conscious market, we have added oat bran products, such as muffins, and low-cholesterol doughnuts," Bill says.

In addition to menu adaptation, it is essential to project a continual image of "newness." "It's a given that our product maintains a high standard of quality," Bob explains, "and the same is true of our physical image. If a shop has a dated appearance, it's then perceived as seedy, run-down, and unclean. That is the kiss of death in this business. And this can happen even when the quality of the food remains high. For instance, how often have you witnessed a successful restaurant lose its trade because the owner didn't invest in a modernization program? Just look at some fast-food operations that dominated a particular marketplace for many years and no longer exist today. That is because their management became complacent. They became content with the status quo.

"This is why we require our stores to remodel every five years. Constant change of this nature has enabled the average Dunkin' Donuts stores to enjoy increased sales of over 20 percent," Bob adds.

The company has also implemented a clever public relations operation that provides the stores with additional and free security. Management recommended to all franchises that coffee and doughnuts be provided free of charge to on duty police officers. "Besides being a public service," Bill explains, "it is the least expensive way for us to buy protection," he says. "Most of our stores are open 24-hours-a-day, and by having police officers as frequent customers, the thugs and crooks stay away. This makes our customers feel secure when they visit Dunkin' Donuts shops. We give the officers all the doughnuts and coffee they want, because they have to consume it on the premises."

The company is continually experimenting with ways to improve by introducing new innovative concepts. The management's quest for constant improvement includes replacing tired techniques with even better ideas. One advantage of having many locations is the ability to test-market in a few stores before moving forward in all locations. The danger of test-marketing in a small mom and pop business is that when new ideas don't work, its entire method of operation is disrupted. In franchising, people don't have to reinvent the wheel.

In addition to test-marketing, there are many other advantages in operating on a large scale. "There is strength in numbers," Bill says, "Our franchises enjoy purchasing power that they would never have if they were operating outside our organization. They have a tremendous advantage over independent operators when they purchase supplies. Our franchises pay much less than our competition for the same materials because we buy in such high volume.

To get the best economy, most Dunkin' franchisees combine their orders by jointly purchasing goods through cooperative warehouses. Through the company's manufacturing contracts, its franchises can buy such supplies as flour, mix, coffee, fillings, shortening, and sugar as well as paper goods at rock-bottom prices.

"When we place an order for 14 million pounds of coffee," Bob says, "we can assure our owners that they are getting a much better price by buying collectively versus independently.

"We employ highly sophisticated buyers," Bob adds. "They are experts who look at satellites for weather patterns and follow the commodities market very closely. They buy when the time is right and at the best price, too."

"I can't imagine a small independent operator being able to afford employing a top management team that we have for our whole system. They can't do with only a handful of stores what we do," Bill states. For a minimal fee, franchisees have the best people in marketing, advertising, and operations all working for them.

"Through extensive advertising, Dunkin' Donuts has become one of the best known names in the fast-food industry, and this didn't come cheap or easy," Bob adds. "We spend over $40 million a year in extensive advertising campaigns on television, radio, and newspapers across the country. And did you ever see a locally produced TV commercial that was in the same league as one produced by a national ad agency? The small independent shop owners can't afford to hire a Madison Avenue agency."

Dunkin' Donuts advertising department has skilled and experienced marketing executives who have received many honors, including a highly prestigious Clio Hall of Fame Award for "Time to Make the Donuts," featuring "Fred the Franchise Owner," starring Michael Vale.

"We are very proud of our advertising," Bob continues. "Our spokesperson, Michael Vale, has been with us since 1982. He is very friendly, and we believe that he truly represents our company's personality."

In addition, the marketing department works with individual franchise owners to determine their personal marketing needs. They coordinate local advertising and sales promotions, which, in turn, generates increased sales.

In 1991, new franchisees paid a $40,000 initial franchise fee and a continuing franchise fee of 4.9 percent of gross sales. While the average producing Dunkin' Donuts store generates over $500,000 a year in sales, the fees are small considering the support received from the corporate office. "Just by virtue of our purchasing system and advertising campaigns, the franchisees often save a substantial portion of the money they have to pay in franchise fees," Bob explains. "In other words, they practically receive our services free of charge!"

There are also many other advantages for being a part of Dunkin' Donuts. "Because of our size, there are many more opportunities for advancement within our organization," Bob tells. "The opportunity for growth is unlimited, so we attract better people."

Hard work and dedication open opportunities for internal promotion; a prime example is Ralph Gabellieri, who has been with Dunkin' Donuts for over 35 years. "I started my career with Dunkin' Donuts when I was 26 years old," Gabellieri tells. "I worked as a doughnut cutter for the first franchise operation. The owner eventually opened up four more stores and promoted me to manager.

"In 1960, I was invited to work for the corporate headquarters as a district manager. Through a succession of promotions, I became a director of operations, a vice president in 1968, and then senior vice president of operations in 1970," he says proudly. "Presently, I am president of Mister Donut, the 500-store chain that Dunkin' Donuts purchased from International Multifoods in 1990. We are now in the process of converting the Mr. Donut stores into Dunkin' Donuts."

According to Bob Rosenberg, the program has been an overwhelming success. "When a Mr. Donut store converts to a Dunkin' Donuts store," he explains, "the average increase in sales has been nearly 50 percent. In fact, one-third of the converted Mr. Donut owners have expressed interest in opening additional Dunkin' Donut franchises. Our success with the Mr. Donut conversion has encouraged us to look at acquiring other chains as well."

The advantage to franchising over company-owned stores is far more than just an opportunity for growth. Bill Rosenberg likes to repeat a conversation he once had with a bewildered acquaintance in the mid-1950s. Rosenberg was asked: "Why do you want to franchise? Why don't you own these stores? You can make more money if you own your store than if you let the franchise operator make all the money."

"It might be so if you run one or two stores," Rosenberg replied, "but you can grow a lot more rapidly if your business franchises. Just think, if I had a store in Chicago and the manager there is short a baker and two servers for a shift, what is he or she to do? Let's say the manager calls up his wife and says 'Darling, I've got a problem here. The baker and two servers didn't show up. Will you come down here with our daughter and son and help me?' His wife will reply, 'I should come down in the middle of the night to help that fat guy in Boston? No way.'

"Now if the fellow in Chicago was a franchise owner, and to buy the business he had to borrow money from relatives and the bank, the conversation would be much different. The owner would call his wife with the same problem, but her response would be, 'I will be right down, honey.' And she runs down with the kids and they help him out because it's their business, and they have their money on the line. It is not the fat guy's business, it's theirs." The now lean and athletic-looking Rosenberg grins, "I used to be that 'fat guy' in Boston, but that was 50 pounds ago."

Carlos Andrade is a good example of a successful Dunkin' Donuts franchisee. Andrade immigrated to the United States from The Azores in 1973 when he was 15 years old with little formal education and worked as a baker for his brother, Manny, who owned a Dunkin' Donuts franchise in Warwick, Rhode Island. When he was 22 years old, after working his way up to a management position, Carlos bought his first franchise in Raynham, Massachusetts, with Manny's help. Carlos now owns nine franchises that do over $10 million in sales a year and employ over 220 people.

"Dunkin' Donuts has always been aggressive in providing opportunity to its franchisees. With the encouragement of the corporate office, we now buy real estate and build our own stores," Andrade tells. "I sell the operation, while leasing the property." The extended Andrade family, which includes brothers, sisters, in-laws, cousins, aunts, and uncles, collectively owns 225 units in New England, Florida, and Montreal, Canada. The Andrades have prospered beyond their wildest dreams and, as such, represent the attainment of the American dream.

Dunkin' Donuts has served its franchisees well, and accordingly, the franchisees have proven their loyalty to the company. In 1989, a Canadian financier was buying stock in the company at a rapid pace. When he had accumulated 5 percent, he announced that he wanted to take over the company. "We resisted," Bob recalls, "but it was the gallant effort of our franchisees and employees who saved us from a hostile takeover.

"The franchisees placed huge ads in *The Wall Street Journal* in protest, and that bought us nine months to think of alternatives," he adds. "Ultimately, we were forced to sell, but we were fortunate to identify another buyer overseas with high integrity, who shares our values and views. We have a great relationship with our new parent company, Allied Lyons."

Allied Lyons, of Great Britain, purchased Dunkin' Donuts and kept management intact, allowing it to have full autonomy. Since the acquisition, Dunkin' Donuts has continued to prosper. Now, Allied Lyons is developing a partnership arrangement between franchises of recently acquired Baskin Robbins and Dunkin' Donuts franchises.

"We are now sharing several locations with Baskin Robbins, and we are looking at ways we can grow and mutually benefit each other," Bob tells. "We are sharing our facilities and personnel, giving us a competitive advantage. Our businesses do not conflict, as they have different peak hours. We have opened 5 cooperative Baskin-Dunkin' ventures already and have 50 more in different stages of experimentation. So far, it seems to be working."

While Dunkin' Donuts today is the epitome of an American success story, it has had its share of problems, as witnessed by the dramatic fall of the price of its stock in the early 1970s and a hostile takeover attempt in 1989. In this respect, its struggle to survive resembles the life of its founder, Bill Rosenberg. Although to look at him today, a robust man with a booming voice, it is difficult to imagine that he is a survivor of three bouts with cancer, three hip replacements and is a diabetic.

In 1971, a doctor discovered Bill had lung cancer. "At that time, less than 5 percent of its victims survived for five years. I was told that it was only a matter of months before I'd succumb," Bill tells. "I was fortunate. I endured a major operation when they removed one of my lungs, and the problem has not reoccurred. Then, in 1977, I was diagnosed with lymphacitic lymphoma, a cancer of the lymph nodes. That was corrected through surgery and radiation treatments. A few years later, my doctor discovered that I had a malignant infection in one of my ears, which was also remedied. On top of everything else, I'm an adult diabetic.

"Every morning I wake up and remind myself how lucky I am that I am still alive," Rosenberg says with a broad smile. He attributes his survival to his never-ending desire to be active. "When I was sick, I got involved in horse racing and bought a farm. I became a top breeder and started the International Horse Racing Association. Between this and Dunkin' Donuts, I kept busy all the time. I think I licked the cancer because I kept my mind active. I never let the cancer get me down," he adds.

In 1980, Bill and his wife Ann made a gift of Wilrose Farms, their magnificent horse-breeding complex in East Kingston, New Hampshire, to the University of New Hampshire. It became the first conference center for the continuing study of franchising and small business administration. The Rosenbergs also established a family foundation that donates money to medical and educational charities. The foundation finances the William Rosenberg Chair in Medicine at Harvard Medical School that funds research at the Dana Farber Cancer Institute, where Bill is an honorary trustee. The Rosenbergs also fostered an educational foundation for franchising through the International Franchise Association that promotes programs at various universities for certification and accreditation in franchising similar to degrees awarded to certified public accountants. Cancer and franchising are two causes that Bill cares about and identifies with personally.

In his retirement, Bill and Ann divide their time between their homes in Boca Raton, Florida, and Cape Cod, where they enjoy sailing their new 46-foot yacht and taking 5-mile-long walks. "I have had three hip replacement operations," he explains, "and some doctors think it's a miracle I can walk today." Bill remains in the business as chairman emeritus of Dunkin' Donuts and is active in franchising with the International Franchise Association, the organization that he founded in 1959.

"When I started Dunkin' Donuts, franchising was a comparatively new thing. Howard Johnson, Holiday Inn, A&W Root Beer, and Dairy Queen were some of the earliest, well-respected pioneers," Bill tells. "Franchising was growing rapidly, and, consequently, there were some operations trying to make a fast buck. People complained about them, and they made the rest of us look bad. Legislators began talking about passing laws that would make it impossible to operate franchises.

"In the 1950s, it was so difficult that if you wanted to place an advertisement in *The New York Times* or *The Wall Street Journal*, you were not allowed to use the word 'franchising'!"

In 1959, Bill attended a "Start Your Own Business" show in Chicago. "I never heard so much grumbling in my life!" he tells. "Everybody was disgruntled and dissatisfied and complaining that the new legislation was making franchising very difficult to do. Many people had become involved with shady franchise operations and lost a lot of money. They contacted their legislators, who in turn, with little knowledge of franchising, lumped the entire industry together. We were going to be legislated out of business if we didn't act fast.

"I knew there were many good companies out there—I had one—but there was no one to represent us and speak for franchising as it truly was. The legislators heard only the complaints. There was no one telling the positive side of franchising.

"No one wanted anything to do with us, so I felt it was necessary to establish an association to police ourselves and to let people know that we were legitimate businesses," Bill adds. "Also with an association, there is an invaluable exchange of ideas for members to share with each other."

"Had the International Franchise Association not been formed," Rosenberg emphasizes, "there wouldn't be any franchising today. It would have been legislated out. There were people who were wrong for franchising. Yet they were doomed to fail and they did. The blue suede shoe operators were ruining a wonderful idea. Fortunately, the IFA represented the legitimate and professional side of franchising and it helped save the industry."

Today, franchising is a healthy, thriving industry, which owes its present prosperity to the early pioneers like Bill Rosenberg who endured hard times to clear the path for others to follow. Of course, through his commitment to ethics and standards, Rosenberg has been amply rewarded. This is vividly witnessed in Dunkin' Donuts' success. The company has expanded to over 3,000 stores worldwide, including Saudi Arabia, Indonesia, Thailand, Korea, Singapore, Europe, Brazil, the United Kingdom, Europe, and Japan, with systemwide sales in excess of $1.2 billion. Dunkin' Donuts accounts for approximately 12 percent of all doughnuts sold in U.S. restaurants, making its sales greater than the combined total of its retail competitors. The company has come a long way since it sold its first franchise in 1955, and, in the process, it has made many believers out of nonbelievers. Its franchisees believe in Dunkin' Donuts, too. Today, approximately 90 percent of new store openings are owned by existing franchise owners.

"Thirty years ago while promoting the International Franchise Association, I said, 'The difference between capitalism and socialism can be franchising, and believe me, within a quarter of a century, the socialist countries will be into franchising.' And that is just what is happening," says the Dunkin' Donuts founder.

"In my humble opinion, franchising is the absolute epitome of entrepreneurship and free enterprise, and is unquestionably one of the most dynamic economic factors in the world today."

Chapter 4

DUSKIN COMPANY, LTD.

Service for People, People for Service

"**D**ust control" hardly suggests the romance of international franchising. Yet that process is the foundation of a company unique in the annals of franchising. In 1993 the Duskin Company, Ltd., will mark 30 years as franchising's premier advocate in Japan. The celebrations, to be held at the company's handsome new headquarters in Osaka, will emphasize Duskin's continuing commitment to franchising and to the "prayerful management" of its founder, Seiichi Suzuki, a devoted Shintoist.

What distinguishes Duskin in the franchise industry, thought of worldwide as an American phenomenon?

- The company pioneered franchising in Japan.
- The company is both a franchisor (of its own product lines)

and a franchisee (licensing know-how and trade names from American companies).

- Duskin's late founder is the only non-American installed in the Franchising Hall of Fame.

- The company is employee owned, and it has no plans to go public.

- The company recently was named one of Japan's top 20 companies in two areas: environmental consciousness and commitment to meeting customer needs.

- Its present chairman, Shigeharu Komai, has guided the company in a dozen new directions and seen it become one of Japan's top 500 companies and its top franchising organization—without ever veering from the philosophical precepts on which the company was founded.

The core of Duskin's operation is its "Aino-Mise" Division. Over 2,000 franchisees employ a friendly army of *leader-san*, almost all housewives, who deliver Duskin's leased cleaning materials to one quarter of the country's households every four weeks. Consider what it would take for a single company to have representatives knock on 56 million U.S. doors every month! Aino-Mise delivers cleaning cloths, mops, mats, and every kind of cleaning tool through its franchised distribution system. (If you can get hold of a catalogue—catalogue sales are a relatively recent addition to Duskin's sales techniques—you might place an order; the products are well designed and efficient.)

More familiar names today fit under the Duskin corporate umbrella: ServiceMaster, Mister Donut, Fog City Diner, Café du Monde, Joe's Stone Crab Restaurant, and others. Yet this fascination with American franchises is transmitted to the Japanese market by an altogether Japanese corporation. Today Duskin is a modern $2.3 billion company that looks toward the twenty-first century as an opportunity, in Mr. Komai's words, "to become the No. 1. service company in Japan."

Duskin's growth grew from a casual meeting, in 1961, when Seiichi Suzuki made his first trip abroad. The young man was the chief executive officer of Kentoku Co., Ltd., a small wax-manufac-turing company based in Osaka. He had been working on some cleaning products of his own design when he met a Canadian small businessman, Lou Mendelson, whose principal business was a linen supply company. Suzuki's interest was caught by a second venture the Canadian owned, a cleaning supply and dust control business. Suzuki already was assessing dust control as an international busi-ness. Visiting the United States, he saw new cleaning products—chemically treated mops and dusters—first developed and marketed by AT&T.

The international experience was a catalyst for the product line Suzuki had begun to develop, and he applied for patents for a new line of cleaning equipment. Within two years of his return to Japan, he left Kentoku and set up Duskin Co., Ltd., a privately owned and operated service organization. (In Japanese, Duskin means Dust Control.)

This newly introduced product line literally revolutionized home cleaning in Japan. The young company tested its operations in various regions of the country for two years in both residential and commercial locations. Suzuki learned that renting chemically treated mops to households for cleaning tatami mats (rice straw mats tradi-tionally used to cover the floors of Japanese homes) was more convenient for customers than was sending them out to be treated and that American-type mineral oil-based chemicals damaged the tatami mats. The business that became Aino-Mise has operated as a leasing business since the beginning, and Duskin began its tradition of developing its own improvements tailored to the Japanese market with a solvent made of soluble oil that cleaned the tatami mats without damage.

Franchising came to the attention of the young entrepreneur in the early years of the company. In the 1960s U.S. franchising was riding a roller coaster of success and expansion, and something in Suzuki responded. Given a book on franchising, the entrepreneur recognized that franchising could help his company expand quickly while offering would-be entrepreneurs with limited capital the chance to become independent businesspeople. Suzuki chose to franchise not primarily for financial reasons but because of the level of services independent contractors would provide to Duskin's customers.

"Mr. Suzuki was also very enthusiastic about the possibility of helping others and that is why he became interested in franchising," said Shigeharu Komai, the president and chief executive officer of Duskin. Mr. Komai worked with Suzuki at Kentoku and joined him at Duskin in 1963, devoting his entire adult career to the company. "At the same time, the company was short on capital, so we were able to avoid a loan from a bank by franchising and collecting initial fees. Mr. Suzuki invited his friends and other acquaintances to join his system as franchisees. Twenty people agreed to do so, making Duskin the first company in Japan to franchise." The combination of franchising with new technology spurred Duskin's rapid expansion throughout Japan.

Duskin was the first Japanese company to come to the United States to learn more about the franchising industry. "Mr. Suzuki realized he needed to know more about franchising, so several of our staff members were sent to America," recalls Komai. "During this process, we met many people—giants in franchising—such as Bill Rosenberg, founder of Dunkin' Donuts, and Marion Wade, founder of ServiceMaster—both of whom today have been inducted in the International Franchise Association's Hall of Fame."

In 1969, Duskin became the first Japanese company to be registered as an official member of the International Franchise Association. According to Komai, this was a major turning point for the young enterprise. "Our involvement with the IFA is responsible for our growth," the CEO explains. "We made a lot of friends through the IFA and were able to develop relationships with other companies. Our drive to learn more about franchising turned out to lead to some very good business opportunities for us. Originally, we didn't have any thought or intent of taking business back to Japan. However, through personal relationships we established with people such as Harry Winokur and Marion Wade, our business expanded. We were friends before we ever talked to these companies about business. This was very important to us. Even today, we never go into a business relationship with a partner company without 'personal face'—an expression we use in Japan that expresses personal relationships and respect."

Duskin's first expansion was a natural extension of its dust control business—the purchase of Continuous Towel, with its patented continuous towel concept, and later, the exclusive franchise rights in Japan for ServiceMaster—a residential and commercial disaster restoration and carpet cleaning company. Duskin could have opened carbon copies of these businesses and avoided paying royalties. Instead, each time, it chose to franchise. The decision, according to Komai, came from Suzuki's wish to deal fairly with American companies. "He was a very religious and honorable person who wanted to pay for the knowledge he received. We didn't want to copy the businesses and not compensate the people who taught us. Our approach to our business partners has helped our company grow and be successful because we received a lot of respect back from the international franchise community."

In 1970 in the process of learning about franchising in the United States, Komai recalls being introduced to the founders of several franchises, one of whom was Harry Winokur, who started the Mister Donut chain. "One day, after I returned to Japan, Winokur telephoned Mr. Suzuki and said, 'We are interested in expanding in Japan; we think there will be interest in our product.' Of course, we were not really interested in the doughnut business because we were too busy developing and improving our dust control, ServiceMaster, and Continuous Towel companies that were our bread and butter business. Besides, doughnuts didn't sell very well in Japan.

"Suzuki could have said no by phone or letter, but since Winokur had been very kind to Duskin, teaching us about the franchising industry, Mr. Suzuki invited Mr. and Mrs. Winokur to Japan," Komai continued. "Suzuki wanted to show him the marketplace, where there were already many places to buy doughnuts. He felt that there wasn't any room for another doughnut shop in Japan."

"So when Winokur arrived, we held a meeting at which we placed several of the doughnuts available in Japan on a huge table. Mister Donuts' founder took one of the doughnuts, broke it in half, and said, 'This is not a doughnut. None of these was made with the same mix as ours.' Doughnuts in Japan were hard, heavily sugared, greasy things, and of course Mr. Suzuki and I were surprised. So I asked him, 'If this isn't a doughnut, what is one like?' Winokur answered, 'Try these,' and offered me one of his. I tasted it and was shocked. It was like nothing I had ever tasted before. Also, Japanese doughnuts were sold at bakeries. There were no exclusive doughnut shops like there were in the United States."

With that taste of the potential, Suzuki and Komai traveled to Miami to see an operating Mister Donut shop for themselves. Both businessmen were impressed; they also recognized the chain could appeal to Japanese teenagers, who had few places to hang out.

During the course of negotiations, Suzuki and Komai could well have headed home empty-handed; the initial fee proposed by Mister Donut's owner, International Multifoods Corp. of Minneapolis, was $425,000—an amount greater than Duskin's entire equity at that time.

Ultimately, Suzuki accepted the huge initial fee because he was willing to pay whatever necessary for the knowledge Duskin would receive—about doughnuts *and* franchising. Mr. Komai, like his predecessor, is comfortable with Duskin's eagerness to borrow ideas from the United States. As he puts it, "It's better to take a proven concept from a foreign firm than to struggle from nothing. Americans are geniuses of creation and the Japanese are geniuses of imitation.

"But at that time, we were not used to paying for something that we couldn't see. We were paying for intangible know-how," he continued. "This was a new thing for the Japanese—to pay so much money for knowledge. Suzuki was the first man in Japan who was willing to pay for something intangible, and it represented an immense involvement, considering how small Duskin was. There was another significant risk: it was the first move toward diversification from cleaning services to food service at a time when Duskin was on its way to becoming an integrated service company.

"Mr. Suzuki's personal aspiration for diversification was to enable us to offer different business opportunities to franchisees," Komai adds. "It was not a selfish motive, but rather one for our franchisees. Then, too, Mister Donut might have gone to someone else. Additionally, he thought it was very important philosophically to experience the same pain and difficulty that our franchisees would have to go through, in paying their fee to us. We were the franchisor, but at the same time, we were a franchisee to Mister Donut of America. As a franchisee ourselves, we were able to understand the pain of the franchisee who had difficulty deciding whether he should pay or not. Since our initial fee to Mister Donut USA was very expensive, we were confident we could charge our franchisees an initial fee to help Duskin. In return, of course, they got their businesses."

Franchising the Mister Donut concept in Japan was a rocky road. The market was crowded, and Duskin had to compete for good franchisees. They opened separate shops, designed with a 1950s flavor, including "golden" oldies, American furniture, and Elvis Presley posters. After 20 years in business, Duskin has an 85 percent share of the doughnut business. Today the company operates over 650 Mister Donut units in Japan, and in 1989 it acquired the rights to operate Mister Donut in 11 other Pacific Rim markets.

CEO Komai is proud of the cultural change Mister Donut introduced in Japan. "Mister Donut turned the image of the doughnut from a blue-collar snack food into a pastry that everyone enjoys." Even more important to the company, he noted, was "the decision to introduce a new system—a tremendous leap forward for us. In those days the Japanese service industry was 20 years behind that in the United States. We're still 5 years behind in some functional ways, but today we've caught up or may even be ahead on the human side."

Duskin continues to study the U.S. market in its search for other service businesses. Not all new franchises travel well. Its company-owned Long John Silver units are one example. "Long John Silver didn't work as we and the American company had hoped, so we didn't franchise it," recalls Akira Kojima, general manager of Duskin's business development. "The product didn't go well with our Japanese taste or eating habits, so we pulled out. But we learned a lot from that experience. For example, we learned how to quick freeze and how to quick thaw. These procedures have been applied to our existing restaurant operations. So it wasn't a complete waste.

Mr. Komai always says even a very serious mistake can lead to a future success. It was a great learning experience. People learn most when they fail. So it's not a failure as such."

Duskin's policy with each new business is to open a pilot company-owned store to test the market and protect its franchisees. The company also owns and operates 10 percent of all stores. Only when the concept works and is profitable does Duskin sell franchises. The company also uses its owned units to train new employees and franchisees. Kajima Duskin offers the most effective schooling for its franchisees.

Expanding Aino-Mise and adding new service concepts, Duskin became Japan's major franchising operation. Today the company produces and distributes a wide range of consumer household products and has multiplied its exclusive agreements with American franchisors. The "Duskin Tree" now has several primary branches:

- Hygiene
- Clean care
- Management support services
- Food service
- "Rent-all"

The Clean Control Business Group today has over 1,000 franchised units providing coordinated hygienic services for commercial locations. This branch encompasses Air Control, Linen Service for industrial facilities, and the Uniform Service Divisions.

The heart of Duskin Co., Ltd., remains the quirky and unique "Aino-Mise" ("May I Help You" outlets) sales system, which brings goods directly to customers rather than selling from fixed locations. The rental system remains central to the Duskin operation. Leader-san commissions equal 25 percent of their sales. The same approach services some 1.5 million commercial businesses every two weeks. Not surprisingly, Duskin uses this vast, franchised, door-to-door retail network to extend its product line.

The Care Service Group includes ServiceMaster; Merry Maids; Terminix; Duskin Home Health Care, an in-home care system; Duskin Healthcare Corporation, a hygiene management service for hospitals; Bright Cleaning, which cleans residential and commercial blinds and chandeliers; and facility management.

Duskin today also dominates the contract cleaning of households, businesses, and hospitals through more than 639 franchisees, the result of a series of tie-ups initiated in 1970 with ServiceMaster, including its subsidiary, Merry Maids, the first house-cleaning system introduced to the country. Initially, the house-cleaning business was a tough sell in Japan—housewives felt ashamed not to be cleaning their own houses. Traditional values changed as more women entered the work force. Duskin's ServiceMaster division (which now includes Terminix) has experienced phenomenal growth and success. Eight years after its founding, there were more than 250 ServiceMaster franchisees in the country, and, by 1989, that number had grown to over 500, servicing more than 170,000 customers. Duskin pays the American company a royalty of 2-3 percent of sales.

William Pollard, chairman and chief executive officer of Service-Master, says "ServiceMaster has shared many benefits from our partnership with Duskin. These benefits stem from our collective commitment to values. Both companies are dedicated to providing the best service possible and to following the vision of our founders who were committed to franchising as a primary method of distributing services to the residential and commercial markets. ServiceMaster and Duskin are also committed to providing growth opportunities for their people. We believe it is the dedication of our people that makes the difference."

Duskin has the rights to a number of other U.S. trademark systems, including United Rent-All and House of Lloyd. The House of Lloyd is a gift business; Rent-All is self-explanatory. American consumers, accustomed to renting long ladders and lawn mowers, might be astonished at the range of available goods: Japanese bridal parties typically rent everything (except flowers) for the entire event. The company is particularly strong in food service; today its food division generates 28 percent of company revenues. It franchises and operates or subfranchises a variety of food service groups out of the United States:

- 1950s-style Ed Debevic's of Chicago
- San Francisco-based Fog City Diner
- Studebaker's from Houston
- Café du Monde, a New Orleans coffeehouse
- "Tokyo Joe's" and "Osaka Joe's" seafood restaurants patterned after the legendary "Joe's Stone Crab Restaurant" of Miami

Duskin's New Business Group offers everything from cosmetics to videotapes to shoe repairs. Aga Cosmetics Co., Ltd., markets a line of cosmetic products delivered to homes of customers. Members' Mart is a catalogue selling various products; Kutsu Kobo are franchised units providing quick service shoe repair that carries on traditional German craftsmanship in footwear services. Duskin's House of Lloyd Japan, Inc., sells gifts and toys through home parties, and J. Express Co., Ltd., is the conglomerate's own innovative travel agency. Finally, the systems division offers a reliable support system for all Duskin's franchise operations. On-line computer systems assist production and distribution services—servicing both the customer and the franchisees. Duskin has borrowed a little here and a little there—somehow the result is a modern, very Japanese corporation.

A Duskin division controls the overwhelming share of almost every major franchised industry in Japan. Aino-Mise's dust control line, for example, has a market share of 84 percent of the household services market and 53 percent of the industrial cleaning market. In addition, Duskin's holds 70 percent of market share in the cabinet towel cleaning service, and, through its Service-Master franchisees, it controls a majority share of the residential and commercial cleaning market. Currently, Duskin has 30 operating divisions and 5,444 outlets, including 142 it controls directly. The company's consumer sales totaled an estimated ¥363.6 billion in fiscal 1991.

Each division adheres to six business strategies:

1. Duskin was among the first to recognize the growth potential of services and, accordingly, focused its business activities in that area.

2. Company shareholders and executives agree unanimously that any service provided by Duskin should be the best of its kind in Japan. Company policy states: "Duskin doesn't do what is already being done by somebody else." The company has consistently pioneered new service concepts and is recognized for doing so. Duskin continually studies new business prospects in its search to identify a new service or product that meets the needs of its customers.

3. Duskin is committed to remaining synonymous with franchising in Japan.

4. Duskin provides the same quality of service in every area of the country. If quick profits were its immediate goal, Duskin would ignore the remote countryside and other areas where marketing is difficult. Quick profit has never been a company goal; rather, Duskin is a national company committed to nationwide service.

5. Once Duskin begins a business, its goal is to make it the best of its kind in Japan. Its record of dominant market share demonstrates the company's success in meeting its goal.

6. When Duskin considers a new business, its annual revenue potential should exceed ¥10 billion.

Charting the company's growth by these basic strategies clearly pays off for Duskin. The company is omnipresent in Japan. According to Akira Kojima, "Our dust control division, Aino-Mise, services over 9 million homes in the domestic market. We go to each of these homes every four weeks, 13 times a year. When you add in all our commercial and industrial customers, we service over 10 million customers every four weeks."

Sophisticated graphics, marketing, and media use mark the contemporary approach the company takes to reaching its customers and to staying in touch with the Duskin employee family. "We use very heavy national television advertising," Komai notes. "During each commercial, we announce a toll-free number in Japan. The awareness level of Duskin in Japan is 99.9 percent, *nationwide*. The Japanese home has an average of three television sets, so it is difficult to miss one of our advertisements. Anybody in the country can dial our toll-free number (100-100) to receive information about our services or our products or a referral to one of our businesses. We refer all inquiries to our franchisees located in the callers' region. We can do this because the 5,000-plus franchisees in our system provide a service network that blankets the nation.

"A recent commercial featured very famous and interesting Japanese twin sisters who are 100 years old. They are a perfect illustration of our toll-free number, 100-100." The advertising campaign is complemented by a direct mail catalogue that allows customers to select specific services, after which they can call the 100-100 number and receive a referral to a local franchisee. The catalogue attracts the customer who had one order in mind to the wide selection of services available from Duskin.

The company also communicates with its own employees regularly. Once a month the company publishes a public relations newspaper titled "Sowing the Seeds." With over 1 million copies a month going to its customers, employees, and franchisees, each issue contains an article written by CEO Komai, in which he shares his personal philosophy and Duskin's with the reader.

Duskin has never had any interest in a public offering. It chose not to make money by means of stocks, securities, or even real estate. The company sees that as similar to gambling. Duskin is a privately held corporation and plans to remain so. Any sales of stock is restricted solely to franchisees, company employees and a few select suppliers.

"While other franchise systems may seek either profit or expansion, we have challenged good times and bad together, as a system," Komai says. "We have no desire to make money the easy way. We try to make a profit through our own hard work. We operate basic businesses—our hands get dirty—and we help others. We all strive toward a common goal: 'People for Service, Service for People.'"

The catalyst for the company's success continues to be its orientation to people and their personal growth, based on the "prayerful management" of its founder. Through his dedication to developing the unique business practices that merge spiritual values with good business, Suzuki shaped the concept of "prayerful management" that still imbues the way Duskin does business. Komai, also a Shintoist, though of a different sect, was so drawn to Suzuki while they worked together at Kentoku that he felt compelled to leave his comfortable and well-paid position to pursue the uncertain future of the start-up. This lifelong commitment to principle has been the foundation of the company since its first day in business.

Suzuki's "prayerful management" sets forth "unity of moral and economic aims" as his management creed. Komai has added "management based on virtue" to the Duskin corporate philosophy. Duskin's bywords, such as "Whether our lot today be profit or loss, be spiritually ready for loss," are tempered by positive thinking, expressed in the company's corporate philosophy:

Day-after-day, starting today, each of us has the opportunity to begin our lives anew.

Whether our daily lot is to be faced with profit or adversity, let us be prepared to accept adversity.

Like a planter, with everyone we meet each day let us sow the seeds of joy.

May each and every one of us live a life in this world to the fullest spiritual and material potential.

Duskin seeks spiritual enrichment in addition to financial success. "Profit is the instrument used to measure a company's ability to meet its goals," says the CEO. "The objective of our management is not just to increase profits but also to make the maximum possible contribution to society. This is not much, but it can help to realize the state of mind called blissful living—plentitude of joy and happiness and liberation from sorrow and grief."

Duskin's philosophy is reflected most clearly in its many community activities. In 1981, Mister Donut began to promote the social integration of the mentally and physically disabled. Named "Let's Expand the Circle of Love" Foundation, the entire Duskin conglomerate supports this fundraising effort, which has enabled several handicapped persons to study in the United States.

Another example of Duskin's active role in the Japanese community takes place on "Duskin Thanks Day" every year in mid-November. On this day, which celebrates the founding of the company, employees show their gratitude and appreciation to people and society through "Takuhatsu" or cleaning service. Every employee participates on this holiday in a national community cleanup.

Duskin also sponsors Duskin Pia concerts at headquarters, and each year, in Nagasaki, Duskin presents a "Peace Concert" featuring popular Japanese singer Masashi Sada. These concerts commemorate Atomic Bomb Memorial Day of Hiroshima and Nagasaki.

CEO Komai distinguishes two kinds of profit. "There is desirable profit, and there is gain from speculations. But wholesome profit comes from joy in one's own work, in exchange for which customers give you profit as incentive and reward. Gain is profit that depends on someone losing what you gain. I express my faith out loud because it's the basis of character building in both corporate and private life. Faith should not be used as a management tool, but a prayerful atmosphere always generates positive energy."

Suzuki's corporate philosophy has remained an intangible asset, and, according to Komai, it continues to shape the company's corporate activities. "Because change constantly affects our business environment, Duskin must have a firm, unchangeable foundation. I learned from personal experience that by living according to the ideas expressed in our corporate philosophy, every employee and franchisee can be successful in life and in business. This foundation has contributed vitally to our success as a corporation.

"Duskin's commitment to franchising complements our foundation in service," the CEO continues. "The company's positive growth over the years is a result of our commitment to franchising.

Franchising has made Duskin the dynamic corporation it is today, beyond what is reflected in positive annual reports. Franchising has provided us with a way of life by emphasizing sensitivity to the needs of others. We have a joint goal with our franchises which is to improve the community through 'sowing the seeds of joy.'

"Gratitude and sharing are essential not only for personal growth, but also for our corporate growth," Komai adds. "It underlines our corporate philosophy. Duskin grows when we help others to grow! Through our prayerful management concept, our ideals of service are united with the sharing and growth that comes through franchising—each contributes its own form of originality and blends with the other to form a harmonic whole.

"Everything I have learned through experience about people and business convinces me that we are on the right path to the future and that we have a solid foundation on which to continue to grow," states Komai.

Seiichi Gotoh, an honorary advisor to Duskin and a former executive vice president of Sanyo Electric Company, says, "More important than being proud of only the many beautiful flowers it has in bloom today, a company should be concerned with how many buds it has that will bloom tomorrow." Duskin and its extended family have taken these words to heart.

To give optimal direction to franchising, Duskin is dedicated to merging spiritual values with economics and combining intellectual qualities with technical ability. "Our experiences have taught us that franchising is a system for selling and attaining success," Komai explains. "Our definition of success encompasses both business and life. Our final goal is to be the best people possible; we want to be people who are capable of sharing by placing the needs and desires of others over our own. In recognition of the fact that the success of franchising depends on human beings, we constantly emphasize the slogan 'Franchising is a way of life.' At Duskin, we ask franchisees to avoid the single-minded pursuit of profit and instead unite with us to accept our joint responsibilities to the community."

The Duskin executive staff provides direction and leadership by encouraging a franchisee to achieve success. As the franchisee becomes more successful, the headquarters staff is, in turn, encouraged to expend even greater effort. Defined as its "philosophy of mutualism," the concept is expressed to franchisees that if they do not succeed, neither can the franchisor. On the other hand, the franchisor has a responsibility to guide a franchisee toward success. And yet the franchisee must not become too dependent; each must contribute to the effort.

Since its founding, Duskin has strived to create opportunities for ambitious people who sought an opportunity to be independent. The company views franchising as a superior system that realizes this immense human potential.

CEO Komai describes the three 'P's' of franchising that contribute to a franchise's success. "The first 'P' stands for the *philosophy of mutualism*, the second 'P' is for the *power of the franchise headquarters*, and the third 'P' represents the *people who are gathered together to work for a common goal*. Taken together, the three 'P's' emphasize that the basis of successful franchising is its human resources," he notes.

In seeking new franchisees, Duskin stresses that each must share its philosophy. "Our first qualification for a prospective franchisee is that he shares a similar philosophy with us. We are not concerned with what religion he or she may observe," Komai says. "In selecting a good partner, one you may have for the rest of your life, money and position are not the first priority—it is personality, feeling, the way of thinking that matches with our own that we stress. This is the most important quality in a long-term relationship. So we ask our prospective franchisees: 'Can you share the same philosophy with us for the rest of your lives?' Fortunately, our philosophy has become well-known throughout the Japanese community, so many people understand what we believe in before they apply to work with or for us."

Throughout the past three decades, customer service has been an important part of Duskin's history. Suzuki believed in satisfying the customers 100 percent, and all his business partners must share this belief. "Our partners, employees, and franchisees must have this same philosophy for mutual respect and love as we have," says Komai. "Japan fell behind the United States by 20 years in terms of functional services, but, traditionally, the Japanese have been very service minded. We want to franchise with American companies so we can learn about their system. Still, our first mission is to satisfy our customers. To accomplish this, we are committed to hard work."

Suzuki's concept is broader than customer service. It must encompass service to franchisees. In the way that Ray Kroc's spirit continues to guide McDonald's employees, Duskin employees are continually reminded of Suzuki's prayerful management. All new recruits and major franchisees must perform three days and two nights of public service and spiritual training at Itto-en Chitoku Kenshu, a religious establishment in Kyoto.

This is spiritual training outside the ivory tower. On the first day, workers are sent to houses and are told to clean toilets free of charge. Day two begins on the streets in Kyoto, where they must find a one-day, unpaid job. On the third day, they clean up the facilities of the spiritual camp. By the end of the session, the students have begun to understand selfless service with no reward except personal satisfaction.

Every Duskin office opens and ends each day with a prayer meeting. Striving for management through prayer, all Duskin employees chant the management philosophy and read aloud the best known Buddhist Sutra, the "Prajnaparamita Sutra," which proclaims that "work's most important function is character building."

Duskin doesn't ignore practical training. Once spiritual training is completed, franchisees enter one of a number of training centers, depending on their business affiliation. Mister Donut Business College provides a 40-day training program for Mister Donut franchisees (each pays the per person $4,000 cost). At Aino-Mise Business College, instruction is structured to expand knowledge, skills, and the best all-around approach to total clean care services. The ServiceMaster Training Center, where employees and franchisees receive professional cleaning technique training, is vital to the division. Duskin Seishinkan is a center for conducting workshops, seminars, and other extensive educational programs.

Komai explains that employees and franchisees are expected to continue to attend many of the classes offered at training programs throughout their careers. "Mr. Suzuki always believed in creating—or may I say, developing—our people before developing our product. Duskin franchisees have a franchise coalition or association. Our organization of franchisees is slightly different from an ordinary association," explains Komai. "We created the organization with one thing in mind, which is that, together, we serve our customers. We want our franchisees to think in this manner, so our association reinforces this philosophy. Then the group becomes a unified body for service to our customers. We operate just like any other company without a worker's union."

Duskin operates 80 district offices, each with a district manager and regional managers. Franchisees must get together with their respective managers at least once a month, not only for motivation but also to keep communication open—Duskin transfers information, education, training, and supervision to its franchisees.

The company makes additional opportunities available to its franchisees. A franchisee can be recommended for another Duskin business. Although Duskin sells licenses to each of its franchised businesses separately, a strong franchisee is eligible to operate other company franchises under his or her ownership. A very successful ServiceMaster franchisee, for example, is eligible to buy a Mister Donut franchise. A franchisee who licenses any of the different Duskin businesses can amass a sizable fortune.

Duskin frequently will guarantee a bank loan for a new franchise, but the company does not provide direct financing. A Duskin subsidiary leases equipment and automobiles to franchisees, saving them the higher cost of doing business with commercial establishments.

General Manager Kojima claims it is considerably less expensive to buy a franchise in Japan than in the United States. Royalty rates, however, are approximately the same. "We set aside the initial fees that our franchisees pay us, because we feel this money should be treated as a deposit," Kojima says. "This money is not used to pay the expenses of the company, but is returned to the franchisees if they leave the company."

In April 1969, Duskin became the first Japanese company to be accepted as a member of the International Franchise Association. In January 1987, at the IFA Annual Convention, Duskin's founder, the late Seiichi Suzuki, became the first Japanese to be inducted into the IFA's "Hall of Fame of Franchising" in the same ceremony that honored Ray Kroc of McDonald's, Colonel Harland Sanders of Kentucky Fried Chicken, and Palmer J. Waslien of the Southland Corporation. These four figures were recognized as "being legendary pioneers and leaders in the establishment of franchise business throughout the world." IFA noted that their companies were still prosperous and enjoy good standing in the international marketplace. This international recognition of Suzuki marked a highlight in Duskin's history as well as in the history of franchising in Japan.

In Japan, Komai and Suzuki, franchise pioneers, helped create the Japan Franchising Association (JFA), initially to study the theories of franchising. This led to the publication of "General Principles of Ethics" and, ultimately, a registration system that has assisted the rapid expansion of franchising in Japan. Komai served as chairman of the board of the JFA from 1981 to 1983 and a second term from 1986 to 1989. Komai believes that both franchising and Duskin share common goals, all of which strengthen service to consumers and to Japan's economy. In *The Challenge to Service*, which the CEO wrote in 1987, he expressed these shared goals:

1. Offering services and goods of equal quality at reasonable prices to customers everywhere. This means in any area of the nation, customers are assured of the same dollar value and product quality.

2. Providing management know-how to modernize and systemize small and medium-sized businesses.

3. Making available those products and services that exactly meet the emerging needs of consumers, especially at times when society is undergoing rapid change.

4. Conducting research and development activities that, when successful, are transferred from the franchisor to the

franchisee. This division of labor allows franchisees to concentrate on service to customers without diversions or extraneous responsibilities.

Duskin looks to the twenty-first century to become one of the most integrated service companies in the world, with an unswerving commitment to franchising. As Duskin looks ahead, it upholds its commitment to being the predominant service company in Japan, ultimately offering 100 service systems to its customers, as well as "100 percent quality," and "100 percent people." Anything less than 100 percent in service is zero, according to the Duskin philosophy. The nationwide chain anticipates targeted sales of ¥1 trillion by the year 2001.

As early as 1987 the company began to develop detailed strategic plans to respond to dynamic environmental and other changes. This Challenge 21 plan expresses Duskin's desire to integrate and expand its quality services in a new era. Today work toward Challenge 21 is directed from Duskin's 11-story headquarters building in Suita City, Osaka. Duskin Pia, completed in August 1990, a reminder that it achieves Duskin's utopia. It is a technological and managerial center as well as functioning as a communication link for franchisees and employees across the Pacific Rim. Duskin Pia boasts a health club and a nine-hole rooftop golf course where company employees and their guests can play, day or night.

The Duskin Co., Ltd., a thriving service company committed to franchising, grew from simple beginnings of selling a single product door to door. Today the company exemplifies the diversity and growth as well as the internationalism associated with franchising. Duskin has expanded its original product base many times over and, as a partner with other entrepreneurial companies, principally American, has brought many franchise concepts to Japan.

As the company looks forward to the twenty-first century, Duskin remains dedicated to merging spiritual values and economies. It is unique among the early franchise pioneers—it has sustained its traditional base while becoming a thoroughly modern franchise success story.

Chapter 5

HOLIDAY INN, WORLDWIDE

Nobody Understands the Trials and Travails of Franchisees Like Holiday Inn

In the summer of 1951, while on a family vacation in Washington, D.C., Kemmons Wilson was appalled that the lodgings available along the way from his native Tennessee were dirty, cramped and overpriced. He was disgusted that his family was forced to stay in motels that offered little in the way of amenities and eat in restaurants that served poorly prepared food. During that trip, he recognized clearly the need for more comfortable, standardized, and economical accommodations for travelers around the country. Upon returning to his hometown, Memphis, Tennessee, with the thought fresh in his mind that he had "the most miserable vacation in my life," Wilson vowed to his wife Dorothy that he would do something about it.

"The experience," he says with a frown, "was so bad that as soon as I got back to Memphis I decided to build the right kind of motel, one that would have all the things we missed on that trip.

"I told my wife that I was going to build a chain of 400 motels," he recalls. "She thought I was crazy—and at first everybody else I talked to thought the same thing. But I managed to talk one of the right people into it—the banker."

Wilson, a building contractor borrowed $350,000 from a local bank and began construction on the first Holiday Inn in Memphis. The hotel opened in 1952, and 20 months later, he built three more inns, each on a major highway approach into the city.

"If anybody was coming to Memphis," he says, "he or she had to go by a Holiday Inn to get there."

The original 4 Holiday Inns were tremendously successful, and Wilson was determined to meet his goal of 400. But it would take an enormous amount of money. Although Wilson was doing well, he had neither the money nor the credit to accomplish his goal. So, as an impatient man who realized that the high financial requirements would slow down the growth, Wilson decided to franchise his "inns."

With a background in home building, Wilson believed he could find enough builders to join him in his efforts. "I contacted Wallace Johnson, the president of the National Home Building Association and one of the nation's largest real estate builders," Wilson says, "and asked him to help me recruit builders to build a Holiday Inn in every city in the United States. I offered Johnson a 50-percent partnership, which he accepted.

"We wrote letters to all the home builders we could find, and 63 of them showed up in Memphis for a meeting with us," the entrepreneur continues. "I told the group I wanted to sell my franchises for $500 each and a flat fee of 5 cents per night for each occupied room. Every one of them gave us $500 and said he was going to build a hotel. The first franchise was opened in Clarksdale, Mississippi.

"Then, we decided that we should find other types of professionals to be franchisees. So we recruited lawyers, doctors, and other professionals who had money but would be passive investors. We did everything for our franchisees from providing the plans and specifications to finding the builders and training their managers."

Quickly, word of the franchises' success spread, and dozens of applications for new franchises began to flow in. Wilson chose the most promising candidates and taught them how to build and operate a Holiday Inn. He standardized the architecture and decor and furniture; fixtures were purchased on a large scale and offered to franchisees at discounted prices. Wilson's central office provided operating instructions for hiring employees, and buying supplies, and it assisted with advertising and promotional campaigns. Wilson promised to deliver quality to the public, and as the chain grew he honored his commitment. He wanted to standardize his hotels in the same way that Howard Johnson standardized his roadside restaurants.

"I had complete confidence in my original idea," he says. "I knew that traveling people wanted a lot more than what existing hotels and motels were offering—and they'd pay a reasonable price to get them. So I provided clean, comfortable, attractive rooms; air conditioning; a swimming pool; a restaurant on the premises; a conference room in every hotel; a telephone and television in every room; free ice; dog kennels; free parking; baby cribs; babysitting services; and all at moderate prices. Also available were a children-under-twelve-stay-free policy when kids share a parent's room and accommodations for the handicapped. I wanted people to enjoy staying in a motel."

He insisted on cleanliness, relative uniformity, and careful attention to detail. He wanted to offer a place to stay where all travelers would know ahead of time that Holiday Inn was an acceptable place to spend the night at a reasonable rate.

Holiday Inn offered many standard amenities which were "firsts" in the hotel chain industry, including televisions and air conditioning in all rooms. It was also the first hotel to guarantee room satisfaction or your money back.

The unique guest services of the chain's first hotels established the pattern for the entire Holiday Inn system. For example, in the early years of development, "No Vacancy" signs were not permitted. Wilson's ploy was to bring potential customers into a Holiday Inn to witness first hand how well the operation was run. If the hotel had a room, fine; if not, the staff would find the customer the best available room elsewhere. This simple policy became a standard feature.

While Wilson was concerned about quality, he was also interested in quantity, so he began to concentrate on growth. For the chain to make a really strong impact on the industry, he sought a Holiday Inn in every city. "Of course, at the time, quality was almost natural because everything was so new," explains an early franchisee, Jim Dora, who owns five units in Indiana, "We were constructing all new buildings, so we didn't have problems with quality."

Further expansion required capital, so Wilson and his partners chose to go public. In 1957, the first offering raised over $2 million, which was used to finance additional hotels. By 1964, Wilson surpassed his goal—the total number of Holiday Inns in the United States reached the 500 mark. Holiday Inn had become the nation's leader in hotel construction; at one point, new units were opening every two-and-a-half days, for 16 consecutive years! The greatest concern for management became collecting franchise fees and developing the reservation and marketing systems.

In 1980, Wilson sold his interest in the company on the public market, and Holiday Corp. was developed with Wilson's staff continuing to lead the company. Holiday Corp. became a leading hotel and casino operator and operated the system until February 1990 when Bass PLC, a 200-year-old London-based company with interests in hotels, restaurants, beverage, and gaming, acquired Holiday Inn. Bass had begun a slow-motion acquisition in 1988, when the company paid $475 million for the entire Holiday Inn operation outside North America, plus 13 U.S. hotels.

Bryan D. Langton, C.B.O.E., chairman of Bass's hotels division, was named chairman and chose to relocate the company's headquarters from its birthplace in Memphis to Atlanta, which became its new North American base. The company was also renamed as "Holiday Inn Worldwide."

As an affiliate of Bass PLC, Holiday Inn Worldwide has the financial strength to support its future growth. Bass's extensive resources support the sophisticated technology, aggressive marketing, and strong management capabilities that Holiday Inn Worldwide requires to maintain its industry lead. Specifically, Bass pledged to invest $1 billion to be used for improving existing facilities and developing new products.

"More than $500 million will be put into our U.S. operations, part of which will be used to enhance our portfolio by acquiring hotels with other brand names, such as Hilton, Omni, and Marriott," explains the chairman. "The money will help support Holiday Inn Express via the conversion of existing hotels to Express," he adds. "The rest, some $450 million, will be used to expand the Holiday Inn name outside of the United States."

Michael Leven, president of Holiday Inn's Franchise Hotels Division, is responsible for all franchising in the Americas, including Canada, United States, Mexico, Latin America, and the Caribbean. In addition, he serves as an advisor to franchisees in the Far East, Europe, the Middle East, and Africa.

According to Leven, "Bass has injected enormous amounts of capital into the company, which has dramatically improved the quality of our owned and operated portfolio. Furthermore, the whole system will improve on a technological basis. We have a very productive reservations system which differentiates Holiday Inn from the competition. And Bass's substantial investment will make it even better to assure that we continue to have that difference.

"When Kemmons was here, Holiday Inn was very entrepreneurial, particularly in the beginning," Leven states. "However, as the company grew, it became more and more bureaucratic. In time, Wilson was moved farther away from the day-to-day operations. Bass is trying to debureaucratize the company and make it more agile, to allow every level of the organization to make decisions. We are trying to get back to our founder's entrepreneurial management style. We want it to run more like a small business."

Holiday Inn's innovations and standards have made this franchise system the icon of American roadside hostelries. Over the years, dozens of other hotel chains have attempted to replicate Holiday Inn's successful system, and currently, there are roughly 60 different brand affiliations offered by about 30 companies. Yet, for over 40 years, Holiday Inn has continuously outperformed every other hotel chain, dominating the massive, flourishing midscale market, which accounts for almost 80 percent of all travelers.

The hotel giant has become the most recognized name in the lodging industry, with a size and reputation that has given it an unparalleled position in the midpriced lodging marketplace. In 1991, there were over 1,600 hotels and over 320,000 rooms in 51 countries, making Holiday Inn Worldwide the largest international hotel chain by number of units in the world. Today, one can hardly go anywhere in the civilized world without seeing a Holiday Inn sign. Recent figures reveal that 98 percent of all U.S. travelers have stayed at a Holiday Inn one night or more. Statistics indicate that consumers choose Holiday Inn 3 to 1 over other franchised brands, resulting in higher occupancy levels than the competition.

The company also outperforms every other major midscale franchise chain in customer satisfaction and intend-to-return scores. There is a price perception that a Holiday Inn is affordable, and what's more, the public trusts the Holiday Inn sign.

Gaines Sturdivant and his father, Mike, have been franchise owners for over 35 years. Today, they own nine units located throughout Louisiana, Mississippi, and Florida. "When we joined Holiday Inn, it was a new, up-and-coming product—the first of its kind," Gaines explains. "And, over the years, it has become the choice brand of the middle market because of its powerful marketing tools, reservation system, and size. Now there's practically a Holiday Inn on virtually every corner.

"Holiday Inn offers hotels brand awareness, prepackaged training, buying power, and most important, the financial power to penetrate the huge marketplace," he adds.

Robert Goff, Jr., who has been involved with Holiday Inn since he was a teenager, admits that he was born and bred to work with Holiday Inn. His father, Robert, Sr., became associated with the company in the late 1950s when he bought his first Holiday Inn in

Hot Springs, Arkansas. "Holiday Inn was the first kid on the block," the young Goff explains. "I think it has continued to be successful after all these years because it was able to get the best locations. My father and I have been so happy with the product that we bought three more Holiday Inns, and our management company operates two other units for other investors."

Michael Leven believes that in the future franchising will have a strong presence in the hotel industry. "Years ago, about 10 percent of hotels were chains, and the rest were independents. Today, over 50 percent are chains, and in the future, we predict that 70 to 80 percent will be chain affiliates," explains Leven. "In today's travel environment, the only way you can get enough market penetration and survive is with a chain. Unless independents can go out and get their own business, they can't make it in today's marketplace.

"I think chain affiliation in 90 percent of the cases is appropriate," adds Leven. "Still, there are some situations where you don't need to be affiliated, but I think most will find that the chains will keep growing because the public wants a brand name that they feel secure with."

The benefits for operating a hotel franchise under agreement with Holiday Inn are numerous. The immense size of Holiday Inn with its 1,600-hotel operation is a major attraction to its franchisees, who, in turn, are able to enjoy enormous buying power, which savings are passed on to them. Franchisees are able to purchase supplies at discounted prices through special catalogues that are available to them from participating manufacturers. They receive volume discounts because every hotel in the system is buying from the same catalogues.

Perhaps the company's number one innovation that made its phenomenal growth possible is its reservation system, "Holidex," which was introduced in August 1961. Hailed as state-of-the-art technology, this international reservation system was the first in the industry to offer property-to-property reservation capacity. While the competition has attempted to duplicate the powerful reservation system, Holidex is still considered the best of its kind in the hotel field. To this day, every Holiday Inn is linked by Holidex, which is operated by computer centers linked to terminals in each of the chain's units around the world. Holidex handles more than 20 million calls a year and books over 30 percent of all U.S. Holiday Inn room nights, translating to more than $1 billion in room revenues per year. Serving both the franchisee and the customer, it provides easy and spontaneous access for making reservations. By telephoning via Holidex, reservations are guaranteed without regard to arrival time when an approved credit card is used. Holidex is also valuable to the franchisees' business. A Holidex machine will typically fill up one-third of a Holiday Inn every night. This portion is enough to cover most of the owner's overhead.

"Holidex 2000" is a separate computerized system, connected to Holidex, which provides franchisees with valuable marketing information, such as yield management, market segmentation, demand pricing, night auditing, folio management, and guest profile information. The Holidex system creates a data base based on customer preferences and reservation information which are analyzed by Holidex 2000. This added service maximizes franchisee revenue by recommending marketing, inventory, and pricing decisions based on projected demand which is routinely used to target marketing programs.

Holiday Inn's quality assurance programs are so well known that its customers are able to identify a unit with a certain quality level and image. These high-standard qualities of every hotel in the system provide instant credibility and allow travelers to feel comfortable staying at any Holiday Inn hotel—sight unseen. Holiday Inn's quality assurance programs include "Hospitality Promise" and "Forget Something."

The Hospitality Promise guarantees customers that if they are not satisfied with anything at all at any Holiday Inn, the hotel will either solve the problem or refund their customer's money. The Forget Something program states that if a guest forgets his or her toothbrush, toothpaste, hair spray, or almost any other toiletry, management will supply it at no charge. Also Holiday Inn uses an automatic customer service tracking system that collects data from guests. The corporate office uses this information to rank and rate each of its hotels so that the superior and inferior performers are identified.

In the past, one type of hotel adequately served the majority of travelers. But as the needs of business and leisure travelers dramatically evolved during the 1980s, lodging demands proliferated, and accordingly, consumer expectations changed. In addition to the original or "core" Holiday Inn hotel, three other types were added to the system, serving a wider market. New lines include the higher-standard Holiday Inn Crowne Plaza, the limited facility Holiday Inn Express, and the European Holiday Inn Garden Court chain.

It was the expanding, discriminating travelers' market that inspired one franchisee to come up with a brilliant innovation. Jack Pratt, a franchisee in Dallas, Texas, constructed the first Crowne Plaza in the late 1970s when he built an upscale Holiday Inn hotel with an atrium, three restaurants, and an indoor swimming pool. This was no easy accomplishment because initially, he ran into considerable resistance. When Pratt put the distinctive Holiday Inn sign up in front of the hotel, customers did not understand why they had to pay higher prices than what they were charged at other Holiday Inns. According to Pratt, a customer would come into town and say, "I want to stay at your hotel, but why do I have to pay $90? It is just a Holiday Inn and no other hotel in the chain costs that much!" While a customer might have stayed at another upscale hotel, perhaps a Weston or Marriott with the same amenities, he or she expected to pay more there. But not at a Holiday Inn!

In the beginning, the hotel had a high vacancy rate, and Pratt realized that something had to be done—and fast. Recognizing that the hotel needed a name to distinguish it as a top-of-the-line hotel, Pratt asked the Holiday Inn management for its permission. His request was denied, and he was told not to advertise anything but the standard Holiday Inn name. Pressed, the Dallas hotelier refused orders from headquarters and placed a "Crowne Plaza" sign above his hotel. At first, this was seen as an infringement of Holiday Inn policy, and the franchisee received a warning to remove it—or else. After a series of "discussions," however, management was convinced to give Pratt a chance to operate his hotel under the name,

Holiday Inn Crowne Plaza. The innovative franchisee's hotel was so successful the company decided to expand his idea on a national scale.

Now opening at a rapid pace in major metropolitan markets, business centers, and resort locations throughout the world, the Crowne Plaza hotels are aimed at an upper midmarket. Here, the Holiday Inn traditional standards for quality and service are increased to a higher level with additional features and amenities, including specialty restaurants, health facilities, larger meeting rooms, executive floors, and top-of-the-line room furnishings. From Bangkok to Geneva to Manhattan, Crowne Plaza caters to the needs of discriminating travelers.

In still another market, Holiday Inn has recently introduced a streamlined hotel, providing functional facilities which are both comfortable and economical. "Holiday Inn Express" is a smart choice for the cost-conscious business traveler as well as the enroute leisure traveler. The Express hotels offer bright, comfortable guest rooms, a buffet breakfast, and a Great Room/lobby with a large-screen television. Small meeting rooms and fax machines are also available, though no restaurant is on the premises.

In Europe, Holiday Inn has addressed the growing acceptance of more value-priced lodging alternatives, with the introduction of the Garden Court hotels. This brand is located primarily in smaller European towns and cities for both business and leisure travelers who appreciate good values. The Garden Court hotels are small (100 rooms) and offer guests a European perspective toward modern hospitality with a bistro-style restaurant and bar, a fitness area, and meeting rooms for small groups. A relatively new face on the European landscape, this chain has received immediate popularity.

Leven reveals Holiday Inn's exciting growth plans: "Currently, we want to grow the system with quality. We plan on expanding the new Crowne Plaza line, and by 1993, we should have 100 more to add to our portfolio. Seventy-five percent of these will be conversions. We will also be replacing a considerable number of our older core-brand Holiday Inn hotels over the next couple of years as they leave the system because of age or quality. Ninety percent of these will be conversions.

"In addition, we will construct or convert hotels for our new limited-service Holiday Express brand which stands at the high end of the economy line," Leven elaborates. "Express is expected to grow to 250 properties, of which 75 percent will be a result of conversions. We are also planning to construct 60 to 70 new Garden Courts in Europe."

Conversions, or "reflagging," frequently happen during a specified period in a hotel's contract with its franchisor when the hotel owner is legally permitted to walk away from its contract. The conversion to the Holiday Inn system typically takes six months, which is usually much more expedient and cost effective than new construction, which can take up to two years before opening.

Present Holiday Inn owners have found the company to be such a sound and attractive investment they purchase over 71 percent of all new Holiday Inn licenses sold every year.

The company's reputation is so secure in the industry that in the past few years over 70 hotels with approximately 13,000 rooms have converted to the Holiday Inn brand. In addition, Holiday Inn is the brand choice for most of the top hotel management firms in the United States.

"It is a lot easier to get a decent loan if you are part of a successful franchise group, and none is better than Holiday Inn," says Jim Dora, a Holiday Inn franchisee since 1962.

"Also, it would be really difficult for us to assure recognition by customers who come from far away to my city for the first time if I didn't have the Holiday Inn name. If my hotel were called 'Jim Dora's Hotel,' what would that mean to them? The reliability that the Holiday Inn name brings to my hotels is invaluable. The chain is well known, and customers can rely on our hotels for at least minimum standards of quality," he adds.

The chain's reputation has made it a sound investment. Regardless of the line, a new Holiday Inn hotel will come with a 20-year licensing agreement. Franchisees pay an average royalty of 4 percent of their room revenue, plus a small fee for marketing and reservations. According to Leven, a core brand Holiday Inn should achieve 35 to 40 percent gross operating profit (GOP) levels, while the Express line generates 45 to 50 percent, and the Crowne Plazas earn between 25 and 35 percent.

"The more expensive the hotel, the lower the percentage of gross operating profit," explains Leven. "Of course, it costs more to operate a Crowne Plaza than our other lines, but even though the GOP percentage is lower, the dollar return can be terrific."

To qualify to be a Holiday Inn franchisee, a good prospect must have a strong financial statement and excellent credit. Today, intangible requirements include a proven track record in the hotel business.

"Even though it is not mandatory for a prospective franchisee personally to have hotel background, he or she will need a management company that does have the experience," states Leven. "Otherwise, we won't sell a franchise. We need to know early on that they know what they are doing.

"Today's hotel business is too complicated to be able to run a franchise effectively without experience. Approximately 85 percent of our licensees are active in the day-to-day operations. While an inexperienced franchisee could have been successful when business was in its infancy and there was less competition," says Leven, "that's no longer the case."

Holiday Inn Worldwide is currently embarking on a mission to revamp its entire organization. Every Holiday Inn hotel must meet new standards for customer service and product quality to remain in the system. Langton states that his staff is moving quickly to revise the chain's operating standards to make certain that units do not deteriorate from age and neglect. For instance, it is now mandatory for every unit to make consistent investments to maintain its property. Holiday Inn management has determined that the average renovation periods are 5 years for public spaces, 7 years for guest rooms, and 15 years for exteriors. If a franchisee owner is unwilling or unable to make such investments, the property could go "down a flag" (an industry term that means losing its Holiday Inn license and signing with another franchisor, usually of lower quality).

"I've notified our people that company-managed and franchised hotels will go out of the system if they don't improve," says Langton. Holiday Inn has removed, or deflagged, several company-owned hotels and franchised hotels that could not meet specific standards. Langton admits that he won't arbitrarily purge hotels from the system, and his plans are almost universally well received by franchisees.

Langton became sensitive to the position of franchisees when he was a franchisee, responsible for the operations of seven Holiday Inns in Europe that Bass purchased in 1988.

"The major thrust for Holiday Inn now is quite clear," Langton explains. "That is to improve hotel quality, to improve customer service, and to continue to look at all markets and take opportunities as they come up.

"We are changing the way that we service all the people who pay us for using our brand name on their hotels. There will be more focus on how we will market, more focus on how we advertise, more focus on assisting franchisees to help them with financing, and more focus, if you wish, on how to operate. I want to go to the franchises to train them. I don't want to train anyone in some office or on some block in the middle of Atlanta or Memphis. Let's train on-site. Let's go to the people; let's show them what we mean. Our franchisees are really in business with us. What we must do is become much more effective, to make sure that they are going to get, as we go forward to the twenty-first century, the services that will make them better businesses."

"We aim to be the most effective hotel company in North America," he adds, "by offering our franchisees the support services they require to achieve higher occupancies, higher daily rates, and higher profits."

Bass has developed additional changes that are designed to set the chain on a new course. A new division focusing on quality makes sure that the franchisees comply with appropriate standards. Called the Quality and Design team, it reports directly to the CEO and visits each Holiday Inn once or twice a year to inspect for quality.

"I'm looking for a much more consistent product in the United States," Langton expresses, "This consistency doesn't mean that the roadside property in Opelika, Alabama, will be the same as the Crowne Plaza in Manhattan. It all goes back to price value. I'm looking for our franchisees, and for us, actually to provide the basics better than anybody else, in whichever bracket or segment of the business we are operating. I think that's what the customer will see. When you are a customer at Holiday Inn, we want to make certain that you go away as a satisfied customer."

The franchisees stand behind Langton's decision to enforce strict quality guidelines. "Of course, in any franchise relationship, the franchisor has to be the leader. If they don't show us the way, there's no one for us to follow," expresses Frank Flautt, former president of the Holiday Inn Owners' Association and himself a long time franchisee.

According to Leven, Holiday Inn lost more than 40 hotels as a result of poor quality in 1991. "Some of these had not reached the failure level, but when their license contract expired, they did not renew it in anticipation that the corporate office would ask for them to make a significant investment," he explains. "When an owner determines that the investment is not in his or her best interest nor is it in our best interest to keep the hotel in the system, he or she will convert to another brand.

"We had one person with five small Holiday Inns in New York and Pennsylvania that needed a lot of renovations. The owner chose to convert these units to Days Inn, which was really an economical decision," he adds.

"There is a lot of older product in the system, some of which is very good. Even so, in the next year or so, we will probably lose over 100 properties, consisting of mostly older products that have been allowed to deteriorate. Hotels can be compared to human beings. Just because you are 65, it doesn't make you bad. If you stay in shape and do the right thing at 65, you can be great. It is the same in our system.

"In some cases, an owner cannot afford to make renovations. We are currently in the process of putting together a loan fund from which our franchisees can borrow money to bring their products up to our standards. We also have had situations where there have been significant numbers of guest complaints about a hotel. When the manager and/or owner does not want to satisfy the complaints, we have to drive them out of the system. Sometimes, it has nothing to do with the physical appearance of the hotel, it's a matter that involves their attitude toward the guests," adds Leven.

Jim Dora is a franchisee who is a strong believer in quality and customer service. "I believe that quality is extremely important, not to just please the franchisor and to adhere to its standards, but to deliver the quality to the customer that is expected," the successful franchisee explains. Dora's five Holiday Inns, located in Indiana, prove that his aggressiveness in quality is paying off. They continuously achieve high occupancy rates in excess of 73 percent; an occupancy rate that is greater than the chain's average.

Dora believes that franchises that fail in quality standards should be dropped from the system. "My hotels are in good shape, and I want the customer to expect all Holiday Inns to have the same qualities," he explains. "Poorly operated franchises can damage my business."

"There are not too many people who want to lose their Holiday Inn sign, so they work hard to comply with our demands for quality," Leven stresses. "The motivation is that they invest their money in order to keep the sign. Our sign brings higher rates and more occupancies than the competition. Our franchisees recognized that they have the most valuable sign in this business."

Prior to joining Holiday Inn, Michael Leven was president of Days Inn for six years and before that president of Americana Hotels, which owned a Holiday Inn franchise in Kansas City, Missouri. With experience as a competitive franchisor and a Holiday Inn franchisee, today as president of the Franchise Hotels Division, Leven has worked both sides of the street. With candor Leven tells, "My experience as a Holiday Inn franchisee wasn't a very cordial one because they threw us out! We didn't have the right product quality, so they wouldn't allow us to stay in the Holiday Inn system. I learned that there was a big bureaucracy in the franchise business, and if you weren't fortunate enough to understand how it worked, you couldn't get much done. Now as a franchisor, I know we need to be more sensitive to our franchisees and their needs."

In addition to a Holiday Inn franchise, Leven has managed several other franchised hotels, including Ramada, Best Western, Roadway, Days Inn, and Hilton. "I have a very good feeling for what the franchisee really wants," he claims. "From my own experience, I found that most franchise companies don't treat their franchisees well. There were times when I felt they took my money and could care less about how much money I made. As long as I paid them, that's all they wanted. Then, every now and then they would come around with a big stick and say 'You are doing this lousy,' and they would come down on me. I think they disregarded me as the one who was paying their paycheck. Now I've made up my mind that I am going to build an organization that will be franchisee responsive; knowing that the franchisee is in the same business.

"At Holiday Inn, I have instilled a system of franchisee service and responsiveness known as our franchise delivery system. Here, our main purpose is to encourage communication between the corporate office and the franchisees.

"We are sensitive to the franchisee's needs and requirements, but they still must be in concert with what it is we want to do for the betterment of the whole system. Part of my job is to assure that our guests receive consistent delivery, so I am responsible for franchise training. We are establishing a customer service system and many other training mechanisms into our franchise system that will provide consistency in all our products," Leven adds.

Today, Holiday Inn is recognized as the leader in the hotel industry in supporting its franchisees. The company recently introduced the "Franchise Service Delivery System," consisting of five interrelated components: franchise service managers, road scholars, property executive training, new unit opening assistance, and strategic revenue management.

The franchise service managers are the heart of the new system.

These professionals are experts in all areas of hotel operations. Based in Atlanta at corporate headquarters, an FSM is assigned to every hotel and owner. The FSM's primary responsibility is to enhance the franchisee's success, and to achieve this goal the FSM must be a problem solver. The FSM is the prime contact for the franchisee he or she serves in all dealings with the company, including answering questions about programs, systems, and services. This saves a lot of time and red tape because the franchisees now have to deal only with one person at the corporate headquarters rather than many different departments. FSM representatives are available 24 hours a day and travel to franchises whenever assistance is requested.

Back in 1959, Holiday Inn opened its innkeeping school "Holiday Inn University," in Memphis, for the training of new franchisees and their managers in every facet of the hotel chain's operations. Here, management preached strict adherence to product standards that encompasses service, product quality, design, construction, safety, operations, and technical management. The company recently remodeled the training programs, permanently closing Holiday Inn University, and, instead, has incorporated many of the training programs to be taught on-site.

A program was introduced in 1990, called the "road scholars," which consists of 17 teams of two people, a junior and a senior trainer, who deliver on-site customized training to franchisees. The teams provide hands-on assistance and up-to-date information. The teams visit each Holiday Inn twice a year and conduct workshops on marketing programs, management techniques, and customer service and explain how to use the Holidex system.

A mandatory "Property Executive Training" program held at the new Holiday Inn Crowne Plaza in Atlanta (located next to the corporate headquarters office) is attended by general managers, food and beverage managers, and guest service managers. This program emphasizes all the different areas of operation that are unique to the Holiday Inn system. The lengths of these courses range from two and a half days for the guest service manager, sales manager, and food and beverage manager to five days for new general managers. Certification for all programs is awarded as well as recertification requirements by attending road scholar presentations.

In addition, Holiday Inn's "New Unit Opening Assistance" program provides all training for new staff with tailored programs for Holiday Inn Express and Crowne Plazas. A new opening team visits a new Holiday Inn two weeks before opening and trains the entire staff on all procedures.

"We believe that this is the most extensive and intensive training in the hotel industry," Leven says with pride. "In the hotel business today, to succeed, you have to be able to train your franchisees properly, which most other hotel chains do not do very well. We are the only hotel firm that has on-property training for all its properties." All franchisee training is free of charge with the exception of the cost of materials, which is minimal.

The Strategic Revenue Management Department is a new and unique resource for all franchisees. This department's purpose is to ensure the future competitiveness and effectiveness of the Holidex reservation system. The consultants in this department analyze strategic revenue and inventory systems, recommend changes, and work with senior management to implement the strategic improvements. Using reservation data, they are able to analyze industry trends on yield management and provide direction for future planning. These teams work closely with Holidex, the franchise service managers, and the road scholars in coordinating the information collected at all levels—from property level to owner level. Their research and recommendations directly benefit the entire Holiday Inn franchise community.

Another valuable service to the franchisees is the enormous advertising campaign Holiday Inn executes around the world with an annual marketing investment in excess of $50 million. In addition, Holiday Inn has leveraged advertising dollars by conducting joint promotions with organizations such as Coca-Cola, American Express, Procter & Gamble, Warner Bros., and the National Football League.

The investment has paid itself off with a top-of-mind awareness level that is three times greater than any other chain. The marketing power of Holiday Inn seems to grow as the chain gets bigger and bigger. With 100,000 rooms more than its nearest competitor, its advertising expenditures per room are actually below that of the competition. Also, Holiday Inn has 1,600 hotels, each with a prominent sign in most cities around the world, serving as a constant reminder to the public.

Holiday Inn has become the best known hotel chain in the world with national advertising that keeps the image clear and prominent. The campaign, "Stay with Someone You Know . . . Who Really Knows You," is one of the most effective messages in advertising. The campaign communicates to the public that no matter how foreign a traveler's surroundings are, Holiday Inn is always familiar and comfortable. Extensive studies of the likes and dislikes of its guests were conducted that revealed that two out of three guests were leaving loved ones behind. Knowing this, the company wants the public to know that "nobody understands the trials and travails of travelers like Holiday Inn."

Over the decades, Holiday Inn has developed a special relationship with its franchisees. In 1963, Kemmons Wilson worked with franchisees to create a trade group for its hotel owners, the International Association of Holiday Inns. The association is a vehicle through which the individual licensee can make his or her feelings known to the corporate office. At meetings, franchisees are able to sit down with corporate representatives and discuss company decisions. "The corporate office treats us with respect, and, most important, they listen to us," says franchisee Jim Dora.

"Holiday Inn decided early on that if it was going to sell a licensing agreement for 20 years, and later it chose to change the rules, how can the company do it without working with the franchisees?" says Jim McCauley who has been with Holiday Inn for 18 years and serves as the full-time liaison between the franchise association and the corporate office. In 1983, McCauley was appointed by the franchisees to be the full-time director of their association. Previously, McCauley had worked for Holiday Inn's corporate office for over ten years in franchise relations and developed a strong relationship with both the franchisees and the franchisor. "I have a lot of franchisee involvement, and the company supports us and cooperates with us a great deal," he adds.

McCauley doesn't believe that there is another franchise organization that allows its franchisees to play as big a role as Holiday Inn does. "I am also sure that there isn't another franchise association that supports their franchisor more than we do," he adds, "and this has helped our system work so well."

Gaines Sturdivant agrees: "Of all the franchises I have operated, Holiday Inn has the strongest franchisee organization, and the franchisees tend to have greater input as to the direction of the company.

"Historically, Holiday Inn franchisees have always had an effective communication link and greater opportunity for input which strengthens the brand because the franchisees saw the company's success as being an integral part of its own success. Sometimes our committees make suggestions and complaints that the company may not necessarily want to hear. It may not always follow our advice, but the company's management does listen to us. Other franchisors are afraid of what their franchisees might try to do, and don't allow them to speak out," Sturdivant states.

Robert Goff, Jr., the current president, believes that Holiday Inn is different from most other franchise companies. "They don't have to listen to us, but they do. They could force rules and regulations on us like most other franchisors. Others just tell their franchisees, 'you will do this, you won't do that, and this is the way it is.' There is a mutual involvement with the corporate office here where the franchisee is helping the franchisor to develop the system. There has always been more camaraderie between the franchisor and the franchisee here and a spirit of cooperation than other companies enjoy. No other brand has franchisees who have as much input as we do with our franchisor."

The owners' association has a board of directors in which executives from the corporate office and franchisees are members. There is also a committee system in place which McCauley attributes as the greatest communication vehicle. Here, key corporate executives will sit on the committees with franchisees to discuss changes, for example, in the reservation system, marketing, and advertising. The company-owned and company-managed hotels are also represented on an equal basis with the franchises in the association.

According to Goff, "Many of the company's decisions are made in the owners' association boardroom. The corporate office always asks for our input, and I will admit that we don't always win. But they don't always get everything that they want either.

"A year ago Holiday Inn announced that it wanted to raise the standards of quality for the entire system. In so doing, the company wanted to arrive at a whole new set of standards, rules, and regulations. It came up with a 'wish list' and sat down with the owners' association, and we went over everything, item by item. Working together as a team, we were able to compromise and agree on all items," Goff proudly says.

"From my vantage point, Bass and all the new Holiday Inn management are very charged up, and they are really focused. They are excited about working with us, and they see great things happening down the road," he adds.

"When Bass came in, it saw the association as the key vehicle for communication with the American franchisors. It understands that the association was important from their personal experiences when they were members. When they were Holiday Inn franchisees in Europe, they sent Bryan Langton as their representative to serve on our Board of Directors," explains McCauley. "Langton knew us, and he realized that all our intentions were honest. This gave us a lot of credibility. Now, with Bass as our franchisor, the management is seeking our advice about the changes they hope to make.

"If the corporate office decides to change the rules, they first come to the owners' association and recommend the change. The company prefers not to change the rules of operations without first consulting the association. The owner's association reviews all changes in rules because we represent the franchisees, and this process strengthens relationships and the Holiday Inn system itself," explains McCauley.

Now in its fifth decade of operation, Holiday Inn has a

worldwide reputation. Kemmons Wilson's promise to his wife in 1951 was achieved and was surpassed beyond his wildest dreams. This couldn't have been accomplished without franchising his hotels. Wilson didn't just build the largest hotel operation in the world; he founded one of the most successful franchisor-franchisee relationships in existence. This intimate relationship has played a vital role in Holiday Inn Worldwide's success in the past, present, and future.

"Our formula for success is to have successful franchisees. When your franchisees are successful, the success of the franchisor is assured," says Leven.

"Franchising is truly an American phenomenon," Leven concludes, "It allows entrepreneurs to go into business for themselves and, at the same time, receive the benefit of national branding. In the hotel industry, there is no better way this can be done."

Chapter 6

MIDAS INTERNATIONAL CORPORATION

Franchising a Golden Opportunity

The man with the Midas touch, Nate Sherman, founded Midas International Corporation in 1956. One hundred million mufflers later, and over $1 billion in annual revenue, Midas International manufactures and/or distributes 1,300 different types of mufflers and 17,033 other automotive parts to fit most domestic and foreign cars, light trucks, vans, and antique automobiles. Through franchising, Midas today is the industry's leader, boasting more than 2,000 shops around the world.

Self-described as "just a Nebraska farmboy," Sherman was born in Omaha in 1898. Exhibiting impressive skills of leadership and

115

entrepreneurship at an early age, and while still in high school, Sherman managed several paper routes by employing a team of delivery boys. After graduation, Sherman, too young to be drafted during World War I, became an agricultural broker in Omaha's booming farm trade.

In 1929, the depression hit the agricultural industry hard, and Sherman, married with three young children, moved his family to Chicago, with hope of pursuing a new career. Here, Sherman noticed the country's new burgeoning automobile industry—one that promised many opportunities.

Sherman landed a job as a salvage yard operator where soon he established a solid reputation as a one-man sales force blitzing Midwest jobbers with a line of auto parts. While traveling around his sales territory, Sherman became acquainted with a small metal fabricating business in Hartford, Wisconsin, that had recently announced its bankruptcy. Sherman contacted Joe Marx, the defunct company's punch-press operator and asked if he knew how to manufacture mufflers. Marx replied affirmatively, and they formed a partnership.

Renting a small factory in Hartford, with little equipment, Sherman and Marx began to manufacture mufflers for the three most popular cars of the day—the Model T, the Model A, and the Plymouth. In addition, the new business manufactured nine multifit muffler models with a nest of expanded bushings to fit most other cars. While Marx was busy supervising the plant's production in Wisconsin, Sherman operated the sales end of the business in Chicago.

Headquartered in Chicago in 1936, the partners named their company International Parts Corporation. With Sherman as president, in addition to the mufflers it manufactured, the new company sold a broad line of automotive parts purchased at wholesale prices. Shortly after World War II, International Parts strengthened its base for future expansion in the exhaust field when it purchased the well-known Powell Muffler Company of New York.

In the early days, mufflers were made of metal, and because they were not coated, they were prone to rust. Sherman and Marx worked to improve the muffler's quality and longevity. After considerable experimentation, a chemical was discovered that prolonged the life of the metal. "We were the first to put a coating on a muffler," Sherman would proudly state to his customers.

Although the mufflers represented a small part of International Parts' business, the company quickly became known to have the industry's best product. Unlike the competition, these mufflers were completely welded, not crimped. Sherman was excited to prove his product performed better than the competition's. When a friend who owned a plant once asked Sherman to provide him a blowout-proof exhaust for his accident-prone forklifts, Sherman took one of his mufflers to an Underwriters Laboratory to be tested and to find out if it could withstand back pressure without blowing out. They looked at Sherman with an expression that asked, "who had ever heard of testing a muffler? Luckily, he talked them into it.

Underwriters Laboratory performed a series of tests on a truck chassis. In the process, testers tried to blow Sherman's muffler to bits. The muffler was a little distorted by the pressure, but it didn't blow out. At no place was there even the smallest hole!

Sherman's product won the Underwriters Laboratory approval, a symbol of quality that was very difficult to attain and no other muffler company had ever achieved. Soon thereafter, International Parts began to advertise the mufflers as "the safe muffler" and "the world's finest."

Believing in the high quality and performance of his product, Sherman publicly proclaimed, "I will give $100 to anyone who has a muffler blown out under normal driving conditions." *To this day, no one has claimed his money.* The company published a written guarantee—the first one in the entire industry—that stated the mufflers were "guaranteed against blowouts from back pressure." This guarantee is currently honored.

Once Sherman had a first-rate product to market, his only concern was how to distribute it to consumers. At the time, International Parts sold the mufflers to distributors who in turn resold them to garages, gas stations, and car dealers. As a result, distribution warehouses were very powerful because none of these small businesses carried their own inventories and completely relied on distributors for each order.

According to Chief Executive Officer Ron Moore, who has been at Midas since 1965, "Things changed back in 1953 after Nate attended a meeting in Atlanta with many of our former distributors. They pressured Nate to lengthen his terms of payment, increase their discount, and provide several more residual services. Upon Nate's return, he called a meeting with key employees and said, 'Gentlemen, we are losing control of our business. The warehouses are trying to dictate our level of profitability.'

"While discussing the dilemma, someone at the meeting suggested to Nate, 'I wonder if there would be a way we could go from the point of manufacturer all the way through the point of installation while controlling the distribution channel ourselves. We could eliminate the warehouse distributor and the jobber. By eliminating the middlemen, we could effectively collapse our current distribution network,'" revealed Moore.

Sherman recognized a golden opportunity. He knew the company's muffler sales were climbing steadily; the sale of automobiles was rising to record peaks—39.9 million cars were sold between 1950 and 1956—which translated into just as many potential muffler customers. Although his company's sales were never better, Sherman was not content with a limited market. He envisioned something bigger and more profitable.

Before International Parts, no one paid much attention to mufflers—neither the mechanics or the public. After studying the market, Sherman noticed that the supply and demand gap was widening and that automobile owners would eventually demand a quick-service alternative to the traditional service station. At the time, consumers had to go to a gas station or a garage where mufflers were just a sideline. The majority of these customers didn't know what brand they were getting or whether or not the price was fair. Sherman's idea was brilliant, but simple: "Why not specialize?"

Subsequently, Sherman chose to bypass the distributors and sell directly to the consumers. To accomplish this, he formed Midas Muffler Shops, the first retailer in the industry to offer direct marketing and installation of exhaust systems to the public through franchised specialty shops. In the 1950s, franchising was in its pioneering stage, used primarily in the fast-food industry. Sherman, however, was confident that this system of distribution—a series of individual businesses supported by a central corporation—would work just as well in the aftermarket industry. This seemingly simple concept revolutionized the industry and prompted a string of less successful imitators in the then infant franchising field to do the same.

The name "Midas" came naturally: When the laboratory came up with the solution to coat the mufflers for rustproofing, it did the job well. But Sherman thought it would be nice to dress it up a little, so he put brass flakes into the solution. It turned out to look like gold. The first thing that came to mind was the touch of gold—Midas, as in King Midas, the legendary figure who turned everything he touched into gold. Midas has a double meaning and also stands for Muffler Installation Dealers' Association (an "s" was added to complete the name). It is a five-letter word that's impressive and easy for customers to remember.

Sherman's next step was persuading a service station owner, Hugh Landrum, in Macon, Georgia, to convert his location into the first Midas franchise. In 1955, Landrum agreed to sign on, and to this day, the station continues to operate as a successful franchise.

To test the concept of the speedy service and the Midas Muffler further, Sherman set up two places in Chicago under the name "Muffler Clinic" and assessed the results day by day. No one at the time knew the muffler manufacturer was backing the "clinics." CEO Moore recalls, "Nate tested the concept in a very interesting way. He selected a trusted employee and asked him to go out and buy our competitors' mufflers and put the boxes in the front window so nobody would know the clinic was operated by a manufacturer. The clinic displayed our competitors' mufflers, but they were never used. In the back room, of course, was the product that we manufactured.

"This clinic serviced the customers' cars in less than 30 minutes, while the competition—principally garages and service stations— were taking two to three days to perform the same job. The idea of changing the muffler in 30 minutes was very new. The clinics were extremely successful, and in a short time, Nate knew we were on the right track," the CEO explains.

"Opening our first muffler shop was the biggest gamble I ever took," Sherman later admitted, considering the fact that many of the distributors to whom he had been selling would feel they were being bypassed. Sherman conceded that there was a great deal of resistance from the aftermarket when Landrum's shop opened. It caused quite a stir among his jobbers, in particular, those who had been long-term customers. But he maintained the belief that the company could hold on to the distribution business on its own.

On the other hand, consumers readily accepted his new concept. "We took the hidden muffler . . . and made the customer aware of it. Midas was the first. Midas shops provided the customers with something they needed—fast service, a quality product, and a written guarantee they trusted," Sherman has been quoted to have said.

It wasn't long before Sherman devised an innovative marketing approach: the first guarantee in the industry to promise to replace installed mufflers "for as long as you own your car." The revolutionary guarantee was well received by the public and continues to distinguish Midas shops as consumer friendly.

"Nate wasn't really peddling mufflers or exhaust systems," Moore explains. "He was solving service problems. He promised to service cars in less than 30 minutes while keeping the prices competitive—this offered our customers the convenience of saving time *and* money. This also conveyed an attitude of confidence in the quality of our product. This fundamental foundation is as important to our business as it was way back when. As you look at our program today, we still guarantee the muffler for as long as a customer owns his or her car. Likewise, we guarantee our shock absorbers, friction material, and brake systems for as long as a customer owns his or her car. It is part of our system—our heritage—that goes back to the founding of this company."

Sherman had terrific confidence in his concept and decided to open more shops across the nation. The founder convinced many existing customers to sign on and become Midas franchisees. Within a year, there were over 100 Midas Muffler Shops in 40 states, each owned and operated by entrepreneurs who believed in Midas and Nate Sherman.

Many of the original Midas dealers and, in some cases, their offspring are still active franchisees today. One example is early franchisee John Rodasta of New Orleans. In 1992, at the age of 89, Rodasta signed a new 20-year lease!

"Johnny Rodasta is a real optimist! His new lease will last until he is 109 years old," the CEO tells with a smile. "Because of John's early involvement, his family is the first in the Midas system to have four generations work with our program."

Midas shops were unique. In the 1950s, the Midas shops began the tradition of a "show and tell" marketing concept in which the technicians explained to the customer in the service bay what was wrong with their car and involved him or her in the decision-making process of choosing the services the automobile needed. Also, when the work was finished, the customer was shown what was done to the car and the replaced parts were given to him or her. And, unlike the service stations of the day, each Midas shop provided its customers with an estimate in advance, so the customers could understand the extent of the repair work to be done.

Sherman didn't believe in dropping a price to meet his competitors' rates. "Having the lowest prices in town isn't everything. It can be the quickest way to go out of business," explained the founder. "In fact, in some cases, I even raised a price, but I always gave the customer something extra."

Sherman's shops were clean, well lit, and complete with picture windows that enabled customers to observe the mechanics at work on their automobiles. Furthermore, when a customer purchased a Midas-guaranteed product, he or she could go to any Midas shop in the country for a replacement.

Unfortunately, the greater public still did not know the Midas name, so Sherman began an extensive advertising campaign. In 1955, the first Midas commercials were produced and played on popular radio shows such as *News on the Hour* and *Paul Harvey with the News*.

The decision to advertise was based on the fact that the public

was not familiar with the Midas name. The advertising was successful and the Midas name became quickly identifiable with the installation of mufflers, fast service, and especially its guarantee.

The success of its advertising increased awareness and Midas
began to expand at a rapid rate. Subsequently, there was an emer-
gence of numerous local and regional competitors. Recalls Moore,
"When I came to work for Midas in the mid-1960s, we had around
310 shops. Nate hired a consulting firm who told us that 500 shops
would saturate the nation! Later, a second consulting firm told us
that 875 would be our saturation point. A third study predicted the
end of the muffler replacement business. The consultants thought it
would taper off and really then start to go down and our business
would no longer be viable, so we countered that by introducing
brake and suspension services.

"All of these things eventually proved to be incorrect," Russell
Richards states, a 28-year Midas veteran and senior vice president of
franchise operations and marketing. "We learned that the consultants were underestimating our market as we expanded and added
services. We quickly surpassed 875 and today operate nearly 1800
Midas shops in the United States, of which 110 are company owned.
Plus, an additional 300 locations are under investigation. We don't
discuss a saturation point anymore because we don't know what that
number is! As the population of this country shifts, we have new
market opportunities identified daily."

According to Moore, Sherman was not affected by his tremendous success and managed Midas the same when it had 1,000 shops
as when it had only three. The CEO recalls that Sherman avoided
excesses and the wasteful spending of money at the company.

By the 1960s, Midas was a very successful organization, but
Sherman felt the stores needed to perform additional services. In an
effort to increase their overall market share, the first move toward
diversification was the replacement of shock absorbers in 1960. In
1966, Midas acquired Huth manufacturing, a company that
developed made-to-order bender machines that automated the cutting and welding of exhaust system tubing. The time-saving Huth

bender worked to augment the company's marketing base in the United States and overseas.

Later, Midas bought a large steel processing plant in Chicago and a muffler manufacturing plant in Hartford, Wisconsin. "These two plants continue to provide us with all of our exhaust product," relates Moore. "In order to guarantee our high-quality products, we test and inspect our exhaust components at each of our state-of-the-art plants."

Through the use of the Eagle Line and the Banner Welder Line, two highly automated computerized assembly machines, the plants produce all the mufflers for its domestic and many of its foreign markets, more than 1,000 per hour, to meet consumer demand. The 50 millionth muffler was manufactured on the high-speed production lines in 1983, and, only six years later, the 100 millionth muffler was manufactured. In addition to the plants, Midas operates 13 regional warehouses throughout the United States and 5 in Canada.

Sherman believed that as the automobile industry grew and developed, so would Midas. Russell Richards explains, "We know that regardless of whatever happens with the evolution of the automobile, it will still need a steering wheel, brakes, and a starter. It won't matter if it is running off a battery or if it has a monkey in the back seat peddling. A car will still have to be steered and stopped, and we must be positioned to service those areas. We know that as vehicles become more complex, there will be an even larger role for us. For instance, the introduction of lead-free gasoline and catalytic converters enhanced our business in the 1970s. We knew it was time to add another service."

By 1979, a national brake program was introduced, now accounting for a substantial portion of Midas's retail sales. "Of course, the bulk of our sales are still exhaust, but brakes will take the lead," predicts the vice president.

Recently, in 1988, Midas added computerized suspension and alignment to its service roster, a decision based on the ever-increasing number of front-wheel-drive vehicles, coupled with smart suspension systems and automotive manufacturers' broader use of four-corner struts. According to Richards, the company anticipates that the $3.2 billion suspension market will prove more lucrative than either exhaust or brakes, both of which remain strong, with 24 percent and 13 percent market shares, respectively.

The family-owned company went public in 1961 and was traded over the counter. The initial offer, though small, created A and B shares, but only the A shares were sold to the public while the B shares, with the option of conversion, were controlled by the family and other key members. According to Richards, the purpose of going public was to amass equity for financing expansion. "Of course, there were a lot of benefits from a financing standpoint to raise capital, and to be a publicly traded company."

In the early 1970s, Sherman felt it was time to sell the business, mainly due to his age—he was in his seventies and ready to retire. In addition, his son, Gordon, who worked closely with Sherman at Midas, had opted to leave the business for a new opportunity. Subsequently, Sherman sold his majority interest in the company to Illinois Central Railroad, since renamed the Whitman Corporation. Currently Midas is a wholly owned subsidiary within Whitman's Consumer Products Division.

The financial resources provided by this highly diversified corporation worked to further the company's marketing base. Recalls Moore, "Illinois Central provided us with the ability to expand our network. They gave us the capital that we needed in order to buy locations and to provide warranties and guarantees on many of our other products. Furthermore, they gave us the autonomy to operate just as we always have."

Midas was endowed with the financial ability to spread throughout the United States and the rest of the world. "Today, we are in many foreign markets," declares Richards. "We have 250 shops in Canada, 220 in France, 135 in Australia, 17 in Spain, 4 in New Zealand, 2 in Panama, 2 in Mexico, and so on. We don't sell territories except in the case of New Zealand, where we signed a master franchise agreement because we believe 22 Midas shops will saturate this small country of 3.5 million people.

"We have learned a great deal from our expansion abroad. When we developed Great Britain, our first overseas venture, we made the mistake of sending corporate employees over on temporary assignment to run the operation. The program didn't grow because we weren't developing the native human resources—the domestic talent we needed to grow the program. Finally, a local businessman approached us and offered to buy out the entire operation. Since the program was folding anyway, we agreed to sell. This businessman renamed the shops 'Kwick Fit' and developed his own chain. Today, he dominates the entire U.K. market!

"We knew when we moved into France that we had to develop a program with a French national to suit their own culture. As a result of our planning, our French operations have been very successful," adds Moore.

A variety of support services and guidance is provided by the company to its network of franchisees. Programs include training, marketing, advertising, public relations, and merchandising. To ensure high-quality service systemwide, the company formed the Midas Institute of Technology (M.I.T.) in Palatine, Illinois, in 1974 and the New England Training Center in Taunton, Massachusetts, in 1986. Both facilities provide franchisees, managers, and technicians with classroom training and hands-on experience in every aspect of the business. Free classes are offered to existing franchisees and their employees in business procedures, shop operations and mechanics, and the use of modern equipment and facilities. Smaller training facilities are also located in Philadelphia, Dallas, and Los Angeles.

A mandatory training program at M.I.T. is provided, free of charge, to all franchisees. The participants are responsible for travel and living expenses incurred during the session: Midas pays for all operating costs. Held periodically in the franchisor's training center in Palatine, the formal training program lasts approximately four weeks. Classes offered cover such subjects as techniques of shop management, record keeping, installation of products, and other services rendered by a Midas shop.

To upgrade the technical skills of employees, the company also produces and distributes training videos and instructor's guides to all shops. "Midas has produced the best library of videotapes in the world on brake work, alignment, exhaust, telephone techniques, and so on. There are 35 videos currently available for training," reveals Elie Rivollier, a Midas franchisee in Boston.

Midas maintains six regional offices that assist the franchisees with their operations—Fullerton, California; Independence, Ohio; Chicago; Atlanta, Georgia; Taunton, Massachusetts; and Dallas—each headed by a regional manager. The managers guide the franchisees with their operations. Also working within these regions are approximately 12 area managers and 40 district managers who counsel franchisees and technical trainers who give instruction to franchisees in the field, conducting in-shop classes.

The company manages several warehouses and stores 1,300 different types of mufflers, the majority of which are manufactured by the company. In addition, the company offers and distributes to franchisees over 17,000 competitively priced automotive parts that fit most domestic and foreign cars, light trucks, vans, and antique autos, a competitive edge that a Midas franchise has over an independent shop.

Due to the high demand for Midas products, there is a Midas shop in every county in the country with a vehicle population in excess of 25,000. Known as a viable franchise opportunity, Midas continues to attract entrepreneurs who desire to be part of a successful business with high-growth potential.

"We look for people who have a tremendous drive to succeed. They need to understand the sacrifices that have to be made and know that it takes a lot of time to build a business. It is not necessary to have a great interest in the automotive industry. Someone who is able to operate a McDonald's or a Pizza Hut franchise is capable of operating a Midas shop, too.

"We receive over 2,000 inquiries a year from people all over the world who want to buy a Midas franchise," explains Richards. "After examining their financial information, we can narrow this pool to around 200 and perhaps 20 will eventually become franchisees." Between 75 percent and 80 percent of franchisees are multiple shop owners.

The Midas Dealer Association was founded in 1971. According to franchisee Rivollier, who is the association's president, it was in response to Illinois Central's acquisition of the company. "The dealers felt they needed to have a stronger voice, given the fact that Nate Sherman, who was our friend in the front office, wasn't going to be there anymore," Rivollier tells.

"At first, it was a struggle to be recognized by the corporate office. "It took us some time to establish communication with the corporate office. Eventually, we convinced them that we were worth talking to," adds Myron Gordon, general counsel and executive director of the association. "The corporate office thought of us as just another union, but as the years passed, we have developed a strong, close relationship.

"Now we have an arrangement with Midas that prevents them from taking action that could affect the profitability of the franchises without talking to us first. Although we do not have the power to veto their decisions, we do reserve the prerogative to be heard," explains Gordon.

As CEO, Moore enjoys a close relationship with the franchisees and makes himself available for them at all times by employing an open-door policy. "The franchisees are the ones whose business is on the line. They have a lot at risk, so I listen to what they have to say. Also, they are very bright people. We would be an unenlightened management if we didn't take advantage of that brain power that is out there. The association is very resourceful for us and provides us with valuable information.

"Any program that the corporate office develops with the association will inherently be much stronger than one that might be imposed on them. I'm reminded of an old saying that tells us: 'Force me to do it and I will resist you. Tell me and I will forget. Involve me and I will help you,'" explains Moore.

Now sharing a productive relationship with the corporate management, the association's committees exchange ideas with Midas officials on a regular basis. While the advertising committee meets with the ad agency to plan campaigns, other committees meet to discuss internal problems, shop operations, training, and human resources. Perhaps the most influential committee is the advisory committee that meets with CEO Moore and other key executives to negotiate policy matters. Franchisees are not required to belong to the association, though its membership represents over 85 percent of all franchisees.

According to Moore, "The association fills an ombudsman's role. If the corporate office tells a franchisee to do something, he or she wonders what the motive is. If another franchisee tells him or her to do something, it will have more credibility."

Elie Rivollier, president of the dealers' association, was introduced to Midas at the age of 8, when his father, Lee, opened the family's first franchise in Watertown, Massachusetts, in 1960. After Elie's college graduation, in 1976, he joined his father on a full-time basis, and together, they built their operation to a chain of 15 shops in the metropolitan Boston area.

"Midas has always had a strong dealer network, and over the years, our association has worked with Midas to help build the strength of the franchise system," Rivollier tells. "We try not to be adversarial when discussing issues; instead, we try to be cooperative. I think the reason why we have a very successful franchise program is because the franchisees and the franchisor work very closely together in developing everything from new products and operational issues to advertising issues. There is a lot of input from both sides."

"There have been a few difficult periods between the association and the corporate office. For example, in 1978, the corporate office wanted to structure a new foreign car muffler guarantee; but the association didn't like the way the guarantee was structured so we did not give it our support. The corporate office went ahead with it anyway and unsuccessfully tried to sell it to dealers. When management came back to the association, we worked with them to improve the guarantee. Then, everybody was happy," recalls Rivollier.

Sherman maintained there was one major reason why he expanded Midas with the franchise concept: To open up opportunities for people with jobs to go into business for themselves.

The founder maintained that a person doesn't have to be a college graduate to run a Midas shop or, for that matter, know anything about the automotive business either. Some of the most successful dealers have started with nothing. "There were Midas dealers who were truck drivers, oil riggers, you name it," Sherman was fond of saying.

"Operating a Midas franchise just takes good common sense," Sherman would preach. "I can't think of a simpler or better business to own. It is a cash business with very little overhead. It doesn't require large or expensive equipment or trucking services, and the inventory is on the shelf."

The founder believed that when a person owns his or her own business, he or she has a stake in what happens. "You can be sure that a franchisee will do everything to make sure that his or her shop is successful," he insisted.

Helen Marchick is one of the few women who owns and operates a business in the automobile repair industry. Her experience in a typically male-dominated industry began in the mid-1950s when her husband purchased a former automobile agency and transformed it into a muffler shop called "Mighty Mufflers" in San Jose, California. The shop was successful, and soon, the Marchicks opened two more units.

Interestingly, Helen's father, who owned a gasoline station also in the Bay Area, was familiar with Nate Sherman as they had both spent their childhoods in Omaha. At one point, as a teenager Sherman had even worked for Helen's grandfather in his butcher shop. Her father convinced her husband, Herb, to investigate Sherman's growing new enterprise. Marchick was impressed with Midas's innovative guarantee program and recognized the opportunity to expand his operation through Midas at a minimal cost. Marchick's units were the first Midas franchises in California, and during the course of the next 30 years, he owned units throughout the Bay Area and served as president of the dealers' association for two years.

Although Helen was not working in the day-to-day operations of the business, she was involved in the decision-making process. A homemaker and avid community volunteer, Helen describes herself as the "typical wife of a successful businessman. There was no need for me to pursue a professional career."

After Herb suffered a fatal bout with cancer in July 1990, Helen was faced with a major decision. Should she sell the business or manage it herself? After choosing to keep it, Helen completely immersed herself in the business.

"After Herb died, I announced to the corporate office that I would be continuing the business myself. When they came out for the funeral, I thought they would think I was wonderful and compliment me for taking it over. Well, they didn't, and instead, they were shocked! I knew I had to prove myself.

"I was 56 years old when I took over the business. The first day I went to work, I called a florist and had flowers delivered to the office. The employees were astonished. I wanted everyone to know that there was a woman there now, so I made tremendous changes. My husband told me run the business as I saw fit because he had terrific confidence in me. Subsequently, I completely reorganized the business—management and all. There was no way I could run the business as it was—I had to modify it to suit me."

The road to success has not been an easy one for Marchick. "I recently spent $400,000 remodeling four of my stores, and it was difficult for me to get approval for the loan I needed to do my remodeling program. The bankers wanted to know where I had been working for the last 36 years and doubted whether I could manage the business by myself," she tells.

Owning a Midas shop can be a lucrative opportunity, though the operating costs are higher in the 1990s than when Sherman was running the business. According to Marchick, she stocks an inventory worth $400,000 for her five shops, pays rents averaging $6,000 to $9,000 a month per store, and manages a staff of 45. But Marchick has proved that she is a first-rate Midas franchisee—her annual gross sales are at $4.5 million and are increasing every year.

"Now the corporate office thinks I am wonderful!" she exclaims.

Hugh Boesett began his Midas career in 1978 as a manager for a company-owned store in Dallas, Texas. After elevating to a position as a supervisor for all company operations in the Dallas/Ft. Worth market, he was transferred to the Chicago headquarters as a district manager in 1979. "As a company employee, I was impressed with Midas and learned a great deal. They taught me how to be successful, how to market properly and how to be profitable. But I always wanted to own my own business and Midas gave me that opportunity.

"The company is a well-run organization. Basically, it is a partnership between the corporation and the franchisees. Midas is a franchisor that is sincerely concerned with the success of its franchisees. After serving in a position where part of my job was to help new franchisees to get their stores going, I knew that this was a program that helped people launch successful businesses. Plus, it offered name recognition, marketing, support, training, advertising, and a strong network that almost ensured a franchisee's success."

In 1981, Boesett jumped at an opportunity to purchase two shops in metropolitan Chicago. "It only took me three years to earn back my investment. I am now grossing over $800,000 a year." Currently, Boesett owns four franchises.

"I think Midas management is astute enough to recognize that its success is hinged on successful franchisees. We are the people on the firing line and the ones who respond to the competitive pressures such as the economy, so it is natural that we give them feedback on what additional products are needed. Many of the successful breakthroughs that Midas has incorporated into our program were originally the ideas of franchisees—such as our brake business, foreign car muffler guarantee, and suspension alignment, to name a few," explains Boesett.

The seventh original Midas franchise, a St. Petersburg location, was sold to Jerry Orns in 1956. Currently semiretired, Orns, with the help of his family, has built his business into an enterprise with 28 shops grossing over $17 million annually. The enterprise is now managed by son Lonnie and son-in-law David Kitenplon who supervise a staff of 225.

"Midas was the best decision my father ever made—one that has affected the future of my family. He could have gone in a lot of different directions back in the 1950s, but he chose one of the most successful franchisors in history. The fact that we have grown from 1 store to 28 says it all," son Lonnie says.

"We consider Midas a partner, and through our dealer association, we have remained a partner with Midas in growing our business. I believe Midas is superior to the rest because of our warranty programs and our network of over 2,000 franchised shops in the United States. So if you buy a product in Miami and drive to Los Angeles and have a problem, you are able to go to any Midas shop and have your car serviced under warranty. In addition, since Midas is the franchisor and the manufacturer, we have a lot of credibility about why our products are better than the competition's. While most of our competitors buy their products from manufacturers who are not directly related to the franchisor, Midas has a vested interest in producing good products," adds the younger Orns.

The franchisee is obligated under the franchise agreement to observe specific standards of service enabling every Midas customer to expect to receive the same high standards in service and guarantees at every store. Apart from excellent customer service, franchisees must also purchase from the company a sufficient quantity of Midas-brand and Midas-warrantied products, principally mufflers, shock absorbers, struts, and brake and front-end parts. Midas offers complete guarantees on its mufflers and lifetime warranties on shock absorbers, coil springs, and the friction material of the brake system. Midas's franchisees are bound by agreement to honor all warranties in accordance with the terms and policies issued by the corporate office.

"We are given a very comprehensive standard service policy procedure manual that is easy to read, and very detailed and spells out every area of operating a Midas shop," Lonnie Orns explains. "Midas has regional and local field representatives who frequently visit our stores, yet they allow us a great deal of flexibility in running our business. For example, I can hire as many people as I want, choose my hours of operation, and specify the amount of inventory and the type of equipment I purchase."

Midas does enforce limits: for instance, a franchisee is not permitted to operate another business, such as an equipment rental company, within the same location as a Midas unit.

According to Senior Vice President Richards, "The success of a franchisee is entirely dependent on the amount of business he or she does. This may sound very simplistic, but the drive to increase those retail sales is with the franchisee. Most franchisees understand that a substandard facility is going to decrease retail sales. We require our franchisees to practice their standards of operation, excellent customer treatment, proper inventory levels, appropriate use of our signage, and a clean shop appearance. If a franchisee doesn't have a clean operation and a courteous staff, he or she will start to lose retail sales immediately."

Stemming from Sherman's confidence in franchisees, the company incorporated a policy that prohibits silent investors from owning franchises. As Moore points out, "We require that all our franchisees be involved in operating the business themselves. Also, we don't put a cap on the number of locations a franchisee can own or operate. We are willing to expand with the franchisees who are willing to reinvest in the program and who dedicate their full time and energy to their business."

Franchisees also have control of their pricing. According to CEO Moore, "A store in Greenwich, Connecticut, has higher operating costs than a store in Albuquerque, New Mexico. Before a national advertising campaign is in place, quoting specific prices, we must first seek the approval and participation from a minimum of 80 percent of our store owners in the domestic market."

"Midas will succeed into the future because the industry is growing. The mom and pop businesses will not succeed in the 1990s because the technological advances that are being made will be too overwhelming and expensive for a small business to operate. There are fewer than six major companies in our industry that I believe will prosper, while the smaller inexperienced franchises and independents will disappear," Orns adds.

"Our franchisees are also permitted to develop and own approved sites, but they must sign an agreement beforehand giving the company the option to lease the location if they choose to sell the business, assuring the continuation of the location as a Midas shop," explains Moore.

Midas's in-house real estate department, Midas Realty Corporation (MRC), has a staff of over 65 and includes two dozen site specialists who search for and develop new shop locations.

Franchisees are encouraged to scout for new locations, but before development can begin, the site must be approved by the real estate department.

In addition, there are 15 employees who are dedicated to Midas shop construction, including renovations, refittings, and redecorating. Moore explains, "Although the physical layout of a Midas shop doesn't change, we want our shops to look new and clean, which we believe is more appealing to our customers. A consumer feels far more comfortable taking his or her vehicle into a facility that is clean, well kept, and organized.

"We have to keep in mind that none of our customers is happy to come in to see us while, on the other hand, visiting a McDonald's is a pleasant experience—a happy occasion. When a customer brings a car in to be serviced, it is an irritant—an interruption of his or her schedule. Also, he or she knows the service rendered does not usually enhance the value of the vehicle. All we do is restore the customer's car to the level it should have operated to begin with. So it is not surprising that our customers tend to be highly critical of our store's appearances. In addition, we realize that we're in an industry that's known for its lack of ethics and integrity," adds the CEO.

"We have adopted a Quality Mission Statement that says that the customer is the foundation of our enterprise and every individual in the Midas system is entitled to fundamental respect. We may repair automobiles, but we serve customers. I get a little excited when people describe our business by saying, 'Well, you are in automotive repair.' Well, we're not! We are in the business of serving people!

"Our goal is that each and every customer will leave a Midas shop completely satisfied. Repeat business is critical in today's environment. Perhaps the one precious thing that our competition is after is our customers. If one of our customers has a bad experience at a Midas shop, he will tell his friends that he was disappointed by Midas the company, not just the single unit. So it is necessary that we work very closely with our franchisees to maintain our high standards of service," adds the CEO. "We also want every franchisee, every installer in the system, to have pride when they are putting our mufflers and other products on a vehicle. After all, we think of our muffler as being the 'Tiffany of mufflers,'" says Moore.

New franchisees pay an initial franchise fee of approximately $20,000 for a 20-year term and a site selection fee of $2,500 to MRC. If the franchisee acquires an acceptable site without the assistance of MRC, a fee of $1,000 will be charged for site examination and review rather than the full amount. The franchisee's initial investment for equipment, inventory, working capital, and other expenses necessary for opening an eight-bay Midas Shop is estimated to be about $279,500, though if a suitable existing building is converted, the cost could be much less. The initial product inventory alone is estimated to cost approximately $45,000. The cost of acceptably located real estate is estimated to be between $80,000 and $500,000. Midas does not directly finance a franchisee's purchase and construction of a Midas shop, but will assist in obtaining financing.

Customarily, the financing of the acquisition of the land and erection of the Midas shop is done by MRC or by an unrelated private investor and leased to MRC. The shop is leased by MRC to the franchisee for a term of 20 years, at a monthly rental which typically ranges from $3,900 to $12,000. The standard lease also provides that the annual rent shall be 7 percent of the franchisee's gross sales if that is greater than the specified fixed minimum rent. In addition, the franchisee pays real estate taxes, fire, and extended coverage insurance and performs all maintenance.

The franchisee does not pay any fee, pay for any equipment, or sign the franchise agreement until the shop is ready to be opened. A prospective franchisee does, however, make a $5,000 deposit with his or her application for franchise that is applied toward payment of the site selection fee and the initial franchise fee. The application may be terminated by either party prior to the execution of the lease documents and franchise agreement. If Midas terminates the application for any reason other than the failure of the applicant to execute the lease documents and franchise agreement, the deposit will be returned in full. If the applicant fails to execute the lease and franchise documents or terminates the application, Midas may retain all or part of the deposit as compensation for expenses incurred in connection with the application. A Midas shop is typically opened nine months from the date the application is submitted. In preparing a new shop for opening day, Midas provides supervision in its outfitting and final inspection, the ordering and delivery of the initial inventory of goods, and assistance in planning the opening promotion.

On a monthly basis, franchisees pay 10 percent of gross sales in royalty charges to the corporate office. Half this payment goes to the field support services and training provided by Midas. The other half is applied to the advertising fund, of which 2½ percent is used on a national basis and 2½ percent on a local basis. In addition, franchisees are encouraged to participate in a cooperative advertising program in which the corporate office supplies additional financing on top of what is contributed to the advertising fund.

The company spends over $60 million each year on advertising, making it the second largest Yellow Pages advertiser in the country. As a result of this high-profile advertising, Midas now enjoys high name recognition with consumers and marketing studies indicate that Midas is synonymous with mufflers in 85 percent of American households.

The amount spent on advertising is not the only factor that was instrumental in making Midas into what it is today. As Nate Sherman once said, "The most important part of the business is to take care of the customer. We can spend millions of dollars on national advertising, but it is how the customer is treated inside our shops that really counts. A satisfied customer is the greatest advertising Midas can have, because he tells his friends, who tell others, who in turn, tell others."

The founder was accurate when a long time ago he predicted that owning a Midas franchise would be a good investment for the future. According to the International Franchise Association, dollar sales through franchises in the automotive products and service market have been growing by about 9.6 percent annually, or $1 billion a year. Industry experts agree that this trend will continue to spiral, fueled by car owners' increasing tendency to keep their vehicles longer, requiring that they spend more money on repairs.

According to the Motor Vehicle's Manufacturer's Association, the average age of cars on the road in the United States today, remains at 7.6 years for the seventh consecutive year. Furthermore, studies indicate that the demand for specialty repair service will increase as gasoline stations continue to diminish their service base and as automotive technology becomes more complex. The total number of gasoline stations is declining each year, and 75 percent of gasoline sold in 1991 was through self-service outlets.

So while the domestic automotive field is considered to be one of the most fiercely competitive as well as cyclical industries in America, Midas continues to prosper. Evidently, the company hasn't lost its special Midas touch.

Chapter 7

McDONALD'S CORPORATION

The Franchisor That Has Influenced the Culture of the World

McDonald's Corporation, with over 13,000 restaurants in 65 countries, is the prevailing food and franchising organization in the world. Serving 96 percent of American consumers every year, and 7 percent of the U.S. population on a daily basis, it is the most popular eatery in the country, drawing more customers than its closest competitors, Burger King, Wendy's and Hardee's combined. McDonald's, with total worldwide sales in 1992 over $20 billion, has succeeded beyond anyone's dreams with a method consisting of a simple menu, a speedy food preparation and delivery system based on assembly-line techniques, and above all, a high level of consistency that is found in each of its restaurants around the world.

Franchised in countries around the globe, from Australia, Japan, and Brazil to Hong Kong and Moscow, McDonald's is undoubtedly the all-time premier franchising company.

McDonald's was the vision of a single entrepreneur, Ray Kroc, who recognized the restaurant's potential and turned a single hamburger stand, through franchising, into a multibillion-dollar company—one that has vastly influenced the culture of the entire world and set the standard for fast-food success .

Ray Kroc was born in 1902, in Chicago, Illinois. Only an average student, Kroc was nicknamed "Danny Dreamer" by his family because he would spend hours fantasizing about his passions—music, baseball, and different ways to earn money. As a young boy, Kroc started his career by opening a lemonade stand on the corner of his block, then working in a grocery store, a drugstore, and even running a small music store. Interestingly, even as a teenager, long before McDonald's was even a dream, Kroc would tell his friends, "Work is the meat in the hamburger of life." At age 17, Kroc played the piano around Chicago and enjoyed moderate success, sometimes earning more money in a week than his father. At the age of 18, Ray fell in love and, two years later, proposed to Ethel Fleming, but his parents insisted that he find a steady job before they would give their approval. So Kroc hit the pavement and found a job as a salesman for the Lily Tulip (paper cup) Company.

For 17 years, Kroc sold paper cups for the company and eventually became its number one salesman. In 1939, Kroc found an opportunity to go into business for himself with a new invention, a five-spindled milk shake machine called a Multimixer. Giving up his lucrative position with Lily, he purchased the exclusive national marketing rights with visions of selling a Multimixer to every soda fountain in the country. With a territory extending from coast to coast, Kroc and his team of sales representatives sold Multimixers, one at a time, to the nation's endless numbers of restaurants, soda fountains, and dairy bars. One day in 1953, Kroc received a bit of news from his West Coast Sales representative, William Jamison, that would dramatically change his life and millions of others forever.

Kroc was told that a drive-in hamburger restaurant called McDonald's, in the quiet hamlet, San Bernardino, California, had eight Multimixers, and this was indeed unusual since typically, a restaurant had only one or two. Jamison informed his boss that to save time, the owners innovatively cut a couple of inches off their Multimixer's spindles in order to mix their shakes into 12-ounce paper cups rather than the machine's larger, 16-ounce stainless steel mixers. Unbeknownst to Kroc, Carnation Milk Company, which supplied the restaurant, estimated that McDonald's was selling an incredible 20,000 milk shakes a month.

Kroc was astounded. "Why in the world," he thought, "would a drive-in restaurant need so many Multimixers. After all, each one can make up to five milk shakes simultaneously!" Intrigued, Kroc decided to visit this drive-thru restaurant on his next business trip to the West Coast.

The history of the restaurant traces back to 1937 when two brothers, Dick and Mac McDonald, opened a small drive-in, outside of Los Angeles. By 1940, their business had increased to a point where they needed to move to a larger facility, so they opened a 600-square-foot restaurant in San Bernardino. It offered no indoor seating, but its team of 20 car hops could serve a 25-item menu to 125 cars at a time. By 1948, it generated annual revenues over $200,000 and the McDonald's had earned more money beyond their wildest dreams. That same year they made some major changes. To increase efficiency, they replaced the car hops with self-service windows, allowing customers to place their own orders. They also cut the menu down to only a few items. Each selection was prepared the same, and no deviations from the norm were encouraged. Service was expedient and prices were reduced—the price of the most popular item, the hamburger, was dropped from 30 cents to 15 cents.

By the mid-1950s their sales volume hit $350,000 and the brothers sold 14 licenses, the first one was to Neil Fox in Phoenix, Arizona. Fox's restaurant was more than twice the size of the original in San Bernardino, rectangular in shape, and embellished with red and white painted tile and walls of glass from the counter to the roof. With a kitchen that was completely exposed, the restaurant's appearance was frequently compared to a fishbowl. What was most different about the design of this restaurant was a new feature that would make people take notice—a pair of golden arches running right through the roof of the building.

In 1954, Kroc flew to Los Angeles, rented a car, and drove 60 miles east to see McDonald's restaurant firsthand in San Bernardino so he could understand better why it needed to make so many milk shakes. At first glance, he was not so impressed. McDonald's was an octagonal-shaped restaurant and very small.

At ten o'clock in the morning, Kroc did not notice anything different from thousands of other drive-thrus in the country. But one hour later, Kroc was amazed to see dozens of cars pulling into the small parking lot, and by noon there were over 150 customers waiting in line. This captured his attention.

It was the speed and efficiency of the McDonald's system that mostly impressed Kroc. The restaurant was extremely clean, and the customers were quickly serviced. The menu was limited, and inexpensive, featuring only hamburgers, cheeseburgers, three types of sodas, coffee, french fries, and milk shakes. The 15 cent hamburgers were small, only a tenth of a pound, all cooked the same way, and a slice of cheese cost an extra four pennies. Sodas and french fries were selling for 10 cents, a 12-ounce milk shake was 20 cents.

Kroc waited until the crowd subsided, and around 2:30 P.M. he approached the two brothers.

"When will this die down?" Kroc asked.

"At 11:00 tonight, when we close," replied Dick McDonald.

"Some way I have to become involved in this," the milk shake mixer salesman said enthusiastically. Kroc made plans to have dinner with the brothers that evening so he could learn more about their operation.

That night, Kroc went to sleep with visions of opening McDonald's restaurants all over the country, each needing a multitude of Multimixers. The next day, the McDonald brothers agreed to give Kroc the exclusive rights to franchise copies of their operation all over the United States. They agreed that the buildings would be designed to replicate the prototype in Arizona, complete with its golden arches. The name McDonald's would adorn every restaurant's sign and offer the same menu at each and every franchise.

At the age of 52, when many businesspeople begin thinking about the day when they may retire, Ray Kroc embarked on a new career. Kroc envisioned a national fast-food chain that would stretch across the nation with thousands of franchisees providing high values of quality, outstanding service, and cleanliness. To accomplish this, he would sell franchises, one store at a time, always demanding uniformity, insisting on obedience to his strict rules of discipline. The other restaurants involved in franchising, such as Dairy Queen, were selling territories and pulling in quick profits, as much as six figures for some exclusive territories. Determined that going the territory route was not the answer, he was wary that subfranchising would evolve, comparable to a pyramid structure with layers of operators who would report to *their* franchisors rather than to him. Kroc believed that selling one restaurant at a time would give him the control that was imperative to manage the quality of the operations. Unlike the rest of the franchisors in the industry, the founder elected not to sell equipment or supplies to the licensees, the only exception being a pair of Multimixers for each unit. Kroc thereby avoided a conflict of interest by placing the success of his licensees as his top priority.

On April 15, 1955, Kroc opened his first McDonald's restaurant in Des Plaines, Illinois, outside of Chicago; a partnership with Art Jacobs, a home builder. The store was designed to serve as a model for selling franchises. Kroc's next step was to search for candidates who would be good franchisees. He did not want passive owners or absentee owners who were interested only in making money. He wanted to find franchising entrepreneurs—people who wanted to go into business for themselves and would work hard to succeed. As long as the early licensees followed the rules in their agreement, they could operate their own business, and they would receive support from the corporate office. He opened an office in Chicago, which remained the company's headquarters until 1971, at which time McDonald's moved to its present offices in Oak Brook.

One of the earliest licensees, Sandy Agate, a Chicago pressman, purchased his McDonald's on May 24, 1956. Scraping together the $950 initial fee, together with his wife, Betty, he opened a restaurant in Waukegan, Illinois. On the first day of business, there were lines of people waiting for service. The popularity of the restaurant continued to grow, and even without the use of advertising, the store grossed over $250,000 with net profits of $50,000 in its first year. The Agates were Kroc's type of entrepreneurs. They were hard-working people who personally managed their operations and devoted their lives to making a success of their restaurant. News of the success of McDonald's franchisee quickly circulated; a newspaper quoted Kroc: "Not one franchise has failed . . . we don't see how anyone could," and immediately, inquiries flooded in from dozens of interested entrepreneurs.

In 1956, Kroc hired Harry Sonneborn, a Tastee Freeze executive, to help manage his growing enterprise. Sonneborn envisioned an opportunity to generate additional revenue that could be realized by leasing real estate on a long-term basis. This could be achieved by finding developers to build restaurants and, in turn, subleasing them to licensees. For rent, licensees would pay either a reasonable fixed base amount or a small percentage of store sales, whichever was greater. They would also pay the property tax and insurance.

To Kroc, Sonneborn's idea represented a golden opportunity to earn additional profits without raising royalty rates that licensees paid to the company. McDonald's would also be able to attract worthy entrepreneurs who did not have enough capital and build a restaurant for them! Kroc agreed with Sonneborn's proposal to form a separate real estate company, so, with paid-in capital of $1,000, Franchise Realty Corporation was established. At this point, McDonald's Corporation began to generate substantial earnings. Today, occupancy costs are fixed, with approximately 69 percent of the U.S. restaurant sites and 35 percent of the international sites owned by the corporation, earning McDonald's the honor as the largest owner of retail real estate in the world.

By 1962, there were over 400 McDonald's restaurants in operation, and two years later, there were more than 657 units. Kroc decided the time was right to go public; an offering would provide the company the capital to expand further. Ironically, it was not easy for McDonald's—one of the earliest companies in the young fast-food industry to become publicly owned—to recruit a major investment banking firm to underwrite the offering, because the fast-food operator was perceived as a "here today, gone tomorrow" organization.

On April 15, 1965, McDonald's went public, offering 300,000 shares of common stock. Offered at selling at $22.50 a share, the stock was almost completely sold out on the first day, driving the price up to $30. A few weeks later, the stock inflated to $49. Over 80 percent of the stock was sold to individual investors who were purchasing 100 share lots or less. Since its offering, McDonald's has become one of the most valuable stocks on the market. Currently, the stock has increased in value more than 41 times over the initial offering price, and, today, 1 share purchased at the time of its underwriting in 1965 would be worth more than $4,000.

By 1966, McDonald's had sales in excess of $200 million having sold over 2 billion hamburgers. Not only was the company now pulling in millions in profits, but its founder had finally achieved the necessary buying power to influence the quality and price of the supplies purchased by his restaurants. Kroc's motto for his operators, "In business for yourself, but not by yourself," was particularly applicable to his savvy style of dealing with the various suppliers who provided the restaurants with everything ranging from the beef for the hamburgers to the potatoes for fries and paper cups for shakes. Because McDonald's was buying more catsup, buns, and mustard than the combined orders of most of its competitors Kroc was able to convince suppliers to extend price discounts ranging from 15 percent to 30 percent. Kroc extended this full discount to his licensees, which was in sharp contrast to his competitors, who were either selling their own products to their franchisees or acting as the middle men between the suppliers and the franchises, thereby making a profit at both ends.

Kroc often made reference to what he called a "three-legged stool"—the commonality of interests between McDonald's licensees, suppliers, and the company. He believed that all three entities succeed together. Kroc was determined to develop a strong working relationship with his suppliers, from whom he demanded the same principles as those of his licensees: quality, service, cleanliness, and of course, value. McDonald's worked closely with its suppliers to set high standards of quality with specifications, some which eventually revolutionized the way food products such as meat and potatoes were processed and packaged.

In the early days, McDonald's stores purchased 100-pound sacks of raw potatoes from their suppliers. They had to peel and blanch each potato in the store. Not only was this time-consuming, but the stores had to designate a large space for potato storage. Jack Simplot, one of McDonald's early potato suppliers, knew that the ideal potato for french fries, the Idaho Russet Burbank, was rarely available during the summer months because of the difficulty of maintaining the cool temperatures necessary for storing the harvest. He pioneered a new concept just for McDonald's—"frozen" french fries—and established his own operation which would completely prepare, cut, and freeze the potatoes—his method was more sanitary and easier for the restaurants, and they would need only a freezer for storage. It also assured consistent potato quality year-round. The farmer convinced the chain to try his frozen variety, which eventually became so popular that by 1972, the chain had completely converted to his invention. This innovation made Simplot the largest potato producer in the world, with four frozen potato processing plants. The company's successful conversion to frozen french fries encouraged the rest of the fast-food industry to do the same, and soon over 25 percent of the U.S. potato crop went to the production of frozen french fries.

McDonald's made terrific strides in standardizing and improving the quality of the meat industry, especially when it came to hamburgers. Before McDonald's, there were no standards for hamburger meat, and the government required only that hamburger meat, or "ground beef," not have a fat content of more than 33 percent. This corporation went much farther. Kroc, himself, declared: "A hamburger patty is a piece of meat. But a McDonald's hamburger patty is a piece of meat with character. The first thing that distinguishes it from the patties that many other places pass off as hamburgers is that it is 100 percent beef. The fat content of our regular patty is a prescribed 17 to 21.5 percent and our quarter pounder is 17.5 to 22.5 percent, and it is rigidly controlled."

Fred Turner, who started as a griddle operator with McDonald's at age 23, is now senior chairman of the company. Turner was the company's first operations manager, and in this position helped establish the high standards for all McDonald's products. Excellent ground beef was also a high priority to Turner. He advised his beef suppliers that McDonald's would not tolerate any additives to the beef, such as soy or nitrites, while most of the competition were concerned only with price and paid little attention to the quality of their ingredients.

With an annual consumption rate of over 490 million pounds of hamburger meat, McDonald's conversion from fresh to frozen hamburgers was not an easy accomplishment. To do so required new technology, previously nonexistent. After scientifically developing a new process for preparing and freezing the beef, the chain completely converted to the frozen variety in 1975. Frozen hamburgers have tremendously simplified the operations in the restaurants; they are juicier and bigger and require less time for cooking.

Today, McDonald's employs a highly sophisticated supply system that maintains the superior standard of quality demanded by the company. Interestingly, in spite of this enormous amount of business being transacted, there are no written contracts with McDonald's suppliers. Ray Kroc believed in people's integrity—those who worked with and for him—and always preferred to do business based on a simple handshake. Even after his passing, McDonald's continues to employ this policy.

This was the company's philosophy of sharing a common goal that encourages its suppliers to share technology—a unique situation for competing companies. Then, when a product is developed, McDonald's makes sure that all its suppliers learn how to use the new process. For example, the introduction of Chicken McNuggets in 1983 brought together Keystone and Tyson—two major poultry suppliers—and competitors—to standardize and manufacture the new menu item. Since then, the company has added the McChicken sandwich, chunky chicken salad and chicken fajitas to its menu, making it the second-largest chicken retailer in the industry, behind Kentucky Fried Chicken.

Over the years McDonald's has developed a close relationship with its suppliers that is based on principles of openness, ethics, and trust. The suppliers share a healthy competition; they compete by making improvements in product quality rather than price cutting. According to Robin Johnson, assistant vice president of quality assurance, "We employ an amalgam of chemists, microbiologists, food technicians, and product experts to work with our suppliers to develop the specifications that we believe will give us the best possible ingredients. Our belief is that the suppliers have to be held responsible and accountable for making the product that our system needs, all the way through to the customer. They have to comply with our strict operating procedures so an excellent product ends up in the hands of our customers as we intended it to."

Another healthy relationship is the one that exists between the corporate office and the thousands of licensees around the world. In fact, without the entrepreneurial spirit that is encouraged within the licensee system, the company would not be the success that it is today. Many of the new innovations, pivotal for the company's evolution into the world's largest food service organization, were those of its licensees—entrepreneurs who knew exactly what the consumers wanted. New products that were introduced by licensees became the most important and successful additions to the menu in the history of the company.

The standard traditional McDonald's menu consisting of hamburgers, shakes, fries, and soft drinks was used until the early 1960s when the company decided to expand it to include new items. According to Charles Ebeling, director of communications, "The first move toward menu diversification occurred in 1964, which is a lot earlier than most people think. It was this year that we added the Filet-of-Fish sandwich at the suggestion of one of our franchisees, Lou Groen, in Cincinnati."

Indeed, most of McDonald's successful new menu additions were the innovations of its licensees, which illustrates how the company listens to its front-line operators. Lou Groen owned a McDonald's in a predominantly Catholic neighborhood in Cincinnati, Ohio. Six days a week, his restaurant was filled with customers, but on Fridays, his store was empty. Groen realized that on this particular day, observant Catholics ate fish, which killed hamburger sales. The licensee surmised that a fish sandwich would attract more business on Fridays.

"I've got to have a fish product; otherwise, I can't afford to stay open on Fridays," Groen told management. His request was flatly denied: "We are in the hamburger business, not the seafood business!" The only way the frustrated licensee felt he could convince Oak Brook to see things his way was to prove to them that fish sandwiches could be a profitable business.

Groen developed a sandwich using existing McDonald's equipment made with a piece of breaded halibut served in a hamburger bun. He took his recipe to Oak Brook and made a sample of the sandwich for the corporate executives. After tasting it, they were extremely impressed and granted Groen permission to test-market the product at his restaurant. The sandwich was an immediate success and volume at Groen's store rose 30 percent within a year. Executives from Chicago and licensees from all over the country traveled to Cincinnati to witness Groen's preparation process. Because the halibut had to be hand-cut into two-and-a-half-inch pieces, the company decided to find a better way to make a comparable fish sandwich.

After a year of experimentation, a modified version, using cod rather than the more expensive halibut, was prepared in a unique batter and introduced around the country. In 1963-1964, the Filet-of-Fish sandwich was permanently added to the menu at every McDonald's in the country. The Filet-of-Fish sandwich, an innovation of a single franchisee, became a standard menu item, which 30 years later, continues to be popular at McDonald's around the world.

The Big Mac, now a McDonald's institution, was also the innovation of an enterprising franchisee who also wanted to increase his business. Jim Delligatti, an operator in Pittsburgh, owned a unit in a heavily industrialized area, near several large steel mills. Every day, the restaurateur listened to dozens of complaints from laborers who said their appetites weren't satisfied by a single hamburger or cheeseburger. Delligatti realized the menu needed a "monster" sandwich for these workers, so he developed the Big Mac: a double-decker sandwich containing two hamburger patties, lettuce, onions, pickles, cheese, and a special mayonnaise-based sauce. In 1968, he took the sandwich to Oak Brook and convinced management to taste it. The colossal sandwich was so well received that, after some modifications at company headquarters, it gained a permanent place on the menu.

In the early 1970s, McDonald's operators complained that their restaurants opened every day at 10:00 A.M. but their employees had little to do until lunchtime rolled around. At the time, a fast-food breakfast was nonexistent. Consequently, an owner/operator in Santa Barbara, Herb Peterson, decided to develop a low-cost, hand-held item that could be prepared on existing equipment in the kitchen. Peterson invented a Teflon® utensil for cooking the eggs on the grill that produced a round egg that could easily fit between two slices of an English muffin. After adding a slice of Canadian bacon and cheese, the product was complete.

Kroc loved Peterson's egg sandwich and was ready to test it on a national basis after a name was created. Fred Turner's wife, Patty, suggested calling it the Egg McMuffin, and this name was widely accepted throughout the company. This marked the birth of the Egg McMuffin.

The Egg McMuffin was test-marketed for several years until the Breakfast Menu became official in 1977. Between 1970 and 1977, the company continued to test new products because the Egg McMuffin was not enough to satisfy every customer. Many ideas were suggested. For example, Jim Delligatti, the father of the Big Mac, proposed hotcakes and sausages, and someone else recommended scrambled eggs; with McDonald's coffee and juices, the breakfast menu was now complete. McDonald's breakfast menu opened a new market, making it the first fast-food company to do so. Only ten years later did competitors such as Wendy's and Burger King follow in McDonald's footsteps. Today the breakfast menu contributes significantly to the company's bottom line.

According to Burt Cohen, vice president of licensing, "Experimentation has been very healthy for the system, and we encourage it from our franchisees. Most of the major breakthroughs in our menu line were made by franchisees, and in most cases, they did it while working in conjunction with us. In some cases, particularly in the early days, we told them not to do something, but because the franchisees were aggressive entrepreneurs, they did it anyway and convinced us that it was a great idea."

Since the Egg McMuffin, many other products have been introduced to the McDonald's menu, as the restaurant continues to diversify to accommodate the current needs of today's market. According to Ebeling, the greatest innovation of the 1980s was the evolution of salads. "We tested a salad bar, but this did not fit in with our business of quick service. We are very busy around noon, and customers would be surrounding one little salad bar. Instead of the fast service they usually receive when they order a meal, they would be spending a lot of time making their salads. Also, there was a question of sanitation that became an issue.

"So, after agonizing over the problem, we decided on an obvious solution. We would make salads fresh in the restaurant and prepackage them with a variety of dressings, croutons, bacon bits, and other toppings. We standardized the portions and focused on the quality; we are also able to serve the salad through the drive-thru."

Parallel to the evolution of the salads in the 1980s was the concept of lighter fare at the chain. One recent revolution made by McDonald's which many consumers are unaware of is the switch from blended shortening to the use of 100 percent vegetable oil for all fried foods. More than eight years of extensive research in the laboratory was necessary, testing the right formula of oil so that the crispness and flavor of the standard McDonald's french fry would not change. In addition, customers participated in tests to taste and compare the original and new french fries.

"We don't want to change our standards with regard to taste when we modify a product. When we reduced the salt content or switched to vegetable oil, it was important to us to maintain the product's original flavor," explains Robin Johnson of quality assurance. "We know that flavor is why people come to McDonald's."

Other innovations at McDonald's in the 1980s included the move from whole milk to 2 percent, soft serve ice cream to low-fat frozen yogurt, milkshakes that are 99.5 percent fat free, and reduced-sodium pickles; hamburger buns were fortified with calcium and chicken was added to the menu. McDonald's invented the Chicken McNugget, a product that is now duplicated at almost every other fast-food restaurant in the country and followed by introducing the McChicken Sandwich and the Chunky Chicken Salad. Menu innovation is an important part of McDonald's business, and the company is experimenting with items from pizza and lasagna to new varieties of chicken products. Although few of these new items will earn a permanent place on the menu, consumers will certainly have more choices when dining at a McDonald's in the future.

"There is probably more product development and product testing going on in McDonald's today, both in our test kitchens and in our restaurants, than ever in our past. One of the greatest changes seen at McDonald's in the 1990s is the evolution of a dinner menu," believes Ebeling. "New products in the 1990s include carrot and celery sticks and various development work with chicken and pasta. Also, we are testing pizza in about 500 restaurants around the country."

In addition to a turn toward a more nutritious menu, McDonald's golden arches have turned green in conjunction with the company's policy to be environmentally sound. The first major step took place in November 1990 when McDonald's announced it would discontinue the use of its signature polystyrene clamshell sandwich boxes. The following spring, the company made over 40-odd additional revolutionizing changes, including recycling all its corrugated cardboard, using less paper in its napkins, offering larger ketchup packets (so consumers will use fewer), and testing a refillable coffee mug. The chain has requested its suppliers to use boxes that have a minimum of 35 percent recycled content. None of the changes McDonald's has adopted will inconvenience customers, since most take place behind the counter.

As the nation's largest consumer of packaging, McDonald's choice to recycle is in line with the company's history dating back to its early days, when, in the 1960s, Ray Kroc made an impact on the world in this arena. Because he couldn't stand to waste the space between the round cans that contained the dairy products for his milk shakes, Kroc insisted that his dairy suppliers shift from steel cans and glass bottles to plastic and paper cartons. This left a permanent impact on the dairy industry, which has continued to use plastic and paper today—all because of Kroc. The more environmentally aware McDonald's has won the hearts of millions. This was evident in a 1991 Gallup poll, when American consumers voted the restaurant chain the most environmentally responsible food service organization in the country.

McDonald's would also like to change the customer's perception of seeing McDonald's as a place to only have breakfast or lunch, though the chain already has a billion-dollar dinner market. As Chairman Mike Quinlan has been heard to say, "In the 1990s you will see McDonald's becoming more things to more people in more places."

Some fast-food industry experts think McDonald's may be biting off more than it can chew. After all, in the past, its success was based on a limited menu and fast service. It was this formula that made it the huge success it is today. So for good reason, changing the formula is a bold undertaking. Although the company is still committed to a limited menu concept, expanding the standard menu offers significant challenges, and just how McDonald's customers will react remains uncertain.

"Our dinner program has as much potential as our breakfast program," explains Cohen. "We have a gigantic food-making machine that is underutilized in the evening, and when we figure out the right way to do it, this part of our operation will be huge. It will be like a whole new business with only a small investment for a pizza oven or whatever it is we decide we put into these restaurants for dinner. So our growth potential over the long term is really quite exciting."

"This reveals our commitment to evolution," agrees Ebeling. "Not only have we been evolving our menu, but we have changed our actual restaurant facilities, too. The original restaurant was a self-service drive-in during the 1950s and 1960s. This became a restaurant with indoor seating and a drive-thru in the 1970s and 1980s. Beginning in the 1980s and into the 1990s, we have added what we call 'non-traditional' locations such as restaurants on toll roads; in military bases, airports, train stations, and subway stations; on college campuses and in museums, zoos, office buildings, and hospitals."

McDonald's come in all shapes, sizes, and locations. For example, on the Mississippi River, there is a McDonald's in a floating reproduction of an 1880s side-wheeler, complete with chandeliers. At St. Joseph's Hospital in Phoenix, Arizona, McDonald's has replaced the traditional coffee shop. The Golden Arches can be found next to Westminster Cathedral in London and opposite the Parliament in the Hague.

Probably the most famous McDonald's abroad, in a country where Kroc's standards of Q,S,C, & V have been widely received, is the one in Moscow's Pushkin Square that opened in 1990. This McDonald's is the most popular spot in the city, with even more visitors than the Lenin mausoleum. The 900-seat restaurant is one of the largest McDonald's in the world, and with over 27,000 customers daily, it is so popular that the line for a hamburger and fries is often over two hours long. The restaurant provides a real service to the Moscow community by training and motivating its workers, establishing quality controls, setting realistic prices, and most important, satisfying customers—basic elements that consumers expect and take for granted in the United States. The restaurant also serves as ambassador for America and is a symbol of free enterprise.

"I don't ever foresee a day when we can't develop additional McDonald's in the United States or the world. There will always be new and exciting opportunities," says Burt Cohen. "For example, we are providing children's food on all United Airlines flights originating in Chicago. This is something that we wouldn't have been able to accomplish five or ten years ago, but the technology has gotten to the point where we can do this now."

Cohen believes that McDonald's success as a system is due, to a large extent, to the fact that it franchises. "We do have the capability to run and control the whole U.S. system ourselves, if we were to convert all our restaurants to company operated, but we wouldn't because we couldn't do as good a job as the franchisees. We have always been committed to franchising as a way of doing business," adds Cohen. "Eighty-two percent of our domestic restaurants are owned by franchisees, and we are franchising in each of our major foreign markets.

"If you find a true entrepreneur or someone who understands the concept of risk and reward; someone who has his or her money on the line, with their family's future at stake, he or she will always do a better job than a salaried employee," the senior vice president of licensing explains.

McDonald's has succeeded because it has been able to keep a tight rein on quality control. In addition to selecting the suppliers of food, equipment, and paper products, each of whom met the company's rigorous standards, the company also chooses the locations for its restaurants, constructs and owns most of the buildings, and usually owns or leases the property. To make sure franchisees commit all their concentration on their restaurant's operations, McDonald's awards franchises only to individuals rather than corporations or partnerships.

"We require that our franchisee devote their full time and best efforts toward the day-to-day operations of their restaurant, while many other franchising organizations do not. Our franchisees must live in the area of the restaurant, and they are not permitted to be involved in conflicting enterprises. We don't grant territories or rights of first refusal, and we franchise only one restaurant at a time," clarifies Cohen.

A secret to McDonald's success lies in the meticulous operating procedures for food preparation and service provided by the franchisor to its licensees. A 750-page operations-and-training manual given to each licensee provides specifics on how to run a McDonald's restaurant successfully. The manual spells out all details relating to the chain's fundamentals of quality, service, cleanliness, and value, reminding operators that hamburgers and french fries must be thrown out 10 minutes after they are made if not sold, and windows must be washed every day.

McDonald's is the only major franchisor in the world that doesn't sell anything to its franchisees. "This practice started 35 years ago, when Ray Kroc realized that there was a potential for a conflict of interest. Since our revenues and income derive directly from the success and failure of an individual restaurant, we share a common interest with our franchisees. If our franchisees are not successful, we are not going to be successful," explains Cohen.

"There are many elements that are unique to McDonald's, though we do not think that we are right and other franchising organizations who operate differently are wrong. We have just found that this works best for us," adds the vice president.

According to the company's Licensing Department, McDonald's receives over 20,000 inquiries a year for franchises. "We interview about 2,000 people and place 150 to 200. We require a training program that takes about two years on a part-time basis— about 15 to 20 hours a week. We encourage people to train part time so they are able to change their minds at any time while we can do the same without putting a financial strain on them and their families," adds Cohen.

"Another requirement is that our applicants must be prepared to relocate geographically. To fulfill our system's requirements for franchisees, our inventory of applicants has to be prepared to move geographically. Now, if you tell me you are interested in the West or the Northeast Corridor, we can try to accommodate you. If you tell me you are interested only in Chicago or Los Angeles, we probably won't put you in the program because we are not going to be able to make you happy or meet your expectations. So, generally speaking, we require all our people to commit to moving when the time comes. Also, patience is a virtue because a franchisee who applies now will probably not get one until about three years from now."

McDonald's does not require previous restaurant experience of applicants. "We actually believe that this is a detriment because we have to reteach them things," Cohen explains. "Our training program and techniques are generally acknowledged to be the best in the industry. People get college credit for going to our Hamburger University. Most of the two-year training program takes place in a restaurant. Even if an applicant has never boiled water, we can teach him or her how to run a McDonald's restaurant. It is more difficult to teach an individual how to be a businessperson, so our franchisees need to have a history of success in whatever they have done.

McDonald's does not permit a franchisee to run his or her restaurant by hiding in an office during the lunch rush. The company expects its franchisee to spend time working on the floor, greeting customers, and refilling their coffee. A franchisee must be an aggressive entrepreneur and be prepared to invest two years in the company's extensive training program without a guarantee. "We have a very interesting profile of people applying for franchises, ranging from former military personnel, teachers, police officers, bankers, and lawyers, to professional athletes and accountants," explains Cohen.

"When it is their time to become a franchisee, they have to give it all up. The only thing our franchisees are allowed to do is sell hamburgers. They have to devote their full time to the day-to-day operation of their restaurant. This doesn't mean sitting in a fancy office. This means in the restaurant, working with the crew, helping train management, being the Mr. or Mrs. McDonald's in the community. They should be involved in the local Jaycees or Chamber of Commerce and enter a float in the Fourth of July parade. They must also develop a relationship with the local high school's principal so they can find students to work part time in the restaurant. Each franchise is an intricate part of its community, with over 80 percent of McDonald's restaurants locally owned and operated by independent entrepreneurs who are involved in neighborhood issues," adds Cohen.

Ray Kroc was a firm believer in giving something back to the community, and his dream lives on through his franchisees and corporate employees. This is evident with the renowned Ronald McDonald Houses that provide a home-away-from-home for families of seriously ill children being treated at nearby hospitals. The Ronald McDonald Houses, originally suggested by a franchisee in the Philadelphia area, are sponsored in part by local operators, Ronald McDonald Children's Charities (a not-for-profit organization), and a multitude of corporate and individual sponsors, without whom the houses would not be possible. In addition to the assistance of local operators and their employees, an estimated 12,000 volunteers help manage the Ronald McDonald Houses around the globe, serving more than 2,200 families every night. In the fall of 1991, the 150th Ronald McDonald House, a 20-bedroom facility, opened in Paris, France. Currently, there are also houses throughout the United States, Canada, Australia, New Zealand, England, Austria, the Netherlands, and Germany.

"Our franchisees make it clear that their restaurant is a locally owned and operated business. We encourage a sense of community. Every one of our restaurants must be committed to putting something back into their community. This is the key to our business," admits Cohen.

McDonald's expects the same interaction with the community from their international franchisees, and for this reason, the company requires franchisees to be resident nationals of the country where they operate. "Just as we want a Kansas person to run a store in Emporia, Kansas, we want a British citizen running the store in Stratford-Upon-Avon and a Frenchman in the Lyon McDonald's. We look for a franchisee in the country where we are opening a restaurant," explains Cohen.

McDonald's offers several programs that make owning a McDonald's restaurant a reality rather than a dream for many of its franchisees. For example, the Business Facilities Lease program is an approach that enables McDonald's to bring in top candidates who meet all the qualifications but the capital requirements. These franchisees enter with a limited amount of capital, and instead of buying the signs, equipment, and the core package, they rent everything from corporate headquarters with a purchase option with a predetermined price. Over 50 percent of all franchisees have entered McDonald's system through this program since its inception. "They save every penny possible, and within about two years they are able to exercise that purchase option and convert the deal into what we call a conventional franchise," explains Cohen. "This is a very successful self-financing tool that has been around for more than 25 years."

The BFL program has contributed significantly to many aspiring franchisees who would otherwise face difficulty financing a franchise with any company, let alone McDonald's. A conventional new McDonald's in the United States, with a 20-year lease, will cost approximately $610,000. This includes a $22,500 payment to McDonald's, a $15,000 interest-free refundable security deposit, and a sum of approximately $572,500 paid to the suppliers (this fee includes kitchen equipment, signage, seating, decor, and preopening expenses). According to McDonald's latest statistics, minority owners (including women), represent approximately 25 percent of its franchise base, a number that is destined to grow because over 60 percent of the current applicants to the training program belong to a minority group.

McDonald's training program is a top priority since the company's success depends on the uniform operations at each of its restaurants around the world. The extensive and comprehensive training program is designed to train a candidate in all aspects of operating a McDonald's restaurant and ultimately transforms him or her into a successful licensee.

Lasting approximately two years, the first segment of the training and evaluation program is completed on a part-time basis and requires a franchisee to spend up to 20 hours a week working in a McDonald's restaurant near the applicant's home. In addition, there are five formal classroom sessions, four of which meet in regional training centers. The last session, the Advanced Operations Course (AOC), is two weeks long and is held on the campus of Hamburger University, a sophisticated training facility located at company headquarters in Oak Brook. After applicants complete the two-year program, they are eligible to purchase a license, though they are not guaranteed one.

Known as Hamburger University, McDonald's worldwide management training center offers nine courses, including the AOC, the most popular course, with approximately 3,000 students a year. The AOC covers four major management areas: equipment, operations, human relations skills, and intrapersonal/communication skills.

In February 1961, Hamburger University was established in the basement of an operating restaurant in Elk Grove Village, Illinois. In the beginning, classes were small, but as the number of restaurant units increased, it was necessary to move the training center to a larger facility. It was first relocated in 1968 to a stand-alone facility and doubled in size in 1973; most recently, in 1983, it was moved to its present location. "Each move really reflects the growth that was taking place at the time," explains Randy Vest, former Hamburger University dean. "So as the business grew, so has the facility, the concept, and the way we use it."

The university is located on the McDonald's sprawling 80-acre tree-covered campus and is the envy of corporate training facilities throughout the world. With six modern theater-style classrooms, an auditorium with state-of-the-art technology, four multipurpose rooms, 17 seminar rooms, a library, and four fully functioning equipment laboratories, it is in a league of its own.

The university employs highly sophisticated audiovisual equipment, including both live and remote television. There is even real restaurant equipment. This combination enables students to apply such principles as troubleshooting learned in the classroom in a simulated kitchen in the same facility. With a resident teaching staff of 30, all with experience in restaurant management, the university frequently features key home office personnel who instruct in their areas of expertise.

"We have graduated in excess of 43,000 students and are doing business in some 65 countries, so we sometimes must hire interpreters to translate. Currently, we provide simultaneous interpretation in 20 different languages," reveals Vest. "Our students come from around the world and are either first assistants who are about to become store managers or individuals who are registered applicants and training to become licensees. In addition, we also train corporate employees, purveyor employees, and 'recycles'—alumni members who have been here before," adds the former dean, now McDonald's ombudsman (a go-between for the licensees and the company who is responsible for maintaining the integrity of the system through mediation and conciliation).

"While our students are here, we provide them with information that will be useful, and even more important, teach new skills, allowing them to return to their restaurant with not only competence, but a lot of confidence. Our training teaches four essential elements: the Four C's. In addition to Competence and Confidence, we stress Consistency and Commitment for the business and to the customer."

Although McDonald's does not reimburse an applicant for his or her time and expenses associated with training, it does pay the cost for training materials. Also, during the course of the training, both the potential licensee and McDonald's have the right to withdraw an application at any time. While McDonald's operates several other smaller versions of Hamburger University in Japan, England, and Germany, foreign franchisees are encouraged to enroll in Oak Brook's extensive program.

Over the decades, McDonald's has not only trained its franchisees, it has also provided the largest youth-training program in the country. Remarkably, 1 out of 15 first-time job seekers in the United States found his or her job at a McDonald's restaurant. The chain which has employed 7 percent of the American work force at one time or another has surpassed the U.S. Army as the country's largest job training organization. McDonald's provides invaluable training to America's youth, who at ages 15 to 18, have difficulty gaining employment elsewhere. At McDonald's they learn how to balance work life with school life . . . as well as important life skills including quality, courtesy, efficiency, consistency, cleanliness, teamwork, responsibility, customer service, and even management skills.

Similarly, McDonald's hires senior citizens, who, like teenagers, have difficulty finding work.

In fact, McDonald's trains and promotes employees, regardless of their formal education, sometimes, all the way to the top where half of the corporation's officers are former restaurant managers and employees. For example, Senior Chairman Fred Turner started as a grillman at age 23, while Ed Rensi, president of McDonald's U.S.A, was paid 85 cents an hour while employed at an Ohio restaurant in 1966. Unlike the others, current Chairman Mike Quinlan didn't begin his career working in a restaurant, but joined the "family" at 19 when he landed a job in the mailroom at McDonald's corporate office. By the time Quinlan was 35, he was president, and two years later, in 1987, he was named CEO. It is no wonder the corporate officers at McDonald's like to boast that they have ketchup in their veins. In addition, more than half the store managers began behind the counter or in the kitchens.

To serve as a reminder of the basics of the business they are in, each year in early October, McDonald's celebrates Ray Kroc's birthday, with an event called Founders Day. On this day every year, the Oak Brook headquarters and the other administrative offices around the world shut down so that each corporate employee can spend a day working in a restaurant, performing a variety of duties ranging from flipping hamburgers and making milk shakes to cleaning floors and tables.

In the late 1950s, Ray Kroc announced, "McDonald's is not in the hamburger business; it's in show business." The founder knew that anybody could sell a hamburger, but his chain was different from the rest because of its Speedee Service and exposed kitchens that served as entertainment for the customers. Kroc wanted a significant advertising campaign to inform the general public that his restaurants were unique. He believed a child who loves a McDonald's television commercial would be brought to a restaurant by relatives or friends, parlaying one viewer into three customers.

In 1963, McDonald's aired its first national television commercial. Willard Scott, now the weatherman for NBC's "Today Show," portrayed Ronald McDonald for the first time on television in

Washington, D.C. By 1966, Ronald McDonald was the national spokesman, appearing on network television commercials at a time when virtually no other food service company was investing in national television advertising. Current statistics reveal that Ronald McDonald is the second most recognized character in the country, closely behind Santa Claus.

The inception of national and local advertising coupled with marketing programs at McDonald's has made the restaurant a household name. It was not long before children and adults across the country were singing the newest McDonald's jingle. McDonald's has had many memorable advertising campaigns, but perhaps the most was "You deserve a break today, so get up and get away . . . to McDonald's."

Currently, the chain spends over $1 billion annually on advertising and marketing. Accordingly, McDonald's is the most heavily publicized brand name in corporate American history. While national advertising is important to McDonald's success, over 60 percent of the company's marketing is done on a local level by the franchisees. There are over 165 advertising cooperatives operated by the franchisees who together with the corporate office produce almost 150 new television commercials every year. In addition, to support national advertising further, the operators created the Operators' National Advertising Fund (OPNAD), whereupon voluntary contributions of an additional 1 percent of gross sales are paid from licensees and company-operated stores around the country. OPNAD now provides the bulk of the funds for national advertising.

In addition to OPNAD, the franchisees are further represented by the National Operators' Advisory Board. Organized in 1975 by the company, it was believed that due to the chain's immense size, a committee was necessary to bring operators together to discuss common goals and concerns. With every operator in the United States included as a member, NOAB has evolved into a successful functioning body consisting of two representatives from 40 regions. Elected by their peer operators, each representative serves a two-year term on a volunteer basis. "We find that NOAB is a very effective communication tool," explains Burt Cohen. "There are many associations including ones for each minority group such as the female, Hispanic, and African-American operators, to address issues that they feel are unique to their background. There are also franchise associations in foreign countries."

A steering committee comprised of six operators meets with corporate officers every six to eight weeks, while the entire board gathers three times a year at Oak Brook to spend a week discussing operational issues with every corporate department head and top management. "This is unique for a company our size," explains Joe Davis, former chairman of NOAB. "McDonald's has allowed the board to be a major part of the system. At the meetings, we try to stay away from making decisions that are better for the owner-operator or for the company. We want what is best for the whole McDonald's family—the entire system—and usually we come to a consensus when making a decision."

A classic story of a McDonald's operator, Joe Davis has been affiliated with McDonald's for over 22 years, an impressive tenure considering he is only 37 years old! As a high school student, Davis began his McDonald's career as a crew member at a unit in Miami, Florida. After graduating from Florida State, Davis became a restaurant manager for his older brother, a McDonald's franchisee. In 1980, soon after his 24th birthday, the young manager purchased his own McDonald's restaurant in Russellville, Arkansas.

"McDonald's has provided me with a great opportunity. I started with the company when I was only 15—my first job was with McDonald's—and I have stayed on to this day. Currently, I own five stores in Florida, and it is a very lucrative business, but it is hard work! It is a 7-day-a-week operation, 52-weeks a year!" Davis explains.

While it is the imperative of McDonald's to maintain quality, service, cleanliness, and value in every restaurant, Davis believes that the success of the immense restaurant chain is due to its consistency.

"They are very strict as far as Q, S, C, and V, but from my standpoint, that is why we are so successful," explains the ex-

perienced franchisee. "And although competition has increased substantially over the years, we have the system and the research and
development that places us leaps and bounds ahead of the others.
We are very conscious of the customer's needs, so I believe we will
stay in the forefront of the restaurant business. Also, as the largest
restaurant chain in the world, we are the leader and set the standard
for the entire industry."

With over 22 years of experience, Davis could surely operate
successful restaurants as an independent, yet he chooses to stay with
McDonald's. "Being a part of a franchise organization provides me
with many advantages. If I have a problem with a city's government
over a zoning issue, for example, I can pick up the telephone and
find help within 15 minutes. We have the resources for every problem that may arise, while it might take an independent two to three
months and a fortune dealing with attorneys to come up with the
same solution. Also, I constantly receive advice from other operators
who have experienced the same problems," Davis exclaims.

The franchisee admits having learned many valuable principles
while affiliated with McDonald's. As a teenager, he learned one
important lesson directly from the founder, Kroc, himself. When
running a business, no matter how successful it may be, there is never
room for waste. "When I first started working for a McDonald's as
a crew member, Ray Kroc visited our store. I had heard about him
and never expected to meet him! I was impressed to see him out in
our parking lot picking up trash. He was very particular about a
McDonald's clean image , so naturally, he was upset with the owner
because of the stray wrappers and cups found in the lot. While they
were discussing the problem and the growing expense of refuse, I
happened to be taking a load of trash outside to the bin. I was
surprised when Mr. Kroc looked at me and said to the owner, 'Well,
I will save you money right now.' Then he told me to put some
cardboard in the bin and jump inside and stomp on it to compact it.
Afterward, Mr. Kroc remarked, 'Now that is how you save money!'
It is lesson I never forgot."

Kroc's principles of quality, service, cleanliness, and value have
created the most successful restaurant chain of all time. While the

McDonald's of the past was built on strategy based on a simple menu, the McDonald's of the future is a company that is environmentally aware, conscious of health and nutrition, and one that services all market segments of the population. With a corporate objective that focuses on three elements—opening additional units, maximizing sales and profits at existing restaurants, and improving international profitability—McDonald's enjoys a compounded annual growth rate of 12 percent (over the last ten years). McDonald's, an American institution that has made franchising a household name, is now internationally acclaimed. Still, this multibillion-dollar establishment maintains its common touch, with a corporate motto that simply reads *food, folks, and fun.*

Chapter 8

PIZZA HUT

Franchising America's Favorite Pizza

For years, the debate over America's best-loved snack food was a two-way contest between hamburgers and hot dogs. While it may be hard for today's younger generation to comprehend, pizza wasn't even in the running. Back in 1958 when Pizza Hut was born, many Americans had never tasted a pizza. Those who had were either of Italian descent or lived in a large Eastern metropolitan area such as Boston, New York, or Philadelphia. It was a time when America's heartland dined primarily on meat and potatoes. Today, sales total over $5 billion at over 8,000 locations around the world from Saudi Arabia to Macau.

When college students Dan Carney, 25, and his younger brother, Frank, 19, opened their first restaurant in Wichita, Kansas, it was indeed a highly improbable place to start what was someday to become the world's largest pizza chain. Dan and Frank Carney, 2 of the 12 Carney children, came from a middle-income Wichita family.

Their parents operated a small grocery store three blocks away from the Carney household, where the 12 Carney children spent most of their free time during their adolescence working. "We all had to pay our way through school," tells Frank, "which was good because we learned a solid work ethic, and it taught us good values. Beginning at age 12, I had at least two jobs—one always at the store and another such as working at a local barber shop to pick up extra spending money."

Located adjacent to the family grocery store was the B&B Lunchroom, a dilapidated bar and restaurant. The owner of the property who also owned the Carney grocery store chose to cancel the bar's lease. She approached Dan, then a graduate student at Wichita State University and suggested that he open a pizza restaurant in the empty space. "The property owner had read an article about pizza in *The Saturday Evening Post*," recalls Frank Carney. "The article revealed that pizza was doing very well in New York City, and she was convinced the new food concept would succeed in Wichita because there was nothing else like it!

"Dan came to me for help because he thought I had money. At the time I was just coming out of my freshman year at Wichita State (then Wichita University), and I thought he just wanted me to work with him. So when we went in to sign the lease for our store, my brother told me to give the owner a check. I told him I didn't bring a checkbook, so he should pay it. He didn't have his checkbook either, and when we went outside to discuss our predicament, we realized that neither one of us had any money to sign the $155 lease!

"We were able to borrow the $600 we needed from a fund that was established from a life insurance policy of my father who died when I was ten year old," Frank continues. "The money was designated for my brothers, sisters and me to use for college tuition, so we had to pay it back. Money wasn't the only problem we had in the beginning! Three or four weeks before our first store opened in June 1958, my brother and I realized that we didn't even know how to make pizza. In fact, I had eaten only one pizza in my entire life, although Dan had eaten it many times when he was in the service."

"About the same time, my sister Sally talked to us about a

delicious pizza she had heard about from a neighbor. The neighbor ate pizza with John Bender, an airman from Bloomington, Indiana, who was stationed in Wichita. Dan and I immediately contacted him and he invited us to his apartment for pizza. Little did my brother and I know then but we were tasting what would become known around the world as the first Pizza Hut pizza. We offered Bender a deal—he could buy in with us if the company succeeded," Carney explains.

"It was funny, but years later Bender confessed to us that he had remembered the recipe for his pizza sauce—grind green peppers, onions, and tomatoes—but forgot the dough recipe!

He flipped through cookbooks looking for a similar recipe for pizza dough, and the closest thing he could find was one for French bread. He didn't have time to let the dough rise; so instead, he rolled it out and made it thin. Our original thin and crispy Pizza Hut pizza dough was really French bread!"

With the $600, the Carney brothers were able to lease the 600-square-foot restaurant and buy paint, used restaurant equipment, chairs, and tables. They paid their employees $1.00 an hour, and the brothers worked at their restaurant whenever they had time off from the grocery store.

The Carneys decided it was time to think of a good name for their small business. The sign above the restaurant still read B & B Lunchroom. So with spaces left between the word "Pizza" and whatever else they were going to use, there was only room left for three more letters. Dan's wife thought the building looked like a little hut, so the brothers decided to use that word. It would have cost them more money to have a new sign made than it cost to open their first store! As a consequence, the name *Pizza Hut* is synonymous with pizza all over the world.

During the first summer, the restaurant's business was slow, but after the Wichita State University football team played their first game, Frank invited his fraternity brothers over for pizza—they loved it and word quickly spread around campus. "In the beginning, we charged 95 cents for a small pizza and $1.50 for a large one and only offered a thin-crust," Frank tells. "By the time the football team played their second home game, the restaurant, which also offered take-out, was filled to capacity and continued to stay busy from then on.

"We then knew that we had something that had real potential. We weren't sure how far the business would go, but our attitude was that as soon as we had the money to pay back our mother the $600, we would plan on opening a second store, which we did six months after opening the first one."

The Carney brothers continued to open more stores in the Wichita area, and by the following year, there were six Pizza Hut units. They decided to franchise their seventh restaurant to Dick Hassur, the manager of the third store, their highest-volume unit. "Dick wanted to get into the business for himself and chose to locate his Pizza Hut restaurant in Topeka, Kansas," explains Frank. "We loaned him the money to open his unit— about $2,700. The cost of opening a Pizza Hut restaurant wasn't high in those days, because unlike today, a store could be placed in any building that was in a half-way decent location."

It wasn't long before many college friends and customers from Kansas and neighboring Oklahoma had tasted the pizza and indicated an interest in operating a Pizza Hut restaurant. The Carneys placed two advertisements for franchise opportunities—the only advertisements in the history of the company. "We were not salespeople—we were order takers," says Frank. "If someone wanted a franchise, they came to Wichita and told us what they wanted to do and how they were going to do it.

"For the first five years we were in business, the restaurants had no uniformity. Not two Pizza Hut restaurants looked alike! Also, our business was spotty in terms of success. There were a lot of failures during the first five years, which, in most cases, were caused by poor management and/or poor locations. It wasn't until 1961 that Dan and I began talking about expanding our small business across the country. Funny, but I was in the business so I could pay my way through school. I planned on pursuing a career in engineering. Wichita is a center for the light aircraft industry—Beech, Cessna, and Boeing were each building aircraft here at the time. So naturally, I wanted to be an aeronautical engineer. I was enrolled in the electrical engineering department at the university, but it soon became obvious that I was going in a different direction! I went to school for about four and a half years, and every year, I found myself traveling more in franchising our business. I was taking fewer and fewer courses, and pretty soon, I was forced to make a choice. I decided to pursue a career with Pizza Hut. My brother left his graduate program for Pizza Hut, too. We had a business that was growing, and it was the most exciting thing we could do."

Although it is a huge success, Pizza Hut was not the first pizza franchise chain in the country: Shakee's opened its first store five years before Pizza Hut did and had 100 stores before the Carneys reached 20. It took Pizza Hut ten years to surpass Shakee's—its earliest competition—in total stores and volume. Although both were national pizza chains, Shakee's had a different format. It was an entertainment center with player pianos and pinball machines, while Pizza Hut was more like a neighborhood pizza place. While Shakee's had a very low carry-out business and a very high eat-in business, Pizza Hut had 60 percent eat-in business and 40 percent carry-out. Pizza Hut was not threatened by Shakee's in the early days, and it had no major competition in the Midwest. Still Dan and Frank recognized the need to standardize their operations and upgrade the entire system. The first standard Pizza Hut building opened in 1964.

Frank Carney admits that he and his brother sold franchises to "anybody who had capital and desire—the two main ingredients." Although they did reject a handful of applicants, they were willing to gamble on almost anyone who was willing to help them expand their restaurant concept around the country. The Carneys charged low franchise fees and confess they did not make a profit from franchising until 1965.

"Our original agreement with one of our earliest franchisees, who is still with the system, required him to pay no more than $50 a month in royalty fees. If he didn't earn that much, then the franchisee didn't have to pay it," recalls Carney.

"I remember selling the Kansas City region to a college friend in 1959. We charged him $100 for the whole Kansas City market area, and a maximum royalty fee per store each month was $100. We didn't make any money on this deal. It took us four or five more years before we had operating manuals, a training program, a standardized building, and location criteria. Prior to 1964, we were a loose confederation. It was not a viable franchise system, and that's why we couldn't justify charging higher fees."

In the beginning, many of the Carneys deals were actually written down on napkins and cemented by a handshake. According to several long-term franchisees, the company operated in a casual manner for the first ten years of existence, but it set a great foundation. "Strong relationships were built based on Dan's personality and trust, while Frank was more the businessperson," tells franchisee Bill Walsh.

Dan and Frank chose not to sell franchises one unit at a time, but instead, sold regions. "We decided early on that if someone is going to own one store in a city, they had better own them all, and if they don't want to own more than one store, then perhaps they ought to go to a small town that is only going to need one unit. We didn't want our franchises competing with each other. We didn't want to worry about them having different price structures (since franchisees are free to set their own prices). We always thought of cities as individual markets," explains Carney.

It took three false starts before the Carneys were happy with a freestanding building design. The first with the standard red roof and large picture windows opened in Colorado Springs in 1965 and by 1969 was adopted systemwide. "Once that building had the name 'Pizza Hut' on it, it became a big billboard," tells Carney.

By 1967, Pizza Hut was earning annual profits in the $150,000 to $200,000 range. As the success of the restaurant chain kept climbing, the Carneys raised the fees, but they were still not earning a lot of money from their franchises. This same year, the Carneys decided to upgrade their advertising. Prior to 1967, their early franchising agreements did not contain provisions for national advertising or require franchisees to contribute to an advertising fund. The contracts simply stated that franchisees must spend 2 percent of their gross sales on advertising. "At our 1967 annual advertising meeting, I proposed to the franchisees that they form an association, pay dues, and have the association join the corporate office in planning a national advertising campaign," Frank states. "Enough of our franchisees agreed, and it provided us with enough money to fund professionally-made advertising materials. This association became what is now known as the International Pizza Hut Franchise Holders Association. We agreed to share some of our profits from the company stores in a joint fund for our national advertising."

Pizza Hut's move toward a public offering was the idea of a franchisee. According to the Carneys, when the company had a total of 250 stores, six company-owned and the rest franchised, one of the largest franchise holders, knowing that the Carneys wanted to expand their company-owned operations around the country, suggested they make an offering. "In 1967, this franchisee reminded me that we needed additional operational funds for growth because the royalty fees were not sufficient to finance what we wanted to do," Frank tells. "'Why don't you make a private offer to the franchisees, allowing them to trade their territories, stores and all, in exchange for Pizza Hut stock. Then, when the company goes public, the franchisees will get a big payoff while the company will have the company-owned stores and capital with which you need to grow,' he said.

"I thought it was a great idea, but first we needed to develop a management system that would allow us to operate company-owned stores successfully long distance. To accomplish this, we bought out a franchisee in Las Vegas who had four units. He was a marginal operator, and we thought if his stores were properly managed, they would be more profitable. We placed a few of our people there, made the stores profitable, and developed the type of management system we needed.

"By late 1968, we felt we were ready to make a trade with franchisees. At the time, our private offering with the franchisees was the largest offering by a company that had gone through the SEC for a class B reorganization. One hundred and twenty-nine franchisees—each a different corporation—agreed to trade stock with us! One month later, in January 1969, we made a public offering. The franchisees who turned over their stores to us in exchange for stock became millionaires overnight! Our initial public offering was for $16.00, and three days later, it skyrocketed to $32.75. In addition to our desire to expand, we also now had the needed capital to make outside acquisitions," Frank recalls.

"Surprisingly, many of the franchisees who made the trade had either a great deal of capital or stock and still they came back to us wanting to buy new territories! They had turned their stores into stock, and they were inspired to go out and rebuild their businesses! We were ready to be more aggressive in company-owned operations, and these franchisees were eager to expand our franchised operations. There were a lot of territories where we didn't have stores, so we sold those back to the franchisees.

"After going public, we went from owning and operating 6 stores in Wichita and 4 stores in Las Vegas to owning and operating 129 company-owned stores in 20 different states overnight. Soon, we had 50 more company-owned stores under construction. We had a very fast acceleration of growth—both company-owned stores and franchises were growing quickly. Both grew in their own markets— even today, territories are either all company owned or all franchises. If there was a territory where the company didn't have expansion plans within the next five years, we franchised it.

Pizza Hut was now on its way to becoming the largest pizza restaurant chain in the world.

"A very funny thing happened at that time," Frank comments. "My brother Dan said that he wasn't interested in running our company anymore. It had become too big for him, and he didn't want to manage hundreds of employees and have to go through several layers of management. He explained to me, 'When I see a problem, I want to fix it. I don't want to have to worry about hurting anyone's feelings. I am going to leave as soon as I am comfortable with you running the company!' At the time, I was vice president of franchising, while Dan was president and chief executive officer. Our board of directors approved of the plan, and I agreed to take over as

President and CEO." The older Carney left the business in 1972, but agreed to stay on as chairman of the board.

Under the auspices of the younger Carney brother, Pizza Hut expanded at an accelerated rate. The entire country was sold by 1972, region by region, to a number of franchisees while Pizza Hut retained various territories to operate as company-owned. During the first five years of existence, the company went from 0 stores to over 50; by 1976, Pizza Hut had opened 2,000 stores.

"The company was growing at such a rapid rate," Carney backtracks, "it was out of control. Overnight, we went from 6 company-owned stores to 129, and each had a different accounting system. In August 1969, when July is usually one of the most profitable months operationally, we were losing money. We had no idea what was going on! It took us eight months to realize we were in deep trouble because we couldn't get the accounting together. Nine months after our stock went public, and was selling for over $32 a share, it dropped to $3.75! All of us who thought we were millionaires suddenly weren't anymore. Boy, were we ever disillusioned!

"The problem was that we didn't know what our stores were doing week to week, and when we would finally receive the monthly financial statements, which were delivered 30 days later, we were trying to solve problems that had occurred months earlier. I told my director of operations and my vice president of operations that I wanted all sales figures, including the cost of goods sold and labor, operational, field, and administrative expenses—and I wanted these weekly figures on the Tuesday following the weekend. They came back to me about a week later and said, 'Well, we have it all figured out. We are going to have it to you on Tuesday, but it is going to be nine days late, not two days.' I thought about that and said to them, 'I am disappointed. What I asked for I didn't get. But I think the two guys who will have your jobs next month are going to be the two guys who will give me the numbers on the first Tuesday following the weekend. I would like it very much if you two did it, because I like you and I like to work with you.' And the following week, I had the figures on Wednesday morning. They figured out that the telephone worked faster than the postal service, and they had the stores call in their numbers to area managers, who in turn called in the totals. After a few weeks, I was receiving the information on Monday!

"Within four weeks, our operating expenses (including cost of goods sold and labor) that were previously running at 65 percent dropped to 56 percent. The thing that made the difference was that everyone, at all levels, knew they were being watched and worked harder to keep our overhead as low as possible. We didn't need to fire or hire anybody to improve our system. We just needed to establish controls, and boom, our cash flow returned in two weeks. It was amazing.

"The next thing we did was form a strong board of directors and put together a strategic plan. We decided it was time to focus and control our entire system. Then the stock went from $3.75 back up to $30 and split 3 for 2. Later, we split it a second time 3 for 2. In 1975, *Forbes* magazine rated us one of the nation's fastest growing companies. What was also happening was that pizza was quickly becoming one of America's favorite foods."

Pizza Hut introduced pizza to many cities and towns across the country, and in these places, the restaurant set industry standards for quality and taste. It wasn't until the late 1970s that there was any real competition in most markets, and once again, Pizza Hut ran into trouble.

"Because we made pizza popular, others began to sell different varieties of pizza, and they were taking our market away. At the time, our product didn't rank very high, while the others' pizzas were better at the same price. We were forced to review all our products and threw a few of them out—such as Taco Pizza and 'Thick 'n Chewy' pizza," Carney explains.

"We didn't win back our market until we introduced our Pan Pizza. We tested the pizza in a company-owned store and sales jumped 25 percent. After we tested the first advertisement, and placed the new pizza in 25 different markets, the average sales jumped from 25 percent up to 100 percent—overnight! When we rolled out the Pan Pizza nationwide in 1980, it was a resounding success. Many of our franchisees were skeptical and cautious at first because they didn't want the burden of making two types of pizza dough. But as soon as they saw the sales results from the test markets, the franchisees began offering Pan Pizza at their restaurants too," the founder explains.

In 1968, Pizza Hut moved into the international marketplace when it opened stores in Canada and Mexico one year later. The Carneys learned a valuable lesson early on, after their units in Mexico were losing terrific amounts of money. "We discovered that we couldn't enter a foreign country without knowing the language and expect to be successful. We need local management who understand the culture. Our first Mexican units were owned by an American franchisee who couldn't keep his employees from stealing the cash.

"We bought the units from the franchisee and sent a Spanish-speaking Cuban refugee (who worked for one of our franchises in the United States) to Mexico to clean up the business. After only four weeks he had the cash flow running smoothly again and was depositing the money in a bank," recalls Carney.

Pizza Hut's next international venture was in Australia. Moving into Australia was a lot easier than the Mexico endeavor primarily because it is an English-speaking country.

In 1977, Carney sold the business to PepsiCo because he wanted to strengthen his business. "We looked at all our growth options," he tells, "and I wanted to build a diversified food service company that could make a couple of key acquisitions. We talked to Sambo's and Hardee's among others, but not many of them were interested in a straight merger. I couldn't convince them that a merger was the right thing to do. After testing the waters we had the choice of staying by ourselves or finding a major partner who would allow us to make acquisitions. So we made a list of criteria of what the company had to have before it would make a suitable partner. Instead of just announcing we were for sale, we said we were looking for somebody who fits our criteria. It was imperative that we run the company as we see fit, and they would provide the financing. PepsiCo, Inc., was a natural choice because they had a stable balance sheet, excellent growth and paid good dividends. They had all the important things we wanted for our shareholders. We looked at 25 companies who fit most of our criteria, and we boiled the number down to 10 and then 4. We then decided that PepsiCo, Inc., was our top choice and gave them a pitch.

When PepsiCo, Inc., became the parent company of Pizza Hut, the conglomerate chose to keep the Pizza Hut headquarters in Wichita. "We were PepsiCo's first food service company. They had dabbled outside the industry for a while in areas that were no good for them," Carney explains. "For example, they acquired North American Van Lines and a sporting goods company—businesses that were not marketing related products to their main thrust—their soda pop. They already owned Frito-Lay, Inc., and we told management that Pizza Hut, in addition to PepsiCo, Inc. Bottling, would be a natural third leg to the stool. Management understood our business because they were involved in food service." After leading the company for another three years, Carney left Pizza Hut in 1980 with tremendous personal net worth to pursue other interests.

As a member of the PepsiCo family, Pizza Hut is part of the largest restaurant system in the world. The giant international organization owns and operates 20,000-plus units of Pizza Hut, Taco Bell, and Kentucky Fried Chicken.

Steve Reinemund, president and CEO of Pizza Hut, joined the company after working for the Marriott Corporation where he was vice president and general manager of the Roy Rogers restaurant division. In 1984, Reinemund joined Pizza Hut as the senior vice president of operations and was moved to his current position in May 1986.

Reinemund explains the many advantages to having PepsiCo as a parent company: "Frank Carney realized that to take the company to the next level, he needed the marketing and financial support of a company like PepsiCo.

"I believe the biggest advantage to being a part of the PepsiCo family is being able to attract the quality of employees we are able to hire because of the many opportunities within the PepsiCo umbrella. I have hired people from other companies where they may have been the chief executive officer. If we were an independent company, talented prospective employees would say, 'Steve Reinemund has 10 or 15 years of work left, so where am I going to go?' People look for opportunities to grow, and this is what PepsiCo offers to them."

Franchisee Mike Dart agrees that the relationship with PepsiCo brought impressive management as well as improving the company's marketing. "Since PepsiCo's acquisition, there has been a strong marketing drive in the organization," Dart tells. "Pizza Hut definitely needed an infusion of new ideas in marketing, and Pepsi-Co, Inc., has brought a great deal of professional management to the organization. Many of the senior executives grew up from the store level to the corporate office and had been here forever, and so they didn't produce many innovative ideas. When you bring in an organization like Pepsi, you attract many quality people who inject fresh thinking."

One top manager introduced to the company by PepsiCo is Dan Paxton, senior vice president of human resources. Paxton has been associated with PepsiCo since 1983 when he served as the manager of management training for Frito-Lay, Inc., and also as director of human resources.

"Every division of PepsiCo is truly autonomous and empowered to make decisions relative to the current competitive structure and strategy within its specific segments and individual markets," Paxton says. "In fact, in the restaurant business, we have a little friendly competition among our divisions in the marketplace."

Expanding Pizza Hut in every possible market has been a main objective of its chief executive officer. "We want to get our pizza to consumers wherever they want it: at home, in the malls, in the airports, in cafeterias—wherever they are," Reinemund explains. His goal is apparent in the mission statement he wrote shortly after taking over the presidency—*Our Mission: To consistently demonstrate to consumers that Pizza Hut is the best choice for every pizza occasion.*

"We needed a mission statement that could be used to challenge everything we do from now on," he explains. "If it didn't fit in this statement, then it wouldn't be something we should be doing. We used to think of ourselves as a company with stand-alone restaurants that served pizza to customers when they came to us.

"So in 1986, we decided to pursue our new mission statement. People may not always want to come to us, so we may need to go to them. Obviously if you want to eat a pizza and we are not there, then you are not going to eat ours. This is really the issue. So, now, our objective is to move from simply being an eat-in restaurant company to being a pizza distribution company," the CEO adds.

A great deal of Pizza Hut's growth in recent years is due to Reinemund's leadership. For example, in 1989, the company's domestic and international units posted net sales of $2.5 billion—up 22 percent since 1988, and operating profits of $206 million—up 37 percent. Repeatedly, Pizza Hut receives the highest recognition in its industry by *Restaurants & Institutions* magazine's annual survey of the American public. Consumers vote Pizza Hut the most popular pizza chain in the country, naming specifically, its top quality product, atmosphere, and cleanliness of its stores as unmatched. Also according to the magazine, Pizza Hut has the highest yearly patronage of any full-service chain.

"We constantly provide our customer's with great service and great pizza, which is why we were named America's most favorite pizza place eight years in a row," says Reinemund. "We are committed to providing nothing less than legendary service—more than just good service."

Pizza Hut's success is an impressive accomplishment since there is an increasingly competitive atmosphere for pizza sales in today's market, where an all-out pizza war is in progress. With strong competitors such as Domino's, Godfather's, and Little Caesar's offering their products at discount prices, it is difficult for others to serve high-quality products at competitive prices.

"There is no question that our product is by far the best in the industry," admits franchisee Bill Walsh, who operates close to 100 units. "The niche players, such as Little Caesar's, a price competitor, and Domino's, a speed/delivery competitor, don't offer pizzas that are as good as ours, although they are very marketable. I don't think they design their product to equal ours, and obviously, they lack the same quality control that we have.

"If I am going to be in the pizza business, I want to sell a quality product. Do we charge more than Little Caesar's? Yes, but in my opinion, we give the consumer a lot more for their money. We may be more expensive, but for what we give them, it is well worth those extra dollars," the franchisee states.

According to Pizza Hut's marketing department, the competition for the company's dine-in service has broadened significantly, particularly in the last five years. It has shifted from mom and pop regional pizza parlors and national chains to other casual restaurant chains, such as Denny's, Shoney's, and Appleby's. As a result, Pizza Hut has made a break from the traditional method in which it served pizza to a full-service restaurant serving high-quality products at moderate prices, plus a strong carry-out business. Pizza Hut now offers a variety of different methods to provide the public with its products. Rather than changing its method of operation entirely, the restaurant chain chose to continue its past operations and introduced new formats of distribution including a delivery service and express, cafe, and drive-thru units.

"In some ways, we don't view ourselves as a national chain," the CEO admits. "We look at every single trade area and ask, 'How can we offer our product in many different forms in an area?'"

Since introducing a delivery segment to the public in 1985, half the pizza chain's total sales come from its carry-out service. A market long dominated by Domino's, Pizza Hut's delivery service was an immediate hit, though it was initially rejected by the franchisees. Many of the company's powerful franchisees balked at implementing what they felt was a risky and unnecessary change.

"Delivery was a major shift in strategy from being a restaurant company to being a pizza distribution company," explains Reinemund. "So it was a struggle to convince our franchisees to go with it. Our franchisees are good businesspeople, so when we showed them that the business proposal made sense, they decided to go ahead with it."

Mike Dart was initially opposed to the delivery segment. "I was

one of the many franchisees who resisted the delivery service because there was an extreme concern about the liability associated
with the driver, cost of insurance, and other problems that might
ensue," Dart recalls, who, with four partners, owns and operates 154
Pizza Huts in Florida and Louisiana grossing over $80 million an-
nually. "As it turns out, our drivers haven't had many serious
complications."

According to Pat Williamson, a ten-year veteran of Pizza Hut,
and executive vice president of development, the company had
massive investments in land, building, and equipment and felt the
delivery service might also compete directly with our eat-in business—cannibalizing their own volume. "But the fact is if we didn't
add delivery, somebody else would take that business, because
many consumers want their pizza delivered to their homes," he
concedes.

"The longer we studied the possibilities, the more interested we
became in adding a delivery service. Now that we have had one for
a few years, we saw that we have expanded our market base. Of
course, to compete with Domino's, we also had to offer to deliver
our pizzas within 30 minutes," Williamson says.

In 1990, the delivery segment accounted for one out of five
domestic system sales dollars. In several established markets, the
delivery segment of the business has grown as high as 60 percent
and has not cannibalized the dine-in business. Delivery has proven
to be a lucrative move for Pizza Hut; the chain currently commands
over 15 percent of the delivery market.

"Dine-in gave us the license to take the Pizza Hut name to other
venues, " explains Reinemund. "We were America's favorite pizza
brand long before we got into delivery, and that gave us tremendous
credibility."

In many regions around the country, Pizza Hut has eliminated
the customer's difficulty in determining which unit to call to place
an order. Instead, a customer needs to dial only a single telephone
number, and with the aid of a computerized system, an order is taken
by an operator and routed to the closest Pizza Hut for immediate

preparation and delivery. In smaller markets, customers dial their neighborhood Pizza Hut restaurant directly.

According to Alan Feldman, senior vice president of operations, the delivery service is not the only new method of distribution Pizza Hut will be pursuing in the future. "A student of the restaurant business knows that in every category of food, whether it is hamburgers, tacos, fish, or chicken, all have gone through the inevitable addition of drive-thrus," Feldman states. "They are able to provide food on demand for people who are in a hurry. This hasn't really happened in the pizza industry yet. We know it will happen, and if anybody is going to do it first, we should be the ones. We have the most license, equity, and best product line, so we are very riveted to provide a quick service for the public."

Filling this need is Fastino's, Pizza Hut's new line of units in the competitive fast-food market. A drive-thru unit, Fastino's specializes in carry-out service and offers no seating. The consumer pulls up to the menu board, places an order, and receives it within 60 seconds. According to Williamson, who is responsible for research and technology, restaurant development, franchising, management information systems, and new concepts, "Our first Fastino's unit is doing very well."

"Fastino's offers a limited line of pizza—only three choices—by the slice with only one crust variety. There will also be a line of pasta products. One reason why we designed this concept was to give our franchisees growth opportunity. We think there will be some cannibalization, but the reality of it is, somebody else is going to take away the business if we don't pursue it. We would rather it be us than Little Caesar's or McDonald's.

"We will demonstrate to our franchisees that Fastino's is a viable concept by operating profitable company-owned units. We will prove these units are financially successful before we expect our franchisees to develop their own," adds Williamson.

The company is also expanding new "Express" units. Located at shopping and strip malls, the Express format offers a limited menu including Personal Pan Pizzas, breadsticks, and beverages. Found in food courts, the counter-service units range from 500 to 600 square feet in size. Since the small units do not require many employees, the overhead is kept to a minimum. The Express units, with transaction times averaging 30 to 60 seconds, serve as an alternative to the quick-service food chains such as Burger King and McDonald's. Pizza Hut Express units also come in mobile trailers that are able to serve as many as 240 Personal Pan Pizzas an hour at locations ranging from schools to factories, airports, and stadiums. The Express units are highly profitable, with sales equivalent or better than those earned at a standard eat-in restaurant while requiring only one-fifth the investment for development.

Another move toward growth is the new cafe concept, a full-service restaurant that is more formal than the typical red roof unit. Recently opened in Wichita, the first cafe unit, a company-owned store, offers consumers a more complete dine-in experience. The cafe's will compete with restaurants such as Friday's, Chili's, and the Olive Garden.

According to Williamson, franchisees were involved in the evolution process of the cafe format. "In developing Pizza Hut Cafe, we created a 'blue ribbon task force' which consisted of key company executives and a small group of franchisees. I think this was a very positive move because we involved franchisees in this project from the start. We hope soon to place our cafe concept in existing Pizza Huts and roll it out in the system nationwide in 1993.

"In my ten years of experience here, franchisees have played a major role in flushing out concepts they didn't believe would succeed. At the same time, franchisees are also involved in improving our new concepts," Williamson adds.

In addition to the new delivery, drive-thru, express, and cafe units, Pizza Hut is also pursuing an innovative distribution option that is greatly expanding its share of the off-premise, fast-food market, one of the fastest growing segments in the industry. The company is "wholesaling" its pizza ingredients to institutions such as schools, hospitals, and military bases, and in turn, the pizzas are assembled and sold to students, hospital visitors, and military personnel. For example, the cafeterias at Syracuse University are baking their own Personal Pan Pizzas with oven-ready dough, cheese, sauce, and toppings purchased from Pizza Hut.

Dan Paxton, senior vice president of human resources, states, "We are currently servicing over 3,000 schools, and we have a very aggressive approach and strategy for contracting with more. There have been some obstacles, the foremost being unreasonable restrictions that were placed on meat inspections, which put us at a competitive disadvantage.

"We have many franchisees who are in schools delivering pizza at lunchtime everyday. There is also a number of company-owned stores and franchise units that are responsible for concessions at high school football and basketball games. This follows our mission that we believe and consistently demonstrate that we are the best choice for every pizza occasion, whether in a stadium, a cafeteria, or an airport dining room. We want to be everywhere in the country with the best product and best service," adds Paxton.

"We are also working very closely with our franchisees in introducing a wide range of pasta products that we will sell retail in each of our business segments," reveals Bob Perkins, senior vice president, marketing. "The truth is that in the pizza business, there are no new products; instead, we added pasta dishes, bread sticks, pastrami sandwiches, and so on. This will be an expense because it will require training our people and purchasing new equipment. There is a lot more involved than just printing the new items on the menu and drop-shipping them. Still, although we are adding new products to our menus, Pizza Hut kitchens and prep areas are actually shrinking in size.

"The franchisees reserve the right to serve or not serve any of our products," Perkins continues. "There are still a few franchisees out there that still don't offer the hand-tossed traditional pizza. There are also some that offer pasta dishes that the company stores don't offer. We enforce standard procedures, and there are standards that are acceptable, based on the franchise agreements. Pan Pizza is a product that is sold by 100 percent of our stores—company owned and franchised."

Before the introduction of the Personal Pan Pizza, Pizza Hut had a small lunchtime business. The restaurant chain took the lead in the lunchtime business by promising to serve its new product to a customer's table in 5 minutes or less. After placing the order, a timer is provided to the customer. If the pizza is not served before the timer stops ticking, the customer is not charged for it.

The quick luncheon service, introduced in 1983, did not run smoothly at first—the average delivery time exceeded 6 minutes. Pizza Hut laboriously worked to meet the 5-minute promise. The company developed a system to achieve its standard and then proceeded to train personnel at its franchised and company-owned units. Now, more than 95 percent of its lunchtime Personal Pan Pizzas are delivered before the timer runs out, and Pizza Hut built a lunch business from practically nothing to nearly 20 percent of its total sales.

"We grew our lunch business by a factor of five times," explains Senior Vice President of Operations Feldman. "We became a favorite lunch alternative for people on the go. In today's world, a one-hour lunch is out; convenience and speed are more of an issue."

McDonald's recently unveiled its own pizza, but according to Perkins, it isn't much of a threat to Pizza Hut's business. "Since McDonald's is primarily a lunch place, our sales are not affected, because only 10 percent of our total business is from our lunch segment. We don't expect to bring about a major impact on the lunch segment. If McDonald's ever succeeds in rolling out a serious dinner menu that includes a wide variety of items—including a high quality pizza and table service—then they could possibly be a threat to us.

"There are really only two positions in the fast-food industry that work. You must either have a high-quality product at a fair price or a cheap product. McDonald's is not in our ballpark. They can position themselves by saying they are inexpensive and have fast lines for lunch, but it will be difficult for them to claim a full service and a more expensive menu for dinner," Perkins adds.

"Our offer for a second pizza for $4 was one of the most brilliant marketing ideas in consumer business in the 1980s. To get the second pizza for this low price, you must buy the first pizza at full price. This is a guest check builder. So instead of coming in to buy one pizza, our customers buy two instead. Before we had this special, only 20 percent of our customers bought a second pie. Now, over 50 percent of our consumers buy two pizzas. The math is staggering. The only problem is that we couldn't patent the price—and now Domino's has the $4 pricing, as do some of our other competitors."

Pizza Hut is the world's largest pizza restaurant chain, with over 8,000 locations in all 50 states and over 1,500 units in 64 foreign countries. With more than 4,300 company-owned units, Pizza Hut is also the largest operator of restaurants in the world, larger than even McDonald's, which has over 2,700.

The Pizza Hut system is 58 percent company owned, while 42 percent of the units are franchised. There is a concentration of ownership because over 40 percent of the franchised units are owned by ten franchisees. Since most of the franchises are owned by a few individuals, there is a smooth network of communication between the franchisees and the corporate office, allowing the company to roll out new products and study the market trends on an expedient basis.

"Today we have about 145 franchise groups," Feldman states. "Many are long-term franchisees who have been with Pizza Hut since day one. Most of our franchisees—we have very few single-unit operators—are multistore operators. They are successful businesspeople who have grown and prospered with Pizza Hut. Many of us at the corporate office would welcome the opportunity to become a franchisee.

"Our franchised territories were structured very differently from most other major franchising concepts that have location-only agreements. Our franchisees own geographical territories, they develop within that area, and they continue to expand it as long as the population warrants further unit penetration. A great majority of the country is owned by franchisees who continue to add new units in their territories."

Franchisees are able to purchase supplies through PepsiCo Food Service (PFS). Over 99 percent of the system's franchisees use PFS for one-stop shopping, where they can purchase everything needed to operate their unit(s) from tomatoes to pepperoni. PFS's charter states that it must be the best source for supply at the lowest cost to all Pizza Hut, Taco Bell, and Kentucky Fried Chicken franchisees, although there is no requirement to purchase from PFS.

"Every now and then, some of our franchisees will buy items that they can find elsewhere at an incredibly reduced price, but the bulk is purchased through PFS," explains Feldman.

Franchisee Bill Walsh believes the royalties are justified by the purchasing power enjoyed by the franchisees. "We save more money on the cost of goods we purchase as a group than we pay out to Pizza Hut, Inc., and this has always been the case. For example, through PFS, we can buy cheese and mushrooms at a lower price than if I were an independent operator buying for one or even five restaurants."

Ironically, franchisees are not required to purchase Pepsi-Cola, and are permitted to carry Coca-Cola if they so desire. "Unlike McDonald's which requires their franchisees to sell Coca-Cola, we do not require our franchisees to sell Pepsi-Cola, although most of them do. About 3 percent of our franchisees sell non-Pepsi-Cola products and while we prefer they sell Pepsi products, it is their decision," Feldman points out.

"We always provide our franchisees with a legitimate business reason for everything we try to convince them to do, whether it is the delivery business, using PFS, or pouring Pepsi-Cola. We inform them of the advantages, and then let them make their own decisions."

According to Executive Vice President Williamson, the relationship between the corporate office and the franchisees has improved over the years. "When sales are good, our relationship with the franchisees is great. When sales are soft, the relationship is never what we would like it to be. But this is true in all franchise relationships. We work very hard to involve franchisees in developing all our new concepts.

"Considering all the issues in franchising today, the relationship we have with our franchisees is well above average. For example, in 1990, the franchisees agreed to renegotiate their contracts, an unusual move that illustrates the current positive climate they have with us. In the contract, our franchisees agreed to individual development schedules for each of their territories. For example, if a franchisee agreed to develop ten delivery units over the course of five years, and does not, then the company is permitted to develop the units as company owned. In my ten years here, we were never forced to do this, and it's improbable that we ever will," Williamson explains.

There is a strong motivation throughout PepsiCo and Pizza Hut that team performance is critical and there are no winners on a losing team and no losers on a winning team.

CEO Reinemund agrees: "I think franchisees are only as successful as the parent company, and the parent company is only as successful as the franchisees. Clearly, the franchisees of the PepsiCo restaurant groups have prospered under the PepsiCo leadership.

"Each restaurant division at PepsiCo is managed as an autonomous entity, although PepsiCo is involved in the discussion of our annual plan, five-year strategic plan, and long-term strategy. We also meet with PepsiCo to discuss employee development within the organization, and who will be the future leaders.

"Frank Carney recently said, 'Franchisees make a company better because they have to pay royalties, and it is different from paying employees' salaries. If they are going to pay you for what you are giving them, they are going to give you their opinion about where you are going. As a result, there are going to be inherent agreements and a lot of disagreements over direction.'

"Over the years, Pizza Hut has been successful because it has had a very balanced relationship with its franchisees. My experience since I joined Pizza Hut is that we have a healthy system which is proven by our renegotiations of the contract with our franchisees five to seven years ahead of time," recollects Reinemund. "It demonstrated the willingness of both sides to compromise to the changing business environment and ensuing contractual changes. There was a lot of give and take on both sides.

"Many of the franchisees who have been with Pizza Hut for over 30 years have invested their life savings in this business. They have a vested interest in the long term success of the company. Therefore, I think that the interchange and discussion that we have with our franchisees are an essential part of our business."

According to Perkins, "Our franchisees have input in almost everything we do. Since the average franchisee has been with the Pizza Hut system for over 13 years, I can count on them as a tremendous source of new ideas. They provide me with advice, input, guidance, and counsel. Our franchisees are the backbone of the system—particularly from an historical perspective. Even though we have slightly more company stores than franchised stores, they represent a huge proportion of our sales.

"I speak to the director of the International Pizza Hut Franchise Holders Association (IPHFHA) three to four times a week, and we meet with the franchisees every quarter," Perkins adds.

Mike Dart began his career with Pizza Hut while studying at Wichita State University. During the summer before his senior year, he accepted an internship with an accounting firm and was placed at Pizza Hut to work on an audit. After returning to school, Dart was contacted by the Vice President of Finance Dan Taylor (later to be Dart's business partner) who offered him part-time employment in the Accounting Department. Dart accepted and started work immediately.

Upon graduation, Dart was offered a full-time position and later served as vice president of financial services. Six months after the PepsiCo, Inc., acquisition, Dart and Taylor bought into founder Dan Carney's business, which owned franchise rights for several Pizza Hut regions. Currently, Carney, Taylor, and Dart, along with partners Bob Moore and Les Rudd, own and operate 154 Pizza Hut units in Florida, Alabama, Georgia, and Louisiana.

"In the early days, franchisees were given the freedom to operate their units in the best fashion they saw fit," Dart tells. "There were not regimented procedures and standards that had to be followed, so there was a lot more flexibility. Because of this, the franchisees developed most of the new ideas that came out of the system that initiated the early growth at Pizza Hut. Currently, the only demands the corporate office has set for our business are that we abide by the standards they have defined for operations, products, decor, and image. Beyond these specifics, we are free to run our business as we see fit."

In 1966, as a freshman in college at Wichita State University, Bill Walsh, now a franchisee, began his Pizza Hut career as an employee at a unit. "At the time, there were only 8 company stores, all in Wichita, and around 152 franchised units elsewhere," he recalls. "I started working for 50 cents an hour and all the beer I could drink. I thought this was a great deal! A few months after I started, I was given my own store to manage. I worked at the restaurant throughout the remainder of my college career, and after graduation I was placed as an area supervisor in West Virginia for six months, and then I was moved back to the corporate office to be the vice president of franchising. In this position, I supported the franchisees—tried to help them make more money and present their opinions to my colleagues.

"I worked at the corporate office until 1978, when I left to become a franchisee. Our company, Daland Corporation, was formed in 1976, when several employees left the Pizza Hut corporate office to become franchisees," Walsh continues. "The two original partners bought 1 unit each and joined forces in creating our company. Two years later, I came aboard their partnership, and they had purchased or opened 24 stores. Our company now has six partners, and we own 96 Pizza Hut restaurants in 12 states. We have built new units and acquired established units from other franchisees. We are the sixth largest franchise holder in the system. Our retail sales in 1992, excluding promotions, were over $65 million!

"There are a lot of great things about being a part of the Pizza Hut system. I believe the company has been successful because Dan and Frank Carney sold franchises for the purpose of growth. They let other people use their own money, time, and effort to grow their system quickly. In addition, the Carneys preferred to have a few franchisees operating 1,000 units rather than having 1,000 different franchisees doing the same thing.

"We have a great deal of freedom in developing new units, mainly because of our vast experience. Although our contract calls for the corporate office to approve of every new location, it is not necessary for us because they know we are more familiar with our counties than any Pizza Hut corporate employee. Plus, the company realizes it saves money by not sending someone out. We do all of our own real estate work—we either buy the land and develop the building ourselves or lease a space—whichever is more equitable.

"There are some things in which Pizza Hut does not allow us flexibility. For example, we have to make our pizzas to a certain spec. We have to meet certain standards for operations, appearance, and cleanliness.

"The current management at the corporate office is very impressive. But, because there are not many long-term employees left at the corporate office, they must rely on franchisee input to give them a historical perspective," Walsh tells. "Longtime franchisees were helpful in 1990 when a new executive suggested we start using the same packaging found at other chains such as Little Caesar's. We call this type of packaging 'sacks and circles'—the pizzas are placed on a round cardboard support and placed inside a thin paper bag. We tried this many years ago, from 1966 to 1970, and the reason why we dropped it was because this packaging didn't hold the heat for long. At a meeting with franchisees, that new executive said 'What we really ought to do to cut costs is to do what Little Caesar's does with sacks and cardboard inserts.' Well, he had no idea that we had already tried it before! He is a bright guy, with an MBA, but he didn't research or understand why we use cardboard boxes."

Marketing Vice President Bob Perkins concurs. "The franchisees' input belongs in everything that we do. Since the average franchisees have been in the Pizza Hut system for about 13 years, I can count on them as a tremendous source of new ideas, advice, input, guidance, and counsel. The franchisees are the backbone of this system—particularly from a historical perspective. We meet with them quarterly and, believe me, we do a lot of listening when they speak!"

A good example of the autonomy enjoyed by franchisees occurred at the Pizza Hut at Red Square in Moscow. When Gorbachev was detained and the coup was announced, Yeltsin and his party were meeting in the Russian Parliament building. The climate was tense, with soldiers barricading the building and citizens gathered in masses, harassing the troops.

The local Pizza Hut operator, "Alex," a native Muscovite, watched the coup unfold before his restaurant, and his first concern was, "My goodness, they are going to run a tank through my store. I'd better get down there and keep an eye on it!" The franchisee telephoned his managers and asked them to meet him at the restaurant. Alex and his managers opened the Pizza Hut in Red Square the next day, as usual, not letting the political chaos deter business.

"Later that same day, when it seemed as if the coup was starting to fail, Alex was even more nervous and surprised when he received a delivery order from Yeltsin's group who badly needed food and drink. Just as any other Pizza Hut would respond to an order, Alex's unit delivered! They took 300 pizzas, 20 cases of Pepsi-Cola, and several gallons of coffee over barricades to the Russian parliament building.

Alex had made an independent decision to provide Yeltsin and his party with all the food and drink they needed for free and continued to do so throughout the lifetime of the coup. As it became evident that the coup had failed, Alex received a personal telephone call from Boris Yeltsin who said, "Thank you very much for coming through and being supportive. I will never forget it."

Dan Paxton, senior vice president of human resources, points out that Pizza Hut is a decentralized business with general managers to serve both company-owned and franchised units. "We focus on markets—the basic building units of our business—such as Cleveland, St. Louis, Detroit, and so on. We manage each of these businesses as a decentralized business unit.

"We are moving from a more control-oriented leadership to a more empowered leadership vision for the future. For us, this means making sure our decisions have the best possible impact on our business."

To maintain a healthy stream of communication between the corporate office and the franchisees, by contract, every Pizza Hut franchisee is required to participate in the International Pizza Hut Franchise Holders Association. The association provides benefits such as a health insurance program, a buying cooperative, and liability insurance.

Originally, the association was responsible for all advertising because the Carneys believed that the franchisees should participate in the entire advertising and marketing process. Several members of the IPHFHA's ad committee (AdCom) meet with Perkins and Williamson on a quarterly basis to discuss the company's marketing and advertising strategy.

"My department is responsible for designing the advertising marketing program which is subject to AdCom's approval. We provide AdCom with the background and statistical research and segment analysis to design marketing programs," Perkins explains.

Perkins emphasizes that AdCom is involved in developing all Pizza Huts marketing and runs the network advertising program. "An average company-owned unit spends 2 percent of its sales on network advertising," he explains. "Proportionally, 2 percent is contributed by franchisee co-ops. In total, the company spends over 7 percent of total sales on marketing.

"There is an old phrase, 'You are what you eat.' Our variation is, 'You are how you spend your money,'" explains the senior vice president of marketing.

"We allow the franchisees a lot of flexibility in how they drive their businesses on a local basis," Perkins adds, "while in our national advertising, we try to lay down broad themes such as emphasizing quality or a price point on a particular pizza or raising the awareness of our delivery service."

Since the late 1970s, the only new opportunities in franchising with Pizza Hut have been extended to minorities. "I think it is important to have a representation of minorities within ownership," Reinemund stresses, "because it is good business. Besides, it gives us input toward decision making and dealing with the minority consumers is an important part of our business. The population of the United States is dramatically changing, and by the year 2000, over 20 percent of the population will be Hispanic. Then, too, there is a much larger proportion of African Americans in the country as compared to 25 years ago."

The company has grown tremendously since the PepsiCo buyout in 1977. "In the domestic market, we have only a 25 percent market share, though we are the leader," admits the chief executive. "It is important that we understand that our customers don't care how big we are. They want their hometown Pizza Hut to provide their favorite pizza when they want it, and if we start thinking about ourselves as being a several-thousand-unit restaurant chain, we are going to lose our customers to a competitor.

"So our objective is to make every restaurant experience for every customer the best anybody can do. We must think of our business on the consumer level every day," clarifies Reinemund.

Reinemund believes that the lion's share of the company's growth will continue to remain in the United States, though plans call for significant expansion around the world. In early 1992, Pizza Hut had 1,600 international units operating in 64 countries. "Obviously, there is a lot of opportunity internationally. In September 1990, we opened in the Soviet Union, and more recently, we opened a unit in Beijing, China, and, it too, is very successful."

While the world's highest-volume Pizza Hut restaurant is in Moscow, the second highest is in Finland. Most international units are larger in size than those found in the United States. As a result, these units, such as those in Sweden and Finland, have annual sales volumes as high as $3 million and $4 million (U.S.), while average domestic system sales per unit are just under $700,000. Pizza Hut recently revealed plans to open as many as 14 units in Poland, Hungary, and Czechoslovakia by 1993. Over half the properties operated internationally are franchised; the remainder are either company owned or a joint venture.

During the course of slightly more than three decades, Pizza Hut has become one of the great success stories in the food industry. The company has come a long way since opening night in 1958 when Dan and Frank Carney gave pizza away to generate interest in their fledgling business. So, now, as Pizza Hut's sales pass the $5 billion mark, company executives brace themselves to meet four major challenges in the 1990s. "We want to double our delivery sales within the next five years, increase our dine-in business, grow and expand internationally, and finally, discover another billion-dollar business," Bob Perkins sums up. Knowing its history, one thing is for certain: Pizza Hut will do its best to satisfy every pizza occasion.

Chapter 9

SERVICEMASTER

The Masters of Service, Serving the Master

Considered the most profitable service company for the last ten years by *Forbes* magazine with annual sales totaling over $3 billion, ServiceMaster is indeed a company that performs. Several reasons set ServiceMaster apart from other companies of its size: specifically, it is principles illustrated by its primary corporate objective—"To Honor God in All We Do."

Providing professional residential and commercial services for cleaning, lawn care, pest control, disaster restoration, maid service, home warranty and appliance repair, and temporary personnel services through a worldwide network of franchises, ServiceMaster is an all-around "service organization"; its subsidiaries operate with very little capital, a lot of talented labor, and dedicated management. With over 5,500 franchisees worldwide, ServiceMaster has a bright future.

ServiceMaster was the vision of Marion Wade. Born in Pocahontas, Arkansas, in 1898 and raised in Chicago, Wade dropped out of school in the eighth grade to launch his career. A man with a diverse background, he played semiprofessional baseball for a few years, sold life insurance, aluminum pots and pans, and even home mothproofing services.

At the outbreak of the depression in 1929, his employer went bankrupt, and at the age of 31 with a family of four, the unemployed jack-of-all-trades started his own mothproofing company, which he managed out of his house. That same year, Wade committed his life to Christianity. As a devout Baptist, he devoted a certain portion of his time each day to Bible study, a practice that he would follow for the rest of his life.

Wade's small business persevered, and by 1945 he employed a staff of two. It was this year that a catastrophe occurred which would change Wade's life and his company forever. While Wade was mothproofing a client's closet, the chemicals he used to annihilate the moths exploded in his face. Lucky to live through the accident, Wade temporarily lost his eyesight and was confined to a hospital bed for several months.

During this time, the entrepreneur began to think about his accomplishments and the purpose of his life and work when he realized something was missing. In his own words, Wade has said, "I was trying to honor God personally, but I had never tried this with my company because I had been trained in the school of competition, which attests that religion and business do not mix." While lying in his hospital bed, the blind man prayed and committed himself and all his possessions (including his business) to the Lord. Of course, skeptical of his sight being restored, Wade also prayed that the Lord would help him recover.

Shortly thereafter, Wade's eyesight miraculously returned, and as he promised, he began actively to honor God through his mothproofing business. This may have seemed like an unlikely way to honor God; however, Wade believed that a person could honor God in many different ways.

After returning to work, Wade explained the company's new philosophy to his employees who readily accepted it. Wade described what subsequently happened: "We began each day with a prayer and an acknowledgment of our commitment . . . We found ourselves undergoing changes in our attitudes toward each other as well as toward the job. We all got along better; there was more willingness to go the extra mile, to work the extra hour, and when disagreement arose, as it inevitably does, we were able to resolve it by a prompt discussion rather than carry grudges and lose tempers . . . . The dedication brought new vitality into the small group. We developed a new pride in doing a good job . . . . Our 'family' business began to grow. Every employee from top to bottom does his job for the glory of God." Wade chose not only to share the commitment to God with his fellow employees, he also felt the company needed to explore it openly with its customers and the community at large.

Later that year, Marion became acquainted with Kenneth N. Hansen, a Wheaton College (Illinois) graduate with degrees in religion and philosophy. Hansen was an interim minister at the church that Wade and his wife, Lillian, attended. Wade's first encounter with the pastor was when they were working together to establish a Sunday School at the church. Hansen told Wade that he planned to be in business someday. Wade admired the pastor's zeal, and told him when he was ready to let him know.

After a permanent pastor was found for the church, Wade offered him a position, but Hansen declined. Instead, Hansen followed a longtime dream to work with a Christian foundation that enabled him to help develop Christian youth organizations. Hansen spent two years with the foundation before he felt ready to work in the marketplace. The former pastor called Wade and asked if an offer was still available. Thrilled to have Hansen as part of the company, Wade placed him in the field, to learn production and sales. After he had accumulated enough experience, it was Wade's plan to place him in a leadership position in the company's headquarters.

"Marion's vision—to serve God in the marketplace—fitted with what my wife, Jean, and I wanted to do with our lives," recalls Hansen. "My work with Marion's company was much different from what I had been doing, yet it offered me the same objectives that I enjoyed with the church."

Through his mothproofing business, Wade was able to meet with customers directly, most of whom were housewives. Wade heard many complaints from his customers who had expensive rugs in their homes, but found it difficult to have them cleaned without taking them in to a professional cleaner, which was inconvenient because the rugs were very heavy. So he conceived a revolutionary approach to rug cleaning: his company would clean the rugs in the customers' homes. Accordingly, Wade expanded his business and added rug cleaning as an additional home service. This service was a natural tie-in with the company's mothproofing services.

Wade visited a major department store in downtown Chicago and conferred with salespeople and managers in the rug department. Wade explained his innovative cleaning services and asked the salespeople to recommend it to their present and past customers who Wade would then solicit. In exchange, they would be paid a commission. It took about six years before Wade was able to convince the store's management that his service would provide a valuable courtesy for its customers and, in turn, enhance the store's service image. Within a year of signing the agreement, Wade's business skyrocketed.

During subsequent attempts to seek new business, Wade approached several carpet manufacturers for their referrals. It was then that he met Bob Wenger, a Chicago-area sales representative for several carpet manufacturers. A fire occurred in a downtown hotel; it all had to be cleaned up—Wade's method of cleaning was so impressive to Wenger, compared to other vendors', that a relationship developed between the two. Wade was also drawn to the salesman, who had a fine reputation for professionalism and integrity. Wenger, he thought, would be a valuable addition to the company.

Two years passed before Wenger could be persuaded to come aboard as a partner. In 1947, Hansen drew up papers incorporating the company as "Wade, Wenger and Associates." With Hansen as the third major stockholder in the newly formed partnership, Wade also distributed stock to his other employees giving them a feeling of ownership. They were also eligible to purchase additional shares.

Wade wanted his employees to know that they were part of a big family and no matter what level they were at, they were working for God. It was in this same year that the small business moved from Wade's house to a store front. There were still fewer than ten employees.

Wade believed that the key to profitable growth was good financial controls. Since financial management was not a great area of strength for the entrepreneur, Hansen was given this responsibility. Wade once said, "Ken had a real feel for finances, and I was happy to give him plenty of latitude. I told him, 'Pay our bills promptly. Give the employees the best wages possible. If there is anything left over after that, I'll get paid.'"

Several weeks after the company was incorporated, it opened a branch in Milwaukee, placing Hansen in charge as the manager. After the branch was operating profitably, additional branches were opened in still other cities.

"I learned one of life's key lessons by how Marion handled a disappointing turn of events by one of our key retailers. The department store chose to go into the rug cleaning business for themselves. Without notifying Marion, the store began to service its rug customers itself, on location, allocating only the excess jobs to us," explains Hansen.

"He was furious that the store had violated the written agreement. The store was servicing all new business themselves, taking many jobs that *our* salesmen had generated. In response, Marion chose to live up to his company's principles and handle the situation in a Christian manner. He recalled a passage in the Bible in which Paul wrote to the Romans, "Recompense to no man evil for evil." Immediately, Wade contacted the store's management and terminated the agreement. Then he went one step farther—he offered to support the store for six months, allowing them enough time to expand their service so they would be able to handle the additional work alone."

In 1948, the partners felt they had a good business and one that fulfilled a niche in the marketplace. Wade, Wenger and Associates possessed unique technology in terms of cleaning techniques and products but lacked the capital to expand. So they made a decision that was to have a major impact on the company for many years to come. The partners decided to expand the business through the franchise method of distribution and offer licenses in areas of the country where the company was not operating.

"Our business expanded at a rapid rate mostly due to the birth of wall-to-wall carpet. At the time, carpet manufacturers were just beginning to produce wall-to-wall, and consumers were having a difficult time cleaning them," explains Hansen, who has since retired and lives in Santa Barbara, California. To this day, he remains in close contact with the corporate office. "We had opened offices in Milwaukee and Minneapolis and planned to expand slowly elsewhere, but having been convinced by the carpet manufacturers and retailers that there was suddenly a great need for our business, we decided that franchising was the way to go."

The first franchise agreement was signed in March 1952. Many of the earliest franchisees were World War II veterans who were students of Wade's in a Sunday School class he taught at his church. Some of these early "recruits" are still with the company today.

"As we opened more offices, the managers and other employees we hired expressed interest in buying their own branches. Wade, Wenger and Associates quickly began to grow," adds Hansen. "I was elected to travel around the country to sell more franchises and assist in training.

"It was never very difficult for me to sell franchises in those days. We provided an obvious opportunity to be a part of a service business to people who did not have major technical skills, a formal education, or much capital. Our objective was to expand through franchising, not to make money selling them.

"I showed the potential franchisees our figures and introduced them to our own people, and they would go right out into the street with our people soliciting new business and cleaning carpets. We were looking for people who would be aggressive at direct selling," adds Hansen. "Initially, we sold our franchises for $250 to $500 and finally $1,000.

"Franchising gave our company a national presence, but we learned that there is a great danger in franchising—some franchisees may feel that they own their territory and no longer want to grow. We had a few franchisees who operated in a beautiful area only to allow their market to freeze. We went through some difficult times because we had to wait to buy them out. We learned a few awfully good lessons, though some were very painful.

"Each time a new franchisee or distributor was signed up with the company, it was a great occasion," recalls Richard Armstrong, senior vice president who has been with ServiceMaster since 1964. "Everybody in the corporate office would do a snake dance around their desks. This tradition has continued with music playing throughout our offices whenever a new contract is signed with a franchisee or a client, although we don't dance anymore. Even today, as a $3 billion company, a single sale or a new individual franchisee is still very important to us, and the music lets every ServiceMaster employee know we are growing and share in the success. We believe this is a valuable concept to keep reinforcing."

Eventually, Wade, Wenger and Associates soon realized that it had expanded too rapidly and was spread very thin. The partners found themselves constantly traveling on the road, training, and visiting franchisees for three and four weeks at a time because there was not enough money to travel back to Chicago on the weekends. Later, the partners would remember the situation as one that could have destroyed the company.

In 1954, to keep up with the demand in the rapidly growing western region, Ken Hansen hired Kenneth T. Wessner, another Wheaton College graduate who had formerly been working as a sales promotion manager for the Club Aluminum Products Company in Chicago. Wessner was placed in charge of the western franchise division, wearing many hats, as regional manager, field sales manager, and general manager.

"I hired 'Wes' because I felt we needed someone who had skill at direct sales and sales promotion. My background was weak in these areas. I heard from friends that Ken was considering leaving his job at Club Aluminum," recalls Hansen. "We had several interviews, and he decided to join our company. He turned out to be a winner in everything he was asked to do. Wherever he traveled throughout the country to work with our branch managers and franchisees, business picked up and became profitable. A great portion of our business growth is attributable to his ability in these areas."

Wessner has many warm memories of his early days with ServiceMaster and recalls the hard work, long trips, and thinning cash flow. "Mr. Wade used to say, 'Fellows, today we have the shorts, but someday we will have the long pants.'

"Money was scarce, so while we were out traveling on the road, we were permitted to call home only once a week for 20 minutes. It became a standard operating procedure to call our families only on Sunday afternoons unless there was an emergency. The rule back then was that we had to travel to support the franchisees. We had to be on the road for at least three weeks, and we were not allowed to fly."

Hansen adds, "While Wes helped manage our franchises, I became the 'fundraiser.' Marion and I raised money by selling shares in our business to friends.

"Luckily, the company was doing well, and we began thinking of other ways to expand our services. At this time, one of our early managers (now a licensee in Chicago) came to me and said 'You know, there are more surfaces to a room than just the floor. There are five more to be exact, and we ought to be cleaning them (walls and ceilings) as well. I heard about a pressure system in pumps and tanks, and we ought to look at it.' So I sent someone up to look at the manufacturer's equipment, and we tested it and thought it would be a great addition to our business. Many of our franchisees immediately chose to go into the wall cleaning business.

"Suddenly, our wall cleaning business tied in with our carpet cleaning business, and we started receiving calls from insurance agents who wanted us to restore homes that had been damaged by fire or water. This brought us a whole new field of business in disaster restoration. It became a major part of our business and changed the company forever! Now, in addition to marketing directly to the customer, we could make promotional calls on insurance adjusters. They would keep calling us back as long as we provided good service. Direct selling was no longer the only way to market our business," Hansen exclaims.

As the company continued to expand at a rapid pace, the associates decided that they needed a new name. Wade, Wenger and Associates was too much of a mouthful, and they thought something more generic would better suit the various functions performed by the company and its franchisees. According to Wade, "We wanted a name which could be applied to the diversified services we performed and at the same time indicate the basic philosophy of the company. The name we chose evolved almost by itself. As a company, we were in the business of on-location cleaning and maintenance services. As individuals and as a company, we were working for the Lord—we were servants of the master. The word 'ServiceMaster' struck us all as perfect in every area." ServiceMaster was an ideal name with its double meaning: *Masters of Service* and *Serving the Master*.

In the 1940s, the corporate objectives became "To Help People Develop" and "To Grow Profitably." Previously, the only corporate objective ServiceMaster observed was, "To Honor God in All We Do."

Armstrong recalls a story which is now part of the company's rich history: "Ken Hansen once said to Marion, 'You know, Marion, if we cap the business off right here, you and I can start taking $40,000 a year out of the business. I am convinced of this.' And without even considering the suggestion, Marion turned to Ken and replied, 'Ken, that is not why God gave us this business. We have got to keep putting this money back into the business so that the people who are committed to it will have an opportunity to grow just as you and I will have the opportunity to grow.' Hansen agreed and proceeded to mortgage his house and belongings to put more money into the company.

Hansen recalls, "As I moved from selling and accounting into managing, I was primarily task oriented because I worked with others. But as I grew into vital union with Jesus, I came to see that I was viewing people as a means to get the work done. I viewed the work as the end to be accomplished. I realized that I was reversing the positions of means and ends which the Bible teaches. It was painful to realize and then acknowledge that this bent is sinful, harmful to others and to myself, and dishonoring to God whom I seek to serve. The living relationship I have with Jesus motivated me to change the way I viewed and treated other people."

Another avenue for business that the company pursued was discovered in the late 1950s by Marion Wade. After delivering a speech to a church group about the excitement and effectiveness with which ServiceMaster representatives did their cleaning work, a Catholic nun in the audience suggested that he look into cleaning services for hospitals. Wade was intrigued by the idea and asked Hansen to study the matter. Shortly thereafter, in 1961, Ken Wessner was enlisted to assist Hansen in analyzing the potential in hospital services and subsequently became vice president of ServiceMaster Industries, Inc. Wessner's initial response to Hansen was, "I really enjoy my experience in the franchise business and I'm not sure I even like hospitals." But once he got involved and realized the potential for growth, Wessner became enthusiastic.

Hansen and Wessner spent two years studying the needs of potential customers. Hansen remembers, "When we began our hospital housekeeping management business, it was based on the cornerstone of hard listening. We heard administrators saying that their time could be used better if they could have professional help for some of the more nonpatient-related functions of their hospitals. We learned that the hospital community was ready for the services of a specialist organization; that would blend itself into their needs. At the same time, other companies heard that a lot of money was going to be spent by hospitals for contract housekeeping, but they approached the business as just more buildings to clean. We were going to take a different approach."

Within two years, Hansen and Wessner had discovered what type of service would meet hospitals' needs, and in 1962, Service-Master secured its first hospital contract for cleaning services at Lutheran General Hospital in Park Ridge, Illinois. The difference between ServiceMaster and the other contractors was that Service-Master developed and sold a system just as they did in their franchised areas. The company placed one or more of its own employees in the hospital to manage housekeeping; however, the individuals actually doing most of the work were employees of the hospital. These employees were trained in ServiceMaster ways, provided with ServiceMaster tools and cleaning products, and motivated by ServiceMaster methods. The hospital gained a higher quality of employee performance with a lower cost for the total service. Wessner convinced hundreds of other hospital administrators that the business of a hospital is in doctoring and patient care while the support services could be handled better and less expensively by ServiceMaster than internal departments. Currently, ServiceMaster counts over 1,000 hospitals in the United States as clients.

ServiceMaster went public in 1962, though according to Hansen, the raising of capital was not the incentive for making a public offering. "We chose to go public in order for the three partners to have liquidity for Marion's estate, in the event the founder should pass away. Bob Wenger left ServiceMaster to return to the carpet business, but he continued to own an interest in the business and serve on the board.

As the company continued to grow and prosper, so did Wessner, and after serving as a director for many years, he became the executive vice president and chief operating officer. In 1973, he was elected president and subsequently chief executive officer.

In his many positions including chief executive officer, Wessner, made many significant contributions to ServiceMaster. Initially writing the manuals for on-site procedures, Wessner was largely responsible for developing additional functions such as laundry and linen services (1967), plant operations and maintenance (1971), clinical equipment management (1975), materials management (1977), and food service management (1981). In addition to hospitals, these management services are also provided to corporations and educational institutions of all sizes. In 1990, the company derived approximately 79 percent of its operating revenue from its management services. One of Wessner's proudest accomplishments during his tenure was the establishment of an in-house M.B.A.-level program with one of the nation's leading experts on hospital management serving as dean.

In 1973, under Wessner's new leadership, the four corporate objectives the company had observed since the early days were officially adopted:

> To Honor God in All We Do
> To Help People Develop
> To Pursue Excellence
> To Grow Profitably

According to Wessner, "The philosophy of a company determines the character and nature of the business it conducts. The climate of a company is created by the concepts of management and life that govern its policies and practice.

"The philosophy of ServiceMaster and the words we use to express that philosophy have been carefully conceived, nurtured, and refined through years of thought, work, and commitment. Our company philosophy is expressed in four objectives. These four statements are the foundation upon which everything we do is built.

"We had always been interested in the training of people and in helping people grow and mature. We were not only interested in their work life but also in their social life, family relationships, and spirituality. I recall Mr. Wade once saying, 'At ServiceMaster we have learned that a person becomes more sensitive to their accountability to God when we give them an opportunity for more responsibility to the company. We make our plans and set the policy at staff conferences. Then the employees go back to their offices to do their jobs, using their own brains and their own skills to make decisions.'"

According to Dick Armstrong, Wade's philosophy is still very alive today, and perhaps even stronger than at any time in the past. "This is because of the strong leadership we have that is committed to the heritage which Marion gave us. Our corporate objectives describe the kind of company we are. Our first objective, 'To Honor God in All We Do,' has an impact on all aspects of our business. It is reflected in the way we treat our customers, how we relate to and treat our employees, and how we conduct our business. It gives us a reference point for what is right and wrong and the kind of people we ought to be.

"We want our franchisees to understand our philosophy, but they don't need to ascribe to it. Our employees and franchisees don't need to share the same convictions, but they do need to know where we are coming from.

"Our business is a tool for helping people grow and develop. Our first two corporate objectives are our goals, and the last two help us accomplish the first two. We don't feel that we can accomplish any of the goals effectively if one were to be excluded. We need all of them. Our fourth corporate objective is driven by our second objective, because if we are going to help people grow and develop, then we need to keep growing as an organization to provide broader management skill opportunities.

"Obviously, our religious orientation is quite different from that of our franchisees in Japan and the Middle East. But they are just as committed to the company's growth and profitability as we are. In Japan, they have taken our corporate objectives and added two more! Our partners in the Middle East admired our corporate objectives because they are employee oriented. These objectives even helped to improve our Middle Eastern workers' living conditions. By giving every employee the recognition he or she deserves, we are able to improve the morale of each worker," adds Armstrong.

"We don't make a big 'splash' about our corporate objectives and the beliefs of many of our leaders of the company, but we are up front about them. I do think it is important that people feel comfortable with our objectives. They are not exclusive; rather, they are inclusive, and we do not reject people because they don't believe in the same things as we do. We try to give people exposure to our objectives, what they mean and why they are important to Service-Master, " explains Chris Oxley, general manager of ServiceMaster International in Japan.

ServiceMaster, with its objectives, has become a major source of fulfillment for its employees. As one of the objectives indicates "To

Help People Develop," the foundation of the company's educational program is to help employees grow both personally and professionally. Through these programs, the franchisees have learned many of the skills necessary for success.

Over the years, education and training at every level have become a ServiceMaster hallmark. ServiceMaster offers its new franchisees an "Academy of Management," a one-week training program at the corporate office. In this program, franchisees learn all the administrative and operational aspects of running their new business. Classes are taught by a corporate staff, including managers in both operations and support services. The franchisee's license fee covers all expenses incurred during the training program while the tuition is paid for by the corporate office.

In 1987, *Management Review* reported,

> *ServiceMaster has given people whose jobs were considered unimportant—janitors, cleaning people, boiler operators, landscapers—new challenges, respect, responsibilities and career options . . . . ServiceMaster offers a system of defined career paths, as supervisors and fellow employees continuously move up to fill their spots in time. This adds a new incentive for maintenance employees to change and improve their work, and eliminates many of the "turf" problems one would expect when hired managers come into an established operation. It also utilizes economy of scale by fully tapping the skills and expertise of workers that no one else has, or can justifiably spend time and money to learn.*

ServiceMaster is proud of the opportunities for growth it has provided to the thousands of people who have been associated with the company. Despite the grunginess of a lot of the cleaning duties, morale is very high. The company is proud of its commitment to training even functionally illiterate workers. The company offers both conventional and unconventional classes to help workers upgrade their skills—a basic step in improving both their self-image and their career potential. To help illiterate or disabled workers master basic tasks and improve their productivity, ServiceMaster often employs the use of color-coded instructional materials and pictorial images in training programs. This may be based upon goodwill, but turnover is minimized and performance is improved, and clients who are pleased to see workers take pride in their jobs are more apt to repeat business with ServiceMaster.

"We have a policy at ServiceMaster that states if a manager or an executive is too busy to teach or work with franchisees and employees, then they are too busy to be a manager. Our managers are servants to the people who work with and for ServiceMaster. This is what "WE SERVE" is all about," explains Bill Pollard, Chairman, the fourth in the history of the company.

In the early 1960s, ServiceMaster expanded its franchised operations beyond North America when it signed an agreement with a licensee in Great Britain (which was eventually repurchased by ServiceMaster in 1976). The next major overseas expansion took place in Japan where ServiceMaster sold the territorial rights to franchise to the Duskin Company, Ltd., which currently operates over 600 ServiceMaster franchises in that country. The on-location franchising network of ServiceMaster continued to grow, and the company began to offer additional services to its clients, including furniture cleaning, disaster restoration, window cleaning, maid services, and pest control.

"Franchising has been a vital part of the growth and development of our business. It is an important partnership relationship in delivering our services.

"Franchising marries the best of an independent businessperson who is working and has a good reputation in the local community with the marketing and technical expertise of a large company. Together, the two partners deliver better service than one standing alone," Pollard continues.

Carlos Cantu, president and CEO of the ServiceMaster Consumer Group, agrees with Pollard. He believes there are some services that are administrated best through the franchise method of distribution. Cantu sites Merry Maids, another provider of service in the ServiceMaster Quality Service Network. Merry Maids has over 550 franchisees providing maid services across North America. The company was initiated in 1980 by Dallen Peterson, who began by operating his maid service business from his home in Omaha, Nebraska. In 1988, to benefit his franchisees and provide them with greater support and more opportunity for growth, Peterson sold his business to ServiceMaster. For continuity and ongoing involvement in the business he loves, Peterson has continued as chairman of that business. Today, Merry Maids is the largest supplier of residential maid services in North America and is a major service provider in the ServiceMaster Quality Service Network under Cantu's direction.

According to Don Anderson, president, ServiceMaster Residential/Commercial Services, the company uses a detailed screening process when evaluating a potential franchisee. Anderson, who began his career with ServiceMaster in 1966, explains, "A franchisee must have the resources to finance the business properly in the initial stages. A healthy cash flow and working capital are very important in starting any new business. We want to make sure that we choose people who can afford to get in the business and have the resources to accomplish that.

"Second, we want to make sure that they have the personality and the emotional makeup that would qualify them to run a business like this and to be able to accomplish the goals that we would hope they could. Our franchisees have an entrepreneurial spirit, a strong desire to run their own business, and a desire to learn marketing and sales skills that are so important to running a business effectively. Their personality and makeup allow them to do that."

As part of the application process, ServiceMaster prefers to interview a potential franchisee in his or her home with the spouse. "We like to interview the husband and wife and observe them interacting with each other and their children. It is extremely important that a franchisee have the support of his or her family members," Anderson explains. "This doesn't mean that the spouse must be in the business too, but he or she must be supportive. It is a stressful period for a person who is starting a new business and spending most of his or her waking hours getting it started, especially if that person is going home to someone who feels he or she is doing the wrong thing.

"Starting a new business can be extremely difficult on a marriage. We want to be sure that we are helping people who can be successful. Franchising is more than a numbers game. You can't put just anybody in the business, even if they have the resources. It is important to ascertain which people will be successful.

"Typically, I think people who buy franchises are people who want to have something with a track record, who don't want to start their own business from scratch. They want to have both a nationally known name and a well-established proven system that will help them be successful. Many people who own a ServiceMaster franchise have never owned their own business before and perhaps didn't even have any real business experience. Our franchisees are from all types of backgrounds," Anderson adds.

According to Chairman Pollard, some of the most difficult times ServiceMaster has had in its long history have been when a franchise is sold to a person who is not suited for it. "I have had friends who bought a franchise and were not successful. I sit down with them, after they have been in business for a year and a half and invested a great deal of money, and we analyze why they had problems. The problems were not because there isn't a good market or that our system doesn't work. Problems usually happen when that franchisee is unable to sell the service. Great technicians can clean carpets until they are as clean as a whistle, but if they aren't able to pick up the telephone or go out and knock on doors to sell the service, they will fail. Every business starts with a sale. Without a sale, you don't have a business. One of our goals is to help franchisees become better salespeople."

ServiceMaster is organized in a unique way that works well for all levels of the company. Franchisees work directly with their local *distributor* who is responsible for their territory. The distributor, who may or may not also operate as a franchisee, purchases and merchandises the cleaning products and equipment manufactured by ServiceMaster and distributes them to the franchisees. They then participate in the franchisees' market with initial and ongoing training support and as the marketing coordinator in sales and advertising. The distributors around the country work directly with

ServiceMaster corporate management and represent the franchisees in their areas.

"When ServiceMaster was first starting, Marion Wade and Ken Hansen realized that they were selling franchisees in far away places, and they may not be able to support those franchisees as well as the ones who were located closer to the Chicago headquarters," explains Bob Groff, a distributor in Seattle, Washington. "That is when they decided they would sell distributorships to experienced people who could help support the franchises in making them successful in return for a portion of the royalty fees.

Bob Groff began his ServiceMaster career in 1975 as a franchisee in Grand Forks, North Dakota. "My wife Sue and I were really impressed with the fact that ServiceMaster had special values and was interested in more than just making a buck. We were attracted to ServiceMaster's principles and the fact that they adhered to them. We felt a real sense of security—something that is valuable to someone who is investing his life savings in a franchise.

"My wife and I built the business from scratch, cleaning carpets ourselves. The business became very successful, and a few years later, we felt it was time to sell and move on. ServiceMaster offered me a position at the corporate office as the regional operations manager and a member of the faculty at the academy. I accepted and became a corporate employee, until 1981 when I purchased the distributorship in Seattle, Washington.

"I felt an obligation to tell Ken Wessner personally that I was leaving my corporate position to take the distributorship. I went to his office and told him that I appreciated my experience at the corporate office and was grateful for the direction he provided me. Then I noticed he had a queer, disappointed look on his face. 'I am really sorry to see you leave. Where are you going to go?' he said to me. 'Well, I am going to be the distributor in Washington,' I replied. He suddenly jumped out of his chair and a large grin appeared on his face. 'Oh!' he said, 'You are not leaving ServiceMaster! That is great!'

"He was very excited for me and wanted to know what the company could do to help. Bill Pollard worked on some numbers, and the company loaned me the money I needed to buy the distributorship.

"In 1981, my first year as distributor, this area had only $533,000 in total revenues. Ten years later, in 1991, with 45 franchisees in the area, the year ended with revenues of about $12 million!

"What I like most about our organization is the ability for people to be associated with it yet still be independent entrepreneurs. If this were a typical corporate setting, when the president says 'jump!' the people ask 'How high?' But in our franchise organization, when the president says 'jump!' 4,000 people ask him, 'What for?'"

Although there is not an association for the franchisees, they do enjoy a successful system that permits them to communicate effectively with the corporate office. For example, CEO Bill Pollard spends as much as 40 percent of his time on the road, part of which he commits to meeting with franchisees, attending their various awards and recognition ceremonies. When back at the corporate office, he believes in an open-door policy.

"I am here to listen to the franchisees and to help them find solutions for their problems. The ability to listen is an important part of my job. I must always keep my ear to the ground and be available."

The franchisees are further represented at the corporate office by an Idea Review Council which consists of ten franchisees and ten distributors who meet with top management at the corporate office on a quarterly basis. During these meetings, ideas are presented and reviewed, such as new systems, technology, training programs, national advertising, and so forth.

"The review council works extremely well, and we receive great ideas from the field during these meetings. During these sessions, the distributors and franchisees have the opportunity to tell us what they think and ways we can improve business. It is an excellent system of communication," explains Anderson.

Unlike most other franchisors, ServiceMaster does not assign exclusive areas of operation to franchisees, and the majority of franchisees own a single license for one unit, usually in the town or the area where they live.

"The reason we have nonexclusive territories is because

everybody has their own individual goals and objectives as to how big they want to have their business. Some franchisees may be completely satisfied by earning $50,000 a year, while another has a goal of $1 million. So rather than operating exclusive areas, we look at what has happened with the individual franchisees and the development of the market potential and place franchisees according to the way the market is being developed," Anderson tells.

"Keeping our franchisees nonexclusive allows for a much better situation for them regarding the development of a market. For example, if a franchisee in one town is doing $75,000 a year in business and is content with that, a competitor may come in to their marketplace and eventually take some of their business away. We would rather have another ServiceMaster franchisee in that town, serving those customers, driving around in the same color trucks as the other franchisee, marketing the same name, and performing the same services than an outsider," he adds.

The average ServiceMaster franchisee in the beginning frequently operates as a working owner out of his or her home. "We don't encourage the new franchisee to have a store front or an office because we want to make sure they keep their overheads low. We want our franchisees to spend their time in the field, marketing and selling and actually performing the work. As the business begins to grow, they will hire employees and additional help as needed," Anderson says.

Although most franchisees operate on a small to medium scale, many have grown into million-dollar businesses. For example, two people in Bob Groff's Seattle area, Wes Mitchell and Steve Losorwith, operate a $2.5 million-a-year ServiceMaster franchise. Primarily a disaster restoration business serving residential homes and commercial businesses, their small franchise has grown into a huge organization and is the largest ServiceMaster franchise in the world. Mitchell and Losorwith employ multiple layers of employees from supervising crew chiefs to a full-time sales force and have their own warehouse where they store equipment and other supplies.

The franchise developed when Losorwith, bored and underchallenged in a 12-year career as a banker, learned about a Service-

Master franchise that was for sale in the Seattle area. "I didn't know anything about ServiceMaster at the time. I didn't even know what business they were in! I was merely interested in the opportunity to own a business so I could control my destiny. Frankly, the corporate objectives were not a driving factor, though they are very important to me now.

"In 1984, I bought the franchise and it took off like a wildfire. It was out of control! There were many things I was good at, but I felt I needed someone that could complement my strengths and take over my weak areas. So, after one year, I invited Wes Mitchell to join me as a partner."

Mitchell began his career with ServiceMaster after completing graduate school in 1971. Having worked for 13 years in the headquarter's office as a franchise regional manager for the western territories, it was in this capacity that he was acquainted with Losorwith. He welcomed the opportunity to be in business for himself.

Together, the two men built their franchise in six years from a $100,000-a-year-business to a $2.5 million one. Now, with over 60 employees, Mitchell and Losorwith are managers and spend less time working in the field.

"ServiceMaster demonstrated to us that management is interested in doing whatever it can to help us be successful and provide us with many opportunities to grow," Losorwith expresses.

Another inspiring story is Terry Burke's, a franchisee who overcame drug and alcohol addiction and found a sense of purpose with ServiceMaster. A Phi Beta Kappa college graduate with a degree in business administration with hopes to some day be an entrepreneur, Burke acquired a drug and alcohol addiction during the 1960s. By the mid-1970s, the honors graduate was working as a laborer on a fruit farm. One day, while driving a tractor, he broke down crying, having realized he had hit rock bottom. At this time, he chose to pursue recovery and soon became involved in a spiritual fellowship.

Never satisfied working for somebody else, the newly recovered Burke had a burning desire to be an independent businessperson. Three years after he began his recovery, during the peak of the urban cowboy craze, he purchased a Western apparel shop in Seattle with a friend. By 1982, the trend was over, so Burke and his partner liquidated their stock. This prompted him to look for a new business. Burke was attracted to ServiceMaster because of its proven track record, impeccable credentials, and more important, its spiritual principles.

"I was thrilled when Bob Groff, my area's distributor told me, 'I will do whatever it takes for you to be successful with our company. I will even work with you on Saturdays,'" recalls Burke.

"I signed up my first contract with a local restaurant. I personally cleaned it every day, seven days a week, from 7:00 A.M. to 9:00 A.M. It takes a tremendous amount of hard work to succeed in business. But I don't look at being in business for myself as working! Working is when I have to go out and work for somebody else," he adds.

Now employing over 40 people, Burke operates close to a million-dollar business. "My life is extremely abundant now because I am with ServiceMaster. I am pleased to be able to help others turn their lives around by providing employment opportunities to many people on welfare or with other troubles. One of my employees was once committed to a mental hospital. Over the six and a half years he has worked for me, he has developed and grown and is now a productive member of society. I have also had the opportunity to help people who are in alcohol recovery.

"I needed more than just a business to keep me straight. I needed something I could believe in that had a purpose, and I found that with ServiceMaster," states the entrepreneur.

Another franchisee, Val Hanson previously had a 33-year-long career with the 7-Up bottling company as a loader, bottle sorter, route salesman, and finally servicing and dispensing equipment to fountains. For Hanson, it was a life-long goal to start his own business, yet he was 52.

"I used to listen to Paul Harvey, while driving my delivery truck," Hanson recalls, "and he always talked about ServiceMaster. I became interested in the company and decided to investigate buying a franchise of my own.

"I was attracted to ServiceMaster because it is a first-class operation. They have quality people and excellent service, which impressed me a great deal. I didn't want to be associated with a company that wasn't reputable and dependable."

In the beginning of his sixth decade, Hanson embarked on a new career, at a time when many of his peers were looking forward to retirement.

"I bought my first ServiceMaster franchise, an existing business. After a few years, I wanted to move to Idaho, so I sold my franchise to buy another one in Coeur D'Alene, Idaho," says the franchisee.

Hanson now employs a staff of 15 and makes more money than he ever imagined was possible. He no longer works in the field, but instead spends his time searching for new clients. "But I still keep my hand in the bucket once in a while. I don't want to forget what business I am in, so I occasionally perform a job myself," he exclaims.

Now contemplating doubling his business over the next few years, Hanson admits, "A lot of people at my age would be cutting back, but I don't want to sit around and do nothing. This business is fun for me and as long as it remains enjoyable, I'll keep on doing it."

ServiceMaster is an attractive opportunity for people such as Terry Burke and Val Hanson not only because of its principles, but unlike many other franchising companies, the start-up fees are relatively low: the on-location and contract service licenses cost approximately $29,000 each. The license fee pays for formal training and includes a week at the Academy of Management at the Downer's Grove corporate headquarters. Additionally, franchisees are provided with operating manuals and assistance from the local distributor in setting up the new business. Anderson estimates that it takes an average franchisee about a year to break even and start earning a profit. "We are currently developing and testing a new marketing and sales program that will actually help a franchisee break even in six months," he explains.

"We do offer financial help and will finance as much as two-thirds of the start-up fees, though we prefer franchisees to have around $10,000 to $15,000 of working capital," explains Anderson.

In addition to any equipment or supplies needed, the franchisees in residential carpet cleaning and disaster restoration also pay ServiceMaster a 10 percent royalty rate (plus an additional

1 percent for a national advertising program while the contract services license has a sliding scale based on revenue).

In addition to the corporate-sponsored advertising program, franchisees are encouraged to plan a marketing program of their own, although there are limitations. ServiceMaster details specific requirements to franchisees regarding how and where they are allowed to market and advertise their services. Franchisees are assigned an area of concentration where they are permitted to advertise.

"But, because our areas are nonexclusive, a franchisee is allowed a degree of flexibility that permits him or her to perform services outside of his or her assigned area. For example, a franchisee might go to a customer's home and clean the carpet. A satisfied customer might recommend the franchisee to a friend who lives in another town. Our system of operation allows this franchisee to work wherever he or she chooses, as long as the work is found through referrals," Anderson adds.

As a supplement to the advertising program, and similar to the Holidex system of Holiday Inn, is a national toll-free 1-800-WE-SERVE line at no additional cost to the franchisees. Already receiving over 9,000 calls a month, the toll-free number is serviced by operators who direct potential customers to the nearest franchisee or company-owned unit in their area.

"Typically, our residential services are performed on a one-time only basis, and customers do not have to sign a contract, although we strive to have regular customers whom we service on a monthly or quarterly basis. We encourage our franchisees to call their customers back. By having a well-established customer base, repeat business provides security to the franchisee's business," reveals Pollard.

With a 95 percent success rate, it is evident that ServiceMaster develops and supports its franchisees, though according to Anderson, "Maintaining quality is a never-ending challenge. We provide the franchisees with training that will give them the level of quality that we demand. We use a variety of mechanisms including our quality assurance program where a regional manager will personally perform a quality inspection on a franchisee's business. The manager will also call on customers and inspect facilities to see how pleased the customer is with the work."

In the business of residential cleaning, the excellent level of quality is extremely important. Bill Pollard expresses, "We are under pressure, in a positive way, to ask ourselves constantly how we can do our jobs better. There is a certain penchant for continuous improvement. There isn't a service we deliver today where the customer hasn't first asked the question, 'Should I do this myself?' Our customers are our number one competition!

"Because our customers always have the option of doing this work themselves, we must be in the business of doing it far better than anyone else. There is a constant tension, in a positive way, for us to ask ourselves how we can perform better. Even as a leader in this organization, I continually ask myself how I can improve in my job.

"We can be pleased about our work, but there is always a better way to do it. We can never be satisfied, and we always look at constant improvement as a learning experience. This is what we mean when we stress pursuit of excellence," explains Pollard.

ServiceMaster has continued to succeed because the standards it promotes are found throughout the system, although its franchisees are allowed a certain degree of flexibility. According to Don Anderson, the most important standard is the Partner's Pledge. "Our franchisees are our partners, and they pledge to us and to their customers and fellow franchisees to always be on time for a job and do the job right the first time. They promise to be properly uniformed and perform their work in a professional manner.

"There are also requirements for maintaining the ServiceMaster identification; for instance, the trucks must be a certain color (the ServiceMaster yellow) and the logo must be used in a specific way. Our distributors and regional managers perform regular inspections to ensure that the franchisees are conducting their business in the way that they agreed to," says Anderson.

One way of maintaining that level of quality is a result of ServiceMaster having carefully researched methods for cleaning and having specifically developed chemicals and equipment. It is estimated that these tools can cut labor costs as much as 30 percent, and at the same time do a superior job. The company spends a great deal of time and money to create the best products possible through experiments performed in its state-of-the-art laboratories.

"All our products are backed by a technical services department, so if a franchisee has a problem they haven't seen before, something that needs special cleaning instructions, they can call a toll-free number and ask us for advice," explains William C. Bond, Ph.D., who is vice president of the Technical Development Department. Bond, who holds a doctorate in polymer chemistry from the University of Florida in Gainesville, was hired by ServiceMaster to oversee all product development, equipment designs, and cleaning processes.

"Our objective is to provide our franchisees with a system that is designed to work and deliver a higher level of quality than could be done by other cleaning processes. Cleaning is a very labor-intensive job. Usually about 95 percent of the cost of cleaning is for the labor and supervision. Only about 5 percent is for the chemicals and equipment. So what we try to do is provide the franchisees with the best chemicals and equipment. This way they get the job done in less time and more productively, which reduces the overall cost of a job. We also price our products competitively. Often, our chemicals may be a little more expensive than other brands, but in the long run, our products are more efficient because the franchisees don't have to clean as often," explains Bond.

"An interesting example is our window cleaning. We are currently experimenting with a window treatment that will reduce the frequency of cleanings. Currently, windows may be washed once a month, and this new window treatment may reduce that to once a quarter. Well, you can imagine the labor savings this will provide!

"Another example is in wall washing. We found that at one time, people were washing walls with a bucket and a sponge or a sprayer and a cloth. It was a useless job. The customer always ended up having to paint the walls at some point. We set out to create a cleaning process that would be as effective as painting and save money, too.

While painting costs about 60 to 65 cents a square foot, washing costs are only 10 percent of that amount. Now, if we could extend the time between painting jobs, we would save the customer money. So we put together a system, including upgraded chemicals and equipment and a new procedure, which provides the customer with a clean wall. The system entails the use of three trowels, one for washing, a second for rinsing, and the third for drying which we put on a cart. Two of the trowels connect to a pump-up pressure spray which allows us to feed detergent into the trowel and spray it on the walls. The pads are attached with Velcro so they are quick and easy to change. This system saves our franchisees 37 percent of the time the old process used to take, and it helps them do a better job of cleaning. We design systems that make our franchisees successful," asserts Bond.

In addition to price, effectiveness, and quality, ServiceMaster develops products and equipment that are more comfortable and dignified for the workers who use them. According to Chairman Pollard, "Cleaning is considered a demeaning job. In part, that's because a worker is down on his or her hands and knees most of the time. To avoid this, we design our equipment to operate from a standing position and is, by the way, just as effective. This makes a big difference in productivity because it increases the dignity of the person doing the job. Dignity is very important to us since it provides a feeling of well-being. What we are trying to do is take cleaning from an art form to a science. We provide systems to our employees and franchisees that will make them successful."

ServiceMaster has turned cleaning into an impressive high-tech business. While the company operates computers that help manage inventories and order supplies, an elaborate information system at the Downer's Grove headquarters even tracks preventive maintenance schedules for equipment in hospital, university, and business settings.

The company is organized as a master limited partnership. With over 40,000 partners in the business, unlike most other large companies which are incorporated, ServiceMaster encourages its employees and franchisees to be partner-owners in the parent company.

Also, unlike many other companies of its size, ServiceMaster has been able to pay more than 50 percent of its earnings to its partner-shareholders each year. "As a service company with a very high cash flow, we have found this to be a very efficient way to operate the company. A principal partnership is one in which every partner owns a piece of the assets in the business while a corporation owns all the assets," explains Pollard. "By 1997, we must convert to the corporate form because the tax advantages of partnership have been eliminated by the government."

As the company continues to expand and diversify, one thing will remain constant: ServiceMaster and its subsidiaries will be service oriented, with a focus on quality and productivity. In 1986, the company acquired Terminex, now the largest pest control company in the country; then in 1988 the company purchased Merry Maids, in 1989 American Home Shield, and in 1990 TruGreen Lawn Care, followed by a 23 percent interest in Norrell Corporation (temporary personnel services) in late 1991. "If you look at our different businesses, each is service oriented and people intensive. This is our niche," explains Pollard. "One of the wonderful things about service is that the better you serve, the more people want your business, so there is always a market with a growing demand."

Today, the company operates with the same philosophy and concepts that it observed in the early days when Marion Wade, Ken Hansen, Ken Wessner, and Bob Wenger were operating the business. As a company that practices what it preaches, its employees and franchisees will continue to grow and prosper.

Chapter 10

THE SOUTHLAND CORPORATION

Franchising Convenience Around the World

By the mid-1920s, Henry Ford's decade-old prophecy that the day would come when every American family would own a car was beginning to become a reality. People were no longer scoffing at Henry Ford, the Father of the Automotive Assembly Line.

Owning a car is now commonplace and as such, is taken for granted; no other invention has had such a profound influence on American life-styles. The coming of the automobile introduced immense changes throughout the nation. No longer were city dwellers compelled to live within the city limits, close to factories and shops where they worked. The population began to spread in all directions with suburbs and new housing developments springing up miles away from the nucleus of the city. As a result, highways were constructed to shorten the commuting time of suburbanites and to connect cities with still other cities. New businesses were born, including gas stations, drive-in restaurants, drive-in theaters, motels, shopping centers—the list goes on and on. As Americans took to the road, their life-styles changed drastically, and a valuable commodity—time—became very important, in particular, the saving of time.

One company that cashed in on the growing popularity of automobiles was the Southland Ice Company, led by a future-minded Joe C. Thompson, Jr., who operated 16 ice docks in the Dallas area. It was a relatively simple business that provided its customers with a needed service: car and truck drivers would pull up beside a loading dock, purchase blocks of ice, and haul it away to be stored in their home ice boxes—this was before the advent of the mechanical refrigerator. Most important, Southland was the first company to offer conveniences to its customers—they also could purchase a few food items and avoid long lines at the grocery store. Other services included being open after hours or on Sunday when traditional stores were closed.

Young Joe C. Thompson, Jr., grew up in Oak Cliff, a suburb of Dallas. His parents had little money, and young "Jodie," beginning at the age of 8, worked at odd jobs after school to help his family. The Thompsons lived next door to J. O. Jones, the vice president and general manager of Consumers Ice Co., a firm that operated several ice plants and retail ice docks in the town. Jones, who had no children, was drawn to the young hard-working Jodie and decided to teach the young man the ice business.

Jodie first cleaned the stables and tended to the horses and mules that pulled the wagons the company used to deliver its ice to homes and businesses. When he became a teenager, he began loading ice onto the wagons. This was hard work, and Jones promised him if he would stick to it, he would succeed. By the time Jodie was ready to leave for college in the fall of 1918, he was helping keep the company's books and was developing a deep, thorough knowledge of the ice business.

After graduating from the University of Texas at Austin, in 1922,

Jodie returned to Consumer's Ice where J. O. Jones had offered him a full-time position with a salary of $150 a month.

In the summer of 1924, Jodie presented his boss with a new merchandising plan to increase Consumers' summer sales. He proposed that Consumers sell chilled watermelons through its retail ice docks. Jones reluctantly gave his approval and Consumers became the first shops in Texas to sell ice-cold watermelon.

Two years later, Jodie was promoted to secretary-treasurer of the company. By this time there were 5 ice plants and 16 retail ice docks; the growing company attracted the attention of a successful businessman, Claude S. Dawley. Dawley was consolidating small ice companies into one large corporation and approached Thompson with an offer. With J.O.'s blessing, Thompson began acquisition discussions. In the proceedings, Thompson was allowed to purchase stock in the new venture, at $10 per share. The young executive bought 2,500 shares in 1927 and was named a full director of the new Dallas corporation—the Southland Ice Company.

Also in 1927, in this position, the 28-year-old Thompson was approached with a second offer, this time by John Jefferson "Uncle Johnny" Green. Uncle Johnny's small ice dock in the Oak Cliff section of southwest Dallas offered still longer hours to its customers. Green's customers knew that they could always rely on him—his shop was open 16 hours a day, seven days a week during the summer. *Now that was convenience!*

In the hot summer of 1927, Green noticed that many requests were coming from customers for such items as bread, milk, and eggs. It seemed a natural to stock such staples, he thought, particularly since these inquiries were made late at night and on Sundays when the local grocery stores had already closed their doors. By offering such a service, Green was certain it would increase customer loyalty. Then, when he saw how well received the new products were, he added cigarettes and some canned goods.

By the end of the summer, Green knew he had a winning idea. Now he was ready to approach young Jodie Thompson. Green proposed that he would sell his new line of products throughout the winter when the ice business was virtually at a standstill, and he was willing to pay for the power bills as well as do the accounting if Southland would furnish the grocery items. Thompson realized that there were many benefits in Green's new merchandising concept—it would increase revenues and profits from ice station operations, and most interestingly it would ultimately provide year-round employment for ice station operators. In addition, it would furnish a much-needed diversification. Thompson was receptive, and the following spring, Southland's portion of the profits was over $1,000. This marked the birth of the "convenience store."

Not surprisingly, Southland's entré into the convenience store business was not well received by everybody. There was a great deal of resistance from local grocery stores. To retaliate, many grocers refused to buy ice from Southland unless they pulled all food items off the shelves. Thompson carefully calculated the amount of lost revenue and determined this amount would be less than that to be gained by selling the food items. Hence, Southland continued to promote and develop the new merchandising idea at its other ice stations.

Another innovation came about in the early days of the Southland Ice Company. One company employee had visited Alaska and was impressed by the Indian totem poles he saw on display. He purchased one, placed it in front of his home, and was surprised that it attracted the curiosity of many people. The employee believed that the Southland Ice docks should be renamed "Tote'm Stores," since customers "toted" away their purchases. Because a totem pole was an attention getter, one was to be built in front of every store. Following approval by the board, the chain, Tote'm, opened throughout Texas, each with a "pole" sign. This marked a first in retail identification, now a standard at retail chains of all kinds around the world.

The advent of the new mechanical refrigerator, which was introduced in 1926, led to the demise of hundreds of ice manufacturers across the country. Thompson realized he needed to explore other avenues to maintain the traffic and sales in his stores in addition to food items. He noticed there was a lot of unused property adjacent to many of his stores, and if gasoline stations were built there, extra customers would be attracted. He soon entered negotiations with an oil company to construct gasoline stations that he would in turn lease to them. After the first agreement was signed, five stations were constructed at the cost of $25,000 each and were rented to the oil company for $8,200 a piece annually.

In 1931, Jodie Thompson was named president of Southland Ice. Two years later, in 1933, the Eighteenth Amendment to the U. S. Constitution was repealed and Prohibition was over. Soon, all but eight states were legally permitting the manufacture and sale of liquor and beer. Thompson realized that drinkers usually preferred their beer chilled, and this would be a good merchandising combination for his ice stores; thus another new marketing concept was born at Southland.

Anticipating the decline of ice plants around the world, Thompson planned to absorb this change by offering still more products through his stores. The stores would charge a few pennies more for providing two services—speed and convenience—and not have to rely on selling ice alone. His insight saved the company, once the top ice producer in the Dallas market, from the demise of the ice industry.

By 1936, Southland's convenience stores were the largest retailers of dairy products in the Dallas/Ft. Worth area, and Thompson was convinced that the company was ready to produce its own dairy products. This same year, Southland opened Oak Farms Dairies, and again, there was resistance from grocery stores. One competitor went as far as opening Oak Farm's milk cartons and putting cigarette butts or lemon juice in them. Incredibly, this harassment did not "spoil" Southland's milk. Within one year, the dairy segment of Southland's business was earning an impressive profit.

By 1939, Southland had 60 Tote'm retail locations in Texas. The company had successfully made it through the depression years. It was observed that the Tote'm stores' profits had greatly surpassed the earnings from the ice operations. In early 1945, Southland began an extensive advertising program, extolling the convenience and other advantages offered by its retail stores: they were open-front, drive-in stores; they were open from early morning to late at night, seven days a week; they sold ice, cold drinks, and groceries; and they offered curb-side service for their customers.

There remained only one problem. Not all the company's stores were named Tote'm. Many of the ice stores that Southland had acquired over the years continued to operate under their former names, such as City Ice. Thompson knew a common identity was needed, and since the various groups were unwilling to assume the name of another, it was decided that an entirely new name would be chosen.

The Tracy-Locke Company, an established Dallas advertising agency, was hired to create a new name. After many hours of deliberation, the advertising executives agreed that if all the stores would agree to stay open from 7:00 A.M. to 11:00 P.M., seven days a week, they could be called "7-Eleven." The suggested name and hours of operation were enthusiastically accepted by the company executives and store operators, a trademark was designed, and the program began. In 1946, the company officially adopted the 7-Eleven name, and a new era in convenience stores had begun.

After a common name was put in place, Thompson believed that the architecture and design of the stores needed to be modified. Originally built as ice houses, the stores were all concrete and not attractive; the new ones had green and white stripes used by the former City Ice stores and displayed a glass open front. They also had twice the amount of floor space. Foreseeing that the life-style of the public would revolve around the automobile, Thompson increased parking lots by five to ten times, and placed them in front of the store rather than in the back. This may seem trivial, but 7-Eleven was among the first retailers in the country to place a parking lot in front of the store. The company expanded its merchandising to include meat and soon was the state's largest retailer of beverages, dairy foods, bread, frozen meats, and crushed ice. The most noticeable addition was the stand-out sign—a freestanding pylon with the name 7-Eleven atop—a descendent of the totem pole previously used to attract customers.

By the late 1940s, Southland had expanded and diversified its operations. It owned 74 7-Eleven stores, many ice properties, and

Oak Farms Dairies. Southland became known as an employer that highly regarded its employees with a CEO who believed employees should be paid a fair wage. Recalls son Jere Thompson, an employee of Southland since 1954, "My dad always believed in hard work, fair pay, and personal contact with his employees. As a child, I used to go with him on the weekends to visit one of the ice plants or Oak Farms Dairies. Dad would put his arm around the employees and talk to them, asking about their families. He was very personable, although he demanded a lot from his employees."

In 1949, annual store revenues were $9.7 million while Oak Farm Dairies had operating profits in excess of $429,000. Thompson's 7-Eleven stores were the originator and leader in the convenience store industry, and it was felt that the time had come to expand outside the North Texas area. Soon, stores were opened in Houston and Austin where they initially struggled because "convenience" was new and an oddity. Gradually, the stores in these other cities gained consumer acceptance.

By 1952, upon Southland's 25th anniversary, the company made the transition from a regional organization when it expanded its operations throughout the immense state of Texas. It was during the early stages of expansion that Thompson realized that the most important factor in the success of the stores was the careful selection of store locations. One of the factors the executives looked at when choosing a location was whether customers who were on their way to a grocery store would have to pass by the 7-Eleven. If they are going to the store for just one or two things, they will tend to go to a 7-Eleven to save time and the hassle of going through a big store to find what they need.

Within two years, the store expansion was a proven success, and Southland felt it was time to venture outside the state. Four stores were opened in Miami, Florida, again initially to mixed reviews by the public. These were the first convenience stores in the state and they introduced an entirely new retail idea. After they were open for a while, they were well received, in part, because the warm weather and the draw of vacationers to the state was compatible with the speed and convenience that the 7-Eleven stores had to offer. In the late 1950s, the company expanded its operations outside of the sunshine belt, first in Washington, D.C., where in 18 months, 20 stores were opened.

In the spring of 1961, Thompson, who had a terminal illness, began to make plans for the future of his company and named his eldest son John to take over as president of the company. At the time of Thompson's death in June 1961, Southland's sales were approximately $100 million.

As president, John Thompson made expansion and growth a top priority, and 7-Eleven soon moved into more states, including Colorado, Arizona, and New Jersey. Next, the company geared itself for the California market where the population and economy were booming. In addition, there was an opportunity—the Speedee Mart stores. This chain of more than 100 units all located in California were all franchised and had a strong management team in place that knew how to franchise their business successfully. Acquisition of Speedee Mart would provide Southland with the expertise and know-how of franchising. With 126 convenience stores and 4 grocery markets, Speedee Mart represented the largest acquisition in Southland's history. But it was not a milestone for this reason; rather, it was the company's first entry into the franchising industry.

Dick Dole, a retired Southland executive vice president, was a district manager for Speedee Mart at the time of the acquisition. "It did surprise me when Speedee Mart was sold to Southland," recalls Dole. "We had become part of a large company that had over 400 stores, while we only operated 125. Southland was very smart to buy Speedee Mart because it gave them expertise in the franchising business."

Speedee Mart's management, including Dole, helped Southland develop a new basic franchise agreement. An applicant was approved and trained under Southland's approach, and Southland would lease or sublease a ready-to-operate, fully stocked 7-Eleven store to the new franchise owner. In return, the franchisee paid for all business licenses and permits and was required to invest an amount equal to the store inventory and pay a modest franchise fee. Unique to Southland's franchise operations, in addition to providing a turnkey store to the franchisee, included paying a royalty based on gross profit, not sales.

Clark J. Matthews II, Southland's current president and chief executive officer, believes that because of its move into franchising, Southland was able to continue to improve the caliber of people overseeing the operation of its stores. Franchisees, Matthews believes, tend to be more customer oriented because their own money is invested in the business and they are thus often willing to try new ideas to improve the store's profits.

"Unlike many other franchisors, we didn't look at the franchising business as a way of raising money for expansion," Matthews states. "Some companies go into franchising as a source of capital for expansion. Then, they may change their approach and start buying back their franchises.

"Our franchisees have done a tremendous job for us, and my personal view is that we would not have been as successful without them," the CEO adds. "In many cases we might not have done as well in our franchised stores had they been company operated."

At this time, Southland decided to use another franchise approach to expand when it developed a franchise concept where it franchised or licensed an entire area to a company to develop 7-Eleven stores. This approach was called "area licensing."

Southland sold its first area license in 1968 to Garb-Ko, Inc., a Saginaw, Michigan-based company. Immediately, Garb-Ko made plans to build seven 7-Eleven units in certain northern and central Michigan markets. Palmer Waslien, Southland's training manager at the time, contributed much to Southland's expansion in the franchising industry by designing the first area license program. According to Waslien, "The whole idea of the license program was to bring in royalties in exchange for licensing our system, trademark, and assistance." Under this approach, a licensee is responsible for building and operating each store within their area, in compliance with the 7-Eleven system. This also allowed the company to expand its 7-Eleven name in areas where the company was not planning any immediate development.

By 1964, there were 1,519 7-Eleven stores in the United States with total revenues of more than $274 million and net earnings exceeding $3.6 million. The Southland Corporation was named one of the nation's 50 largest merchandising firms by *Fortune* magazine. Southland's significant growth continued, and only four years later, the total number of units had more than doubled to 3,537. By the end of 1969, Southland was operating in 38 states, Washington, D.C., and three provinces in Canada.

On August 21, 1972, Southland common stock was traded on the New York Stock Exchange for the first time, opening at $32 7/8 per share. Jere Thompson, the second oldest son of Joe Thompson, then executive vice president, recalls that the company was taken public and was well received, especially in view of the significant expansion of the company that had taken place during the late 1960s and early 1970s, when 7-Eleven was doubling in size every few years. "We needed capital to invest in land, construct the stores, purchase equipment, and buy inventory," he tells. "So we began to sell private placements which included notes convertible into the common stock. Eventually, as those were converted, there were enough outstanding shares to enable us to be listed on the NYSE. Later, there were many splits and dividends."

In 1973, 7-Eleven expanded its area licensee concept into Japan—a great accomplishment considering there were no other convenience stores anywhere in that country. Ito-Yokado, a $7 billion company and one of the largest retailers in the world, operating general merchandise and grocery stores throughout Japan, bought the second 7-Eleven international area license (the first was sold in Mexico in 1971). In its first year as an area licensee, the company opened 25 7-Eleven stores. The stores resembled those in the United States, but offered a different product mix. Items such as dried and fresh fish were sold in great quantities in Japan, and within two years, the Japanese licensee had opened over 100 stores throughout the country. Today, the licensee operates more than 4,600 stores in Japan and Hawaii.

Since Southland entered the franchising business in 1964, the company has had significant growth, maintaining an excellent image and performance record while achieving national recognition as one of the country's leading franchisors. Southland continues to develop three types of 7-Eleven operations—company-operated stores, area licenses, and the individual store franchisees.

Southland, as the owner, is responsible for all aspects of a company-operated store, including the land, building, property and equipment, and store operations. Each company-operated store is managed and staffed by employees of Southland, and sales and profits from all its company-operated units appear in Southland's public financial statements.

A 7-Eleven area license provides an independent business entity with exclusive rights to use the 7-Eleven trademark and system in a predefined geographic territory within the limits of the license agreement. The licensee pays Southland an initial fee that is calculated according to a number of factors, including the geographic territory. The initial fee and an ongoing royalty on sales paid by the licensee for the duration of the area license agreement are for use of the 7-Eleven trademark and 7-Eleven system, training, and start-up services. In addition to the license fee and ongoing sales royalty, the licensee is responsible for every aspect of the convenience store operation, including the land, building, equipment, inventory, staffing, and operation; they must maintain the 7-Eleven image and system; and they must obtain their own financing. The licensee may operate individual corporate stores with its own employees, or it may, under certain circumstances, grant individual store franchises similar to Southland's. Southland, pursuant to the area licensee agreement, provides certain training and technical assistance for the licensees.

Through its individual store franchising program, 7-Eleven provides opportunities for small business entrepreneurs to operate their own business for a relatively modest investment. In addition to a one-time franchise fee, which is based upon the gross profit of the store (during the first half of 1992, the fee averaged less than $40,000), franchisees are required to invest an amount equal to the store's inventory and cash register fund, part of which Southland will finance. In 1991, the total start-up cost to a franchisee ranged from $13,000 to $161,000. In August 1992, in the continental United

States, there were approximately 3,040 franchised stores in Southland's system.

The company maintains an "open account" for all franchisees, including those who have used the company to finance their investment for the inventory and cash register fund. The financing through the open account allows franchisees to repay their loan each month and also borrow additional funds when needed for operational expenses.

Southland is responsible for the land, building, and equipment for both franchised and company-owned stores, an investment that usually ranges from $500,000 to $1 million or more per store. The company then, in a franchised operation, leases or subleases to the franchisee a ready-to-operate 7-Eleven store that has been fully equipped and stocked. Because Southland develops its own real estate, the company is better able to control its fixed costs. In Southland's franchised operations, the company also pays for the utilities and property taxes and provides ongoing store services such as merchandising, record-keeping, advertising, store audits, business counseling, training, and preparation of financial statements.

In turn, the franchisee is responsible for paying out of his or her portion of the store's gross profits: all operating expenses including payroll, sales and inventory taxes, inventory and cash variations, licenses and permits, supplies, certain repairs and maintenance, and other controllable in-store expenses. Unlike most franchise systems, Southland does not require royalty payments based on a percentage of sales. Instead, both Southland and the franchisee have a stake in the gross profit of a 7-Eleven store. Rather than taking a cut off the top of the total sales receipts, Southland's royalty is based upon a share of the gross profits of a store with the franchisee.

On a daily basis franchisees deposit all their store receipts and cash, less any cash expended for purchases on a daily basis, into a designated bank account administered by the corporate office. Southland, in turn, uses these funds to operate the system, including paying for the land and building and utilities, and pays most of the franchisee's bills, which the franchisee sends into an accounting office. Another unique feature in the 7-Eleven franchising operations is that the corporate office also prepares the franchisee's payroll at the direction of the franchisee.

"Basically Southland's financing is very much like a line of credit," explains Charlie Simpson, manager of Southland's Franchise Department. "We administer the payroll out of the franchisee's portion of the gross profit and manage all the money, paying their expenses and then returning to the franchisee the remainder of his or her portion of the gross sales profits."

Mike Davis, assistant general counsel for franchise and international matters, explains how Southland's system provides its franchisees with the record-keeping system: "The franchisee can use a portion of the daily receipts to make certain purchases if they wish, although most of the franchisees utilize Southland's system and pay the bulk of their purchases through our accounting system."

"The advantage of our open account and the financing package is how it allows our franchisees to start receiving deliveries immediately," adds Tom Kanawyer, stores administration manager. "For example, if the store is open in mid-June, the franchisee can immediately order extra merchandise to get ready for the busy Fourth of July weekend. They don't have to go to the bank to borrow an additional $20,000. All they have to do is take the invoices, stamp them, and send them to our office, and we will pay these bills for them. As they reduce their inventory through sales during the weekend, the franchisee deposits cash into the bank. Our system is very fluid, allowing our franchisees open financing, so they don't have to worry about having a lot of capital or a line of credit at a bank during peak promotional periods."

CEO Clark Matthews credits former Southland manager Palmer Waslien for the gross profit split system that the company continues to use today. "Palmer believed that one reason why small businesses fail is because they don't have adequate control of the accounting aspects of their business. He advocated that this would be a valuable service for us to provide for our franchisees.

"Waslien also believed if our royalty was based on a percentage of sales, the company would continuously try to increase sales that would not generate additional gross profit dollars that are so important to the franchisee's success," adds the CEO. "Therefore, if we split gross profit dollars, we would both have a common objective, which would be to make the stores as profitable as possible for both parties. This was a novel idea at that time because there was not another franchise system that used anything other than a percentage of sales." It remains a unique system today.

Waslien's son Glenn, now managing director of 7-Eleven Stores Licensing Group, began his career with Speedee Mart in 1965. "My father was instrumental in designing agreements and agreement changes that allowed the 7-Eleven system to grow," recalls the younger Waslien.

Under this Gross Profit Split System, the financial return to both Southland and the franchisee is tied to the profitability of the store. As a result, Southland maintains much more of a "partnering" relationship—both in a financial and marketing sense—with its franchise business than do most other franchisors. Southland has a vested interest in helping its franchisees control costs as well as increase sales. This is quite different from a sales royalty system in which the franchisor has no particular interest in aiding the ongoing profitability of a franchisee. It also is designed to make small business operation possible for persons who have limited financial resources and business experience.

In most cases, Southland's royalty, which is based upon splitting the store's gross profit, is 52 percent, charged to the open account monthly to compensate Southland for use of the 7-Eleven operating system and trademarks, and also rent, utilities, bookkeeping, advertising, and other services. These services are typically covered by franchisees in other systems on top of what they pay in royalty fees and the wholesale cost of their franchisor's products that they are required to purchase.

To enhance the success of its franchisees further, Southland by policy offers the franchisee an assured gross income, which can be as much as $110,000 a year. In other words, Southland will forgo part of its gross profits from the store to assure that the franchisee can, under certain circumstances, realize an annual minimum gross income as high as $110,000.

If the franchise agreement is discontinued or expires, Southland retains the right to repurchase the franchisee's interest in inventory and other assets as well as continue to operate the store under different management.

According to Charlie Simpson, franchise department manager, 7-Eleven does not necessarily exclude an applicant for a franchise based on a lack of previous retail experience, although such experiences may help. "We are not necessarily looking for someone with prior business or management experience," he explains. "Someone who does not have a business background has the opportunity to learn all he or she needs to know to run a successful 7-Eleven store through our franchisee training programs. Obviously, it is easier if a prospective franchisee has some retail experience, but the most important things we look for when interviewing a prospective franchisee are that he or she has an affinity for people and is able to deal with the public. A person with these qualities can be trained to run a successful store and do very well."

Simpson also explains that 7-Eleven franchisees come from all types of backgrounds. "Our franchisees were formerly taxi cab drivers, managers in a corporate environment, Southland employees who were field managers, district managers, or sales managers—a wide variety. Our franchisees are single men and women and also married couples."

According to Simpson, owning a 7-Eleven franchise is an investment that requires a lot of hard work, but can be a lucrative business. However, it is not a good get-rich-quick scheme. "We don't want absentee owners who want to invest money and just want to look over computer reports. We want all our franchisees to be actively involved in the 7-Eleven business.

"We have many franchisees who operate or franchise more than one store franchise, but only a handful operate as many as five or six stores," Simpson explains. "Most of our franchisees have one 7-Eleven franchise, live in the vicinity of that store and operate it on a hands-on basis."

Tom Kanawyer, stores administration manager, explains that a high energy level and self-motivation are additional qualities that

Southland looks for when interviewing potential franchisees. "A 7-Eleven store is a 24-hour-a-day operation, and anytime you operate your own business, it requires a significant time commitment and a lot of self-motivation.

"We look for people who enjoy working with other people— someone who likes to get out and talk to customers and be involved in the action," stresses Kanawyer.

As part of the qualification process, Southland administers a test to prospects interested in owning a franchise. The test determines, from a psychological perspective, which applicants have tendencies that could allow them to have an opportunity to be a successful franchisee. Then, after acceptance, but before the franchisee is assigned to a store, Southland provides training to teach numerous aspects of the store's operation, including customer service and how franchisees can motivate employees. New franchisee training consists of approximately 100 hours of store experience, plus three weeks of formal training with two weeks spent in a store and one full week spent in classroom training at Southland's training center. Intensive follow-up training is also provided by the franchisee's field consultant. In some areas, Southland uses a franchisee "coach" program.

Southland's franchise system is among the most field intensive in the franchising industry. It provides ongoing seminars that address specific operational issues such as controlling expenses, selection and training of employees, merchandising, and so on. In addition, Southland management personnel continually visit franchisees to counsel and advise them on all aspects of the business.

Kanawyer explains that Southland is very careful to whom it sells franchises—the company wants to make sure that owning a franchise will be good for the applicant as well as for the system. "Our franchise sales are nonpressure. We don't want someone in a store if it is not right for them," he asserts.

Southland's principal source of franchisees is word of mouth from existing franchisees. "About 75 percent of our franchise applicants are referred to us from existing franchisees," claims

Kanawyer. "This tells us that the majority of our franchisees feel very good about our system.

"Unlike most other franchisors, we actually allow our franchisees to 'test-drive' a store before committing on a long-term basis," Kanawyer adds. "We believe it is difficult to explain the experience of operating a 7-Eleven store while sitting at a conference table, so we allow our franchisees to operate their stores for 180 days to make sure this is what they want. If, at the end of that period of time, they want to pull out, we will return their franchise fee, buy back the investment, and part as friends. It is important that they are sure of what they are getting into because we are establishing a ten-year relationship."

"Our goal is to not have one unhappy franchisee," says Charlie Simpson who works closely with Kanawyer. "It is good for us and our franchisees to know that if things don't work out, they can get their money back."

Southland continues to sell franchises because it believes franchisees tend to watch their stores with a more scrutinizing eye than do managers of a company-owned store because the former's own monetary investment is involved, according to Simpson. "Generally, because a franchisee has an investment involved and controls their own labor dollars, their store can earn a higher income than will company-owned stores.

"On the other hand, a franchisee has the opportunity to own a piece of a proven system with a franchisor who understands its consumers, and knows how to select successful real estate locations," Simpson says. "And the franchisee can still own his or her own business while reaping the benefits of the affiliation with an established, reputable franchise system."

"We try to get the best franchisees—if we don't have the best people operating our stores, we will not be as successful as we want to be," Kanawyer states. "We have an old saying, which is, 'You franchise your own problems.' A poor location can cause a store to close, but so can selecting the wrong franchisee at the outset.

"In retailing, location is one of the keys," Kanawyer continues. "If you don't have the right location, the store will fail. An average location with a great operator can create a great store, while an average operator with a great location also can have a successful store.

"For the past decade, we have been trying to build our proprietary business with differentiating factors that make our franchises more valuable, such as our trademark Slurpee drinks and Big Bite sandwiches," adds Kanawyer. "We know that our stores do 15 to 20 percent more volume than another convenience store put on the same location. We have sold stores that were converted to another name and the store went broke. We know the value of our trademark and exclusive products, and they are worth a lot."

Goodwill sales are another unusual benefit for 7-Eleven franchisees. A goodwill sale occurs when a franchisee sells his or her interest in the franchise to another and signs a new franchise agreement with Southland. "Of course the amount depends on how well the franchisee has operated the store, the quality of the operation, and many other factors," explains Glenn Waslien, managing director for 7-Eleven Stores Licensing Group. "Our store goodwill sales have increased ever since the program started in the early 1970s. This is an additional return on the franchisee's investment."

Previously, until the mid-1970s, franchisees had to sell their stores back to Southland in exchange for their original investment, and the company would refranchise it. With the goodwill program in place, franchisees can sell their interest in the franchise to a new franchisee candidate who, if approved by Southland, takes over the business. "There are many franchise laws that regulate the way franchises are able to be sold, so technically, our franchisees sell their rights to the franchise back to Southland, and we refranchise it to the approved prospective franchisee," explains Assistant General Counsel Mike Davis. "Then, the new franchisee pays the original franchisee the agreed goodwill price for their interest in the franchise and remits to us a franchise fee and then we sign an agreement with the new owner."

Another unique feature of the 7-Eleven system is that franchisees have the ability to leave the system at any time. Tom Kanawyer, stores administration manager, points out that a franchisee can turn in his or her store keys and have his or her inventory (less any amounts owed the company) repurchased by Southland. "Franchisees in other systems can't do that because they have an ongoing obligation on the property's lease," he tells. "Every year, a few franchisees realize they are not happy operating their store and pull out. We part ways and send them a check for any amount due them under the terms of the franchise agreement."

Southland also extends to its franchisees a "son or daughter transfer" that basically allows them to transfer their interest in their franchise to their son or daughter and continue the franchise in the family—at no fee. The company also offers a survivorship provision—if a franchisee dies and has executed this agreement, the franchise will turn over to an heir named by the franchisee as long as Southland qualifies the individual.

Recently, the company introduced a long-term rebate for existing franchisees under which it will reward tenure in the 7-Eleven franchise system by remitting to long-term franchisees some portion of the franchise fee paid by the incoming operator. If the franchisee has been in the system for five to nine years, he or she is eligible for 25 percent of the fee; over ten years of operation, he or she receives 50 percent. "This is a way we can recognize our franchisees for some of the sweat equity involved in building their business over the years," says Kanawyer. "They receive this payment in addition to their goodwill fee. These two arrangements are very beneficial to our franchisees. Our franchisees have overwhelmingly thanked us for these well-earned benefits."

In 1992, Southland began implementing several new processes aimed at making 7-Eleven more responsive to customer's rapidly changing needs and preferences. As part of this effort, more formalized, two-way communications systems were set up to transmit information promptly throughout the company as efficiently as possible—with each 7-Eleven store as the focal point of the process.

As part of this new communications process, maintaining high image standards became a joint responsibility of store operators and the company's front-line management. In the meantime, Southland changed its 2 percent gross profit incentive to reward the franchisees who participated in its comprehensive new merchandising process because the company felt so strongly about its potential to impact positively 7-Eleven customer satisfaction and revitalize 7-Eleven stores and profits. This process greatly improves the quality of 7-Eleven's product selection by deleting items that don't sell while stocking more of what each particular store's customer really wants, including products that are new to 7-Eleven or the marketplace in general.

Franchisees are given a great deal of flexibility in choosing what products and brands their stores will carry, as long as they are consistent with the 7-Eleven's image. "We do have certain proprietary products, principally containers that display our trademark, such as cups, that are purchased from an authorized supplier," says Kanawyer. "Apart from these items, the franchisees can buy all other goods from any source they choose and take advantage of the best prices they can find.

"The franchisees are given a lot of freedom, but they are not permitted to sell anything they want—particularly items that would be damaging to our image. They can sell whatever products they want to as long as they conform to our general guidelines," adds Kanawyer. "We do encourage our franchisees to identify the needs of the consumers in their neighborhood. For instance, if they are in an ethnic area and a particular food section makes sense for that store, we will support and help them. We feel it is important to market to the needs of the individual customers in each area. So we are constantly in the process of looking for the right products to service the needs of our customers, and these vary year to year."

Many of 7-Eleven's domestic franchisees are involved in fresh sandwich programs, according to Charlie Simpson, franchise department manager. "Currently, in some of our test markets, we even offer dinner entree programs. We are also testing commissaries for sandwiches. Some of our franchisees already offer fresh-made deli sandwich programs—but this depends on where they are located. In-store delis are not that popular in Texas, whereas in the East, they are a way of life."

A customer cannot expect to find all the same products in every 7-Eleven store across the country, but every store offers fountain drinks, bread, milk products, and scores of other grocery items, as well as beer and wine in areas where they are allowed. "We want our customers to be able to travel throughout the country and fulfill their expectations when they go into a 7-Eleven store," says Southland's Stores Administration Manager Kanawyer. "We want our stores across the country to reflect the same image, although there will be many differences from region to region."

"Our stores offer a wide variety of products, but a customer may not find the same brands," explains Simpson. "For example, our franchisees are able to sell both Pepsi and Coca-Cola fountain drinks, so when a customer enters one of our stores, it is remarkably different from a McDonald's or Taco Bell—not only because our stores offer 3,000 items instead of 30, but if you want a soft drink, you are not limited to one brand.

"We want to provide every customer with good service, a clean, well-lit store, products they want, and a fast speedy checkout," Simpson tells.

"I remember one story that happened several years ago that involved two franchisees and points out that speed of service is burned into our minds," recalls Glenn Waslien, managing director of 7-Eleven Stores Licensing Group. "Hub Hubbard, a franchisee in Yuba City, California, operated one of our most successful 7-Eleven stores. His good friend Weldon Bell was a struggling franchisee operating a low-volume store. Bell's was a new store, but the surrounding neighborhood had not yet been developed. The struggling franchisee worked alone at his store all day long and didn't always have much opportunity to leave to go to the bank.

"Hubbard, who had more flexibility, would stop by his friend's store every day to pick up the day's receipts that he would later deposit into the bank. One day, Hub pulled his car into a parking space in front of the store, just as he always did every afternoon, but was surprised to find that his brakes weren't working. His car rolled along and crashed right through Bell's front door, smashing the glass. Fortunately, no one was injured, and Hub was able to stop his vehicle right next to the cash register where his friend was waiting.

"Hub, who had a tremendous sense of humor, calmly rolled down the window, stuck out his head, and said, 'Hey, Weldon, can you get me a loaf of bread? I am in a hurry!' This shows that convenience is always on our franchisees' minds!" Waslien continues.

Southland's dedication to providing convenience for its customers is clearly evident at every store around the globe. Approximately 95 percent of the 7-Eleven system are open 24 hours a day, seven days a week.

Franchisees may close on Christmas at their option, but they are obligated to be open during all other holidays. Yet the vast majority of franchisees choose to be open on Christmas to provide additional convenience to their customers. Also, even with paying higher holiday wages, the volume of sales and profit that results on these days is far greater than any other day of the year.

Southland is equally concerned with the physical appearance of each store and provides capital to maintain the condition of the properties, engage in remodeling, and update equipment. "One thing that is different about our system," explains Waslien, "is that we allocate a certain portion of our capital budget each year to maintain the image that we want to portray to the public and, in fact, are now engaged in a major systemwide physical upgrade of 7-Eleven stores. This is not an expense that the franchisees have to bear themselves. Franchisees are responsible, however, for the cleanliness of the interior of the store as well as the exterior and the parking lot."

Customer service is an important factor of the success of the 7-Eleven stores, and Southland provides training for both franchisees and their employees. "If the store doesn't provide good customer service, it will be reflected in low sales receipts and gross profit dollars," adds Simpson. "So every day, the customer is telling them whether they are succeeding or not."

Over the last 15 years, Southland has developed a very effective communication system with its franchisees through an advisory council system and other programs. Newsletters and videotapes are regularly dispatched to franchisees. Still, the company's management is committed to meeting personally with franchisees from all over the country to hear what they have to say. "Open communication is the best way in the world to maintain good relations with our franchisees," says Tom Kanawyer.

The most important communication link is between 7-Eleven franchisees and Southland field consultants, whose primary responsibility is as business advisor to franchisees. Field consultants meet at least once a week with each of the six or seven franchisees for which they are responsible, to develop business-building strategies for each store. As the franchisees' primary contact with Southland, field consultants are also trained to help remove obstacles to 7-Eleven stores' success, where possible, by drawing on resources and expertise from within Southland.

In addition, says Kanawyer, "a National Advisory Council of franchisees elected by their peers and Southland management meets several times a year to discuss issues of wide interest. During these meetings, we frequently negotiate with our franchisees and develop new programs to motivate them." In fact, it was through these advisory councils that substantive changes were implemented in the 7-Eleven franchise agreement. For example, one such change was developed during a National Advisory Council meeting in 1983 when the company negotiated with the franchisees to establish a renewal rider. "We created the renewal provision in the existing agreement to give the franchisees the contractual right to renew their franchise when it expires at no fee, as long as they meet certain criteria," tells Assistant General Counsel Mike Davis.

Southland credits the ongoing and open dialogue between its franchisees and management in large part for its successful franchise system. There are many channels that encourage the franchise community to communicate with company management. For example, franchisees meet with their assigned field consultants on a regular basis to discuss ways to improve the franchisee's business, as well as share concerns, questions, and ideas on how to improve the franchise system in general. Franchisees are also free to discuss concerns with the market manager, a division manager, a vice president, or even the president of the company.

In addition, each of 7-Eleven's geographical divisions holds frequent market-level meetings between the market staff and franchisees, while each division has a franchise advisory council that meets regularly.

Southland's top management meets on a regular basis with an independent association of 7-Eleven franchise owners to work together on major issues and opportunities. Southland also has invited 7-Eleven franchisees to participate on corporate task forces to enhance the 7-Eleven system.

A tumultuous period in the history of the Southland Corporation occurred in the late 1980s, when the Thompson brothers took the company private in a leveraged buyout (LBO) in a response to threats that a hostile raider might attempt to acquire the company. The Thompsons sought to protect the company, the trademark, the employees, and the franchisees from a buyer who didn't share the company's philosophy of superior quality, service, and convenience.

"Unfortunately, our timing on the buyout could not have been worse," claimed Jere and John Thompson in an article they wrote that was published by the *Dallas Times Herald* on March 26, 1990. It went on to state: "We had already repurchased two-thirds of the outstanding stock in the company and had begun to sell our high-yield bonds in October, 1987, when the stock market crashed—causing us to have to pay much higher interest rates than we expected.

"Nevertheless, we successfully completed the transaction. However, over the next couple of years, the U.S. economy slowed considerably, the convenience store industry slumped and competition increased, practically stopping growth at all convenience stores. And while our stores continued to out-perform others in the industry, poor economic and industry concerns, combined with our debt repayment obligations, led to projections indicating that by 1991 we could experience a cash shortfall. Therefore, to ensure the long-term viability of the company we built, we had to take dramatic action.... After much consideration, we approached 7-Eleven Japan and Ito-Yokado, our longtime friends and business partners, and asked whether they would consider further extending our business relationship.... What we proposed was a strategic alliance between two of the most powerful retailing companies in the world ... an alliance between partners who shared the same deep commitment to 7-Eleven."

Southland, which filed for Chapter 11 protection only 132 days earlier, was sold on March 5, 1991, to Ito-Yokado Co., Ltd., and Seven-Eleven Japan Co., Ltd., which together purchased 70 percent of the company's common stock for $430 million. Together, these companies form the fourth largest retailer in the world.

"Ito-Yokado approached us in the early 1970s about becoming a 7-Eleven area licensee for Japan because they were interested in the convenience store business and what they perceived could be a very viable business concept in Japan," recalls Tom Kanawyer, stores administration manager. "They are wonderful people who ultimately created a great 7-Eleven organization over there, and we are just delighted that under the circumstances, we were able to attract them to become a majority owner of our company. They bring an expertise in retailing and a specific expertise in the convenience store business.

"Some of the $430 million they invested in Southland was used to pay certain expenses resulting from the reorganization, but the bulk of it, together with our internal cash flow, is funding a capital expenditure program that is being used to upgrade our 7-Eleven stores over the next few years so as to present a fresher, more modern image to our customers.

"We are going to devote the bulk of the funds toward our existing store base to bring all the stores up to a higher level to serve the customer's needs better," adds Kanawyer. "We will have some expansion during the next few years in markets where there are good opportunities, but our emphasis will be on existing stores. We are interested in our existing stores growing to be more profitable and a place that our customers enjoy."

A rewarding discovery made during the LBO/brief Chapter 11 period and the resulting sale to Ito-Yokado was that the franchisees stood united with their franchisor. Shortly after the LBO, Southland franchisees eagerly accepted the "Year 2000 Amendment" that underscored their loyalty to the company. This amendment to the existing franchise agreement lengthened every contract, free of charge, to the year 2000, regardless of when it was due to expire. During the bankruptcy virtually all the franchisees continued to accept their obligations, confident that the company would soon escape its troubles and return to a healthier condition.

"During our Chapter 11 reorganization period, for example, the franchisees could have attempted to establish their own terms with their vendors, perhaps paying for goods with cash if they wanted to rather than going through the corporate system," recalls Simpson, franchise department manager. "The fact that they opted not to do that and stood united with us helped us keep the whole system together, whereas had they gone their own way, it could have developed a problem in finalizing the plan.

"If we had a large group of franchises who didn't trust us, it would have been a serious problem for the company," Simpson points out.

"Fortunately, the average customer walking into a 7-Eleven store anywhere in the country wouldn't have known that we were in bankruptcy," Kanawyer reveals. "I never heard of any of our stores even running out of inventory as a result of the Chapter 11. It was a phenomenal effort by people from the store level on up to the organization, and it was masterfully done."

A constant problem for all retailers is the threat of robbery. One innovative idea in place in all 7-Eleven stores was suggested by a franchisee: the Cash Controller, now a widely recognized and effective crime deterrent. "Today it is called the Tidel cash controller—a device that allows the clerk to deposit all the cash in the time-controlled register, which then drops into a safe," recalls Jere Thompson.

"If the clerk needs change, he or she must push various buttons, but then must wait a preprogrammed time, such as 90 seconds for the change," describes the co-vice chairman of the board. "Most robbers are not going to want to wait that long to get the money.

"A robbery took place at one store where a fellow came in, put

$20 down, and asked the clerk to get a pack of cigarettes," recalls Thompson. "When the clerk returned to the counter, the customer was holding a gun and demanded all the money from the register. After waiting the allotted time for the safe to dispense a limited amount of cash, he took the money, grabbed the cigarettes, and ran out. The clerk was amused to discover that the robber had carelessly left his $20 bill on the counter, but had only stolen $17 in change! We made money on this robbery!"

An FBI report recently published claims that crime rates have decreased at convenience stores because of the many programs that have been instituted around the country. "Since we implemented a robbery prevention and violence program in the late 1970s, we have seen a significant reduction in our robbery rates," recalls Mike Davis. "This is something we are continuously trying to control. We are testing different things around the country, and we are proud of the strong program we have in place. In fact, several states have legislated our Cash Controller, making it a requirement for late-night operators."

"At present, our future looks bright," concludes Matthews, Southland's president and chief executive officer. "We are in a position to provide our customers with the kind of store they want and the services and products they demand. Our new majority owners have provided us with an exciting future, and we will continue to concentrate on our core business—7-Eleven convenience stores."

Today, the company that invented the industry of convenience retailing is now part of everyday life in neighborhoods throughout America and around the world. In spite of this presence, millions of customers think of their neighborhood 7-Eleven as "the little corner store," never realizing it is 1 of over 13,000. As the industry leader for more than six decades, the Southland family consists of approximately 3,000 company-owned units in the United States and Canada, 3,100 franchise-operated stores in the United States, and over 7,350 7-Eleven stores owned and operated or franchised by area licensees in parts of the United States, Japan and 17 other countries, as well as Guam, Puerto Rico, and the Virgin Islands.

Like so many great international corporations, 7-Eleven has had its share of vicissitudes throughout its long history; still, it is a company rich in tradition that epitomizes the free enterprise system at its best.

Index